Millennial
History

Izzy –
Keep the Faith !

Steve

MINDSTIR MEDIA

Published by Mindstir Media, LLC
45 Lafayette Rd | Suite 181 | North Hampton, NH 03862 | USA
1.800.767.0531 | www.mindstirmedia.com

Printed in the United States of America
ISBN-13: 979-8-9855339-7-2

Millennial History

STEVE JACKSON

To Donna, my loving, shining North Star!

UNITED STATES

Foreword

AS A WORN-OUT BEN FRANKLIN exited Independence Hall after four months of helping to craft the new nation, he was stopped in the streets by a female citizen.

"What kind of government had the Founding Fathers created?" asked the lady in the street just outside of the hall in Philadelphia.

"A republic ma'am, if you can keep it," replied Franklin.

The same message was repeated to the American people almost two hundred years later by President Ronald Reagan. In a famous speech, Reagan warned America that "Freedom is never more than one generation away from extinction."

Keep this message in mind especially as you read the latter chapters of this book.

Introduction

NEARLY EVERYONE WANTS TO MAKE SENSE of the world around them. This would include even the most primitive of cultures and societies dating back to antiquity. The nature of man is to seek order, not chaos. How one achieves this psychological state can occur in as many ways as there are human beings inhabiting this planet. When I first started teaching, I used to believe that the chaos some kids could cause was because they did not want to be in the classroom. As I learned more, I began to understand that the restlessness of youth was a plea to me to help them make sense of the world. School years were always toughest in September but would get better as they began to buy into you as a teacher and as a resource for answers to life beyond the classroom.

My uncle was a renowned physics teacher in every high school that he taught. His notoriety extended well beyond numerous teacher-of-the-year awards. President Reagan saw fit to have him join the President's Council for Education in the 1980s. I can only imagine what his full impact in the educational world would have been had he not succumbed to cancer at age fifty-nine. My uncle derived his sense of order from the hard science of physics, where concrete scientific laws led directly to a disciplined and orderly life. His genius extended beyond academia into mastering piano, stand-up comedy, entrepreneurship, and to becoming a terrific role model. He was a true Renaissance Man with extraordinary talents in every field in which he endeavored.

Though I may have been bequeathed my uncle's teaching gene, I did not inherit his genius. My path to order came through the study of history, an incomplete discipline as many events were never recorded. Fortunately, I had some training in geology and paleontology that have reinforced many of history's perceptions.

I am going to share my Weltanschauung (world view) with you. Most of the subject matter contained in this book I was required to teach in a two-year sequence in middle school social studies class. If you are in the millennial generation, you may never have been exposed to some of what you are about to learn. Indeed, history is often interpretive in regards to "facts" and "acts," but this is my thesis and it has served me well. I hope that this book will help you make sense of the seemingly never-ending chaos that threatens to swallow us up each and every day.

One more point to be made here. Because the scope of this book covers many millennia, details will be necessarily superficial, much like a survey course you might have taken as a freshman in college. I do feel that I will be able to tie the threads of history together into one cohesive story that will expand your frame of reference of the world going forward. As a quick anecdote, one time in high school geography class, I asked a student to locate the city of Chicago on a map. The student was staring intently at the continent of Africa to find the city. Yikes!

How do you know where you are going when you don't know where you have been? Here we go!

Contents

CHAPTER 1

Dawn of Man

THE OLD TESTAMENT OF THE BIBLE puts forth one theory for the origin of mankind. It said that God made man in his image and placed him in the Garden of Eden. Adam was the name of the first man, and Adam's rib was transmogrified into the first woman named Eve. Eve ate the forbidden fruit of Eden and was cast out of Paradise along with Adam into an imperfect world. Eventually, they produced offspring and over the millennia subsequent generations populated the world. Their exploits are detailed throughout the Old Testament, with one of the last offspring to be named Jesus of Nazareth. Many people accept this as gospel as to the creation of man and the proliferation of the human race. The Bible does not designate how many years ago Adam and Eve were created. It only states "In the beginning..." Those who subscribe to this theory are called Creationists.

On the other hand, Evolutionists have a completely different narrative as to the appearance of mankind. According to the Evolutionists, mankind underwent a long series of changes before becoming the homo sapiens we are today. Millions of years ago, they theorize, there was a Primordial Soup that they define as a solution rich in organic compounds in the primitive oceans or bays of the earth from which life is hypothesized to have originated. Those organic compounds were made up of amino acids that are the building blocks of proteins that would evolve into atoms and over time into cells. They probably rained out of the sky, part of the hydrologic cycle. These cells combined to eventually form larger and more complex organisms. These larger organisms grew both lungs and gills. Food was obtained on land, then the organisms retreated back in the water for protection from would-be predators. In short, your earliest ancestors probably crawled out of a swamp!

One fact Creationists and Evolutionists can agree on is that no matter the origin of mankind the Earth sits in the perfect orbit to sustain life as we know it. If the Earth's orbit was a million miles closer to Venus, we would be incinerated; if we were a million miles closer to Mars we would freeze to death. Did God place Earth in the right spot or was it the law of chance at work? You make the call.

The Age of Dinosaurs

For millions of years before man would exert hegemony over the earth, the apex predators, aka dinosaurs, ruled the natural world. With developing earth lush with food sources, these amphibians that crawled out of the swamp grew into mobile behemoths eating everything in sight and not allowing the humanoid population to proliferate quickly, to say the least. The reign of the dinosaur lasted for eons but eventually otherworldly and geologic forces brought about their demise. Paleontologists posit that about 66 million years ago a gigantic asteroid impacted the Yucatan Peninsula in Mexico. Under the Yucatan is an impact crater (Chicxulub Crater), where the asteroid hit. What was once a warm, lush area where dinosaurs roamed unabated was quickly turned into a wasteland where 75%

of the species were wiped out, eliminating the food sources and breeding grounds of the former apex predators. Worse than that, the entire continent if not the Earth itself was plunged into an instant ice age. Virtually overnight an entire species was wiped out, but other organisms survived.

Mammals were able to adapt to increased radiation levels. New species began to appear at the end of the ice age. Those species included bats, whales, horses, and especially primates. The fact that these new species sprung to life and have been with us ever since is supported by Charles Darwin's treatise on the theory of evolution called Origin of the Species that involves adaptation to changing environments with the end result of the "survival of the fittest." In short, adapt or die!

Evolution of Man

It is an accepted premise in the scientific world that man was associated with the ape—the primate that was able to adapt to a new post ice-age world. Look at the physical similarities. Both have stereoscopic (rotational) vision and both have the ability to walk in an erect manner. Want more proof? Hold your arms out straight and look at your fingers. They naturally hang downward. This is an evolutionary reminder that your primate ancestors once lived high up in trees, swinging from tree to tree perhaps to elude predators. Adapt or die! The major difference between man and the ape, not counting speech, is that man developed a thumb, which allowed him to build objects and modify his environment. This gave mankind a huge evolutionary advantage over the primates.

Many eons ago men and primates bifurcated (split) into two distinct species. New evidence shows an association between the ancestors of man and ape, but over time the two became less like each other.

So how do we describe the first humanoids? Mankind has gone through many stages of evolution to become what he is today, again adapting to his environment. The first of our type was probably much bigger and stronger, having to fight off predators while living in a hostile environment. They also did not walk in a totally erect upright manner like we do today. Paleontologists would call them savages—cavemen if you will. With their thumbs, they were able to fashion clubs and spears that they needed for protection, and as they became nomadic hunters and gatherers they used them to subdue beasts for food. They certainly had no language skills and probably lived in bands (ten or fewer people). Anthropologists think that about 120,000 years ago the earliest bands roamed around the Nile River in Egypt. The discovery of fire probably advanced the savage to the next stage of evolution.

Anthropology (the study of man and his culture) would describe the next phase of evolution as the barbarian stage. Barbarians were not as large as savages and less hunched over. Barbarians had limited language skills not much beyond grunts and groans, though later those described as barbaric like Attila the Hun had developed some language skills. The barbarian cultures did probably stumble onto an advancement called horticulture, which was primitive farming without irrigation and fertilization. They figured out that the seeds of plants would regenerate if they were put back into the ground. The barbarians were the first to breed and herd animals for food. The bones were made into utensils. The Great Plains Indians of the United States in the 1800s used the buffalo in the same manner. Barbarians dwelled in small villages where there was strength in numbers. Barbarians were aggressive and warlike and the village was dominated by the strongest man or men. Later as they roamed and conquered other bands, small "kingdoms" came into being.

A number of factors evolved the barbarian culture into what I will call the age of modern man. Advanced agriculture freed up large blocks of time to do other things. Before agriculture, finding food to survive was a 24/7/365 day mission. One of the greatest inventions ever, the wheel, was invented in Sumeria (Middle East) about 3500 B. C. This allowed populations to be mobile and as a result "cities" sprung to life. These cities needed order, so centralized governments had to be set up. Communication skills increased greatly now with alphabets that led to written and spoken languages. The first businesses and industries were born during this period.

There is a final factor that hastened the development of man, the domestication of dogs that probably began as early as 30,000 years ago but continued into the new agricultural societies. There was a bifurcation of grey wolves and dogs into two species. The dogs looked to men for protection from larger predators, then helped men to slay those predators. This union of dog and man led to increased stability and prosperity of the now thriving and less threatened villages. Notice the difference in how a dog generally reacts to a human as opposed to another dog. The dog will generally wag his tail and smile at human beings but will sometimes growl with a rigid tail at the sight of another dog. Do you know why? In their DNA they still have a recessive gene that sees another dog as competition for food the way it was before they befriended man and were domesticated. Much like your hanging fingers, dogs have an ancient connection to their ancestors.

CHAPTER 2
Cradles of Civilization

A CRADLE OF CIVILIZATION IS A LOCATION where civilization is understood to have originated. A cradle of civilization is the progression of society to agriculture, industry, invention, and advanced communication skills. There were several such cradles, but anthropologists and archaeologists indicate that Africa was the first area from which humans migrated to other areas. This migration probably occurred between 50-75,000 years ago. From oldest to youngest, the cradles of Civilization are as follows:

1. Mesopotamia (including Egypt and the Fertile Crescent)
2. China
3. India
4. Mesoamerica (Mexico and Central America)

Mesoamerica developed independently from the other three, as did the aboriginal tribes of Australia that trace back as far as the African emigrants. Mesopotamia was located in Western Asia or the Middle East, if you will, between the Tigris and Euphrates

Rivers and encompassing the countries of Iraq, Syria, Turkey, and Kuwait, also known as the Fertile Crescent because of its shape and the ability of the land to be used for agriculture. The Egyptian culture is the oldest culture in the world, predating China by almost one thousand years. Much of what we know about ancient Egypt was deciphered by archaeologists, who were able to decode the hieroglyphics (picture alphabet) that were prominent in caves and near the tombs of the Egyptian Pharaohs. The Egyptians believed in reincarnation and included a Pharaoh's possessions in the tomb for his use when he was reborn. The huge pyramids that are an architectural wonder were built specifically to be tombs for the Pharaohs! One crop that is grown and used prominently in the U.S. today had its origin in Egypt—cotton. As previously noted, the first written language, cuneiform, began in Sumeria. Most of their written records had to do with business transactions. Other inventions of this culture were the wheel, chariot, gunpowder, sailboat, the plow, the concept of time, astronomy, astrology, mapping (cartography), mathematics, urbanization, and glass. It is amazing to me that all these advances were discovered thousands of years before the birth of Christ!

The Chinese cradle of civilization is about a thousand years younger than the Fertile Crescent. The earliest Chinese developed near the Yellow River, which is the English name. The Chinese refer to the river as the "mother" river. Similar to Egypt, the Chinese had thousands of years of rule under family dynasties. That China is run by a virtual dictatorship today should come as no surprise. For a good part of their history, like their rival Japan, they were cut off from Western culture that left them far behind in technological development until the 20th century. However, the ancient Chinese culture contributed the following: silk clothing, tea production, kites, noodles, the wheelbarrow, porcelain, iron ore, the seed drill, natural gas drilling, and most importantly the first beer 9,000 years ago. I'll drink to that!

The Indian civilization, which thrived in the Indus Valley, yielded several contributions to modern culture. Perhaps the most important was the numbering system based on the concept of zero, which the entire world uses today. Indian cultures were the first to distill water and take the salt out of ocean water and create fresh drinking water. India is also credited with advancing speech, and in fact their language symbols along with Latin and Greek formed the basis of many European languages, including English. Sanskrit was the name given to the early Indian language. Other discoveries include yoga, buttons for clothing, cataract surgery (6th century), and prefab and movable home construction.

As you can see, many of the products, ideas, and technologies we utilize today in our global culture have their roots in antiquity. I would define antiquity as the period before the birth of Jesus Christ. Before I discuss the contributions of Greece and Rome, I think it would be wise to speak about cultural diffusion. Cultural diffusion comes from the study of anthropology and means the sharing of ideas, technologies, languages, etc. from person to person and from one nation to another. It should not take you long to see that many things we use in the United States today came from places far away and a long time ago. Keep this term in mind as we study Greco-Roman ancient history and identify many aspects of their cultures that we utilize today.

The Rosetta Stone

Known as the ultimate codebreaker, the Rosetta Stone is viewed as one of the most remarkable finds of the ancient world. It was discovered in Egypt in 1799. The top and middle sections of the stone are carved with hieroglyphics and demotic—a variation of the Egyptian text. The lower section is in Greek script, which ultimately acted as a codebreaker for the upper sections. A series of scholars were involved in the race to decipher the hieroglyphic code, but the breakthrough is credited to Jean Francois Champollion. He used the Greek portion of the text to reveal the secret language of the pharaohs.

CHAPTER 3

The Glory that was Greece

THE CLASSIC GREEK SOCIETY, which was the envy of the known world at the time originated in the eighth century before Christ and lasted until the first century before the birth of Jesus, was finally conquered by an envious Roman Empire that immediately culturally diffused many of their ideas. Before its own conquest, the Greek Empire expanded, aided by the conqueror Alexander the Great, who waged an undefeated campaign of war and conquest across Mesopotamia all the way to India.

Other conflicts both internal and external led to the weakening and eventual downfall of Greece. The Persians—today's Iranians—twice conquered Greece, but after the Battle of Thermopylae (made into the movie 300) were finally vanquished at the Battle of Platea. Later on, a civil war between Athens and Sparta, the two biggest city-states in Greece, laid the groundwork for the eventual Roman conquest. To make a long story short, Athens was the urban multicultural liberal state of Greece, located on the coastline. Sparta was the militaristic, more conservative, and less democratic province located inland. When Athens attempted to expand its influence throughout the remainder of Greece, it drew the ire of Sparta and thus the nearly thirty-year war (Peloponnesian War) was initiated with a resulting Spartan victory. Unfortunately, the golden age of Greece would be diminished as advances of culture and democracy came to an end in Greece. Therefore a weakened Greece would be no match for a growing Rome, which had its eyes on the entire Greek Empire, not just the country of Greece.

The glory of Greece actually involved two components; that of sound mind and body. Although the Athenians were more literate and the Spartans more physical, they both embraced the idea of body and mind development. Depictions of Greeks in Renaissance art and in Hollywood movies portray bodies that would be the envy of many.

The true glory of Greece is what they bequeathed to the generations following their demise. There are many, but I decided on a modified top ten list that covers advances in science, education, history, math, and government.

In the area of science, the Greeks invented the first water mill, which uses water power for the production of lumber, paper, and textiles. They invented the first odometer used to calculate mileage traveled. They also devised a primitive alarm clock (don't you hate it!), Aristotle initiated Zoology, the science of animal classification. Hippocrates discovered the cause and effect of germs and disease and was awarded the moniker "Father of Medicine." He believed in the confidentiality of his patients with the result that today's doctors adhere to the "Hippocratic Oath" as they become licensed. Greek astronomers were the first to put forth the theory of Heliocentrism—that the Earth revolved around the sun, later confirmed during the Renaissance. Previously men were told that the sun revolved around the Earth, but Heliocentrism proved that man was not that divine or powerful. Archimedes discovered the roots of geometry and invented pulleys and levers. He mused that if he had the capacity he would build a lever pulley system that could have pulled the continents back together.

In education, Socrates used the Socratic method of question and answer—still for my money the best way to teach a classroom. The Greeks were the first long-distance runners, sometimes warning of foreign invasion. Thus the marathon became part of the annual Olympic Games held in the city of Athens.

In the realm of government, the Greeks gave birth to the concept of democracy originating in the city-state of Athens. The Greeks practiced a form of democracy known as pure or direct democracy in small villages where the people voted directly on the laws. Due to populations today in the millions, we use representative or indirect democracy, where representatives make laws with the approval of the voters. Draco Codified the first laws in Greece (the Draconian Code). The disclaimer was that these laws were too harsh and put people to death for rather minor infractions. Similar to British law centuries later, when debtors were thrown into jail for small debts and therefore not given the ability to get out of jail. It is thought that Draco based his code on the Babylonian king Hammurabi who put forth the Hammurabian Code of Laws in Mesopotamia many years before Draco in Greece. The most famous tenet of the Hammurabian Code was equal but brutal justice. "An eye for an eye." Thieves had their hands cut off. If you killed someone's son, your son would be put to death. Many Greeks began to ask for the repeal of the Draconian Code, and in the 6th century B.C. Solon the Lawgiver overhauled the code, which led to more lenient punishments and paved the road for the liberal democracy that would take root in Athens. The last item on my top ten list is the introduction of the Greek Alphabet, which was a forerunner of the Roman Alphabet we employ today in English. You may have encountered the Greek alphabet if you were anywhere near a fraternity initiation in college. One of the Herculean tasks of a fraternity pledge in those days was to recite the Greek Alphabet three times before a lighted match would burn you.

One final topic before we leave Greece was the influence of Greek mythology. Though the Greeks made more headway in science than any other culture, they still looked for ways to make sense of their world and provide answers for vexing questions. One of their answers was to create a hierarchy of Gods that were able to manipulate human beings like puppets. A belief in many Gods is known as polytheism. Polytheism was present in many non-modern cultures, including Rome that succeeded Greece. The Gods were made to look like man and woman but were much larger and could transform themselves into other life forms to carry out their plans that often involved revenge against their humans for alleged slights. The Greeks invented an entire Zodiac chart of astrology based on the alignment of the stars and constellations to help them understand and predict the Gods' potential machinations against them. Today most people know what their astrological "sign" is and what attributes it allots to you. Perhaps some of the information does ring true for you.

Mythology is always based on some elements of truth, and I would encourage anyone to read a book on Greek mythology. Here are some examples used commonly in our culture today derived from Greece. You have probably read Aesop's parable about the tortoise and the hare and the warning affixed to the Trojan Horse. How about the danger of opening Pandora's Box and the fatal flaw of Achilles' Heel? Lastly, two gigantic U.S. companies employ Greek names. Nike is named for the Greek Goddess of victory, and Amazon is the name given to a mythical race of powerful female warriors.

CHAPTER 4

The Grandeur that was Rome

THERE IS MORE OF A WRITTEN RECORD of Roman history than Greek history. This is because the Romans admired the systemic organization of events recorded by the Greek historian Herodotus, who chronicled the wars between Greece and Persia in great detail. Cicero, a famous Roman avatar, in first-century Rome was so impressed that he gave the title "Father of History" to Herodotus, who had lived about 500 years before the Roman Empire. Before written history, oral storytelling was the way traditional knowledge was passed along to succeeding generations. This is why I refer to history as incomplete, as many events were not recorded and therefore could not be confirmed. Paleontology and archaeology have helped to fill in the gaps of knowledge, but a good part of the earth's history is unknown. Dust in the wind, a lyric from an old song...

According to both legend and written history, the Roman Empire began in 753 BC and ended in 476 AD. Legend has it that two brothers named Romulus and Remus got into an argument over who would be the king of the nascent Roman kingdom. Romulus slew Remus and "Rome" was built on the seven hills overlooking the Tiber River. Homage to the empire can be seen in the 1960's TV series Star Trek, where the Romulans dressed in traditional garb became periodic enemies of Captain Kirk and his crew. The empire went through many changes in government from dictatorships to a Republic and back and forth before being overrun by combined barbarian enemy forces in 476 AD.

The grandeur of Rome has to do with the size of its empire and the immense architectural and construction projects. The old saying "all roads lead to Rome" is not without merit. The Romans amassed the second-largest empire in the world, only surpassed centuries later by the British Empire that had the advantage of newer technology and awareness that there was no shortage of places to conquer. The Roman Empire took over the lands once controlled by Greece, then marched and sailed west into continental Europe as far as the British Isles. The Romans plundered these lands of all their resources and returned to Rome with the booty. All of this wealth was put to use. Over a million miles of modern concrete roads were built where possible with mile markers. The Roman engineers built huge aqueducts to transport fresh water into the city, then built large sewers to get rid of the dirty water. Sanitation and safety from plagues were high on their list of priorities.

Roman engineers developed the concept of grid cities with intersecting streets and avenues much like any other major city in the United States or elsewhere. Rome was famous for its arches that spanned streets and framed the homes of the rich patrician class of people in Roman society. The archway that spans the Mississippi River near St. Louis is an ancestor of Roman architecture. Like the Greeks, the Romans built huge and beautiful columns for their government buildings and entertainment centers. In the U.S. look at our government buildings in Washington D.C. or the many beautiful college campuses that employ columns and arches. This may be cultural diffusion to the highest degree. Because of the great wealth of Rome and without any fear of foreign invasion, the population of Rome exploded especially during the era known as Pax Romana (Roman Peace) where the Roman legions (armies) were not at war and people of many nationalities got along well with little civil strife.

Why did this gargantuan, seemingly unchallenged and indestructible empire crash and burn? Permit me to begin the answer with an analogy. As I grew older and became a homeowner, I became somewhat of a gardener, a gene that was nurtured by my maternal grandmother. Anyway, I developed a green thumb when it came to the growth of plants and flowers but by the fall, many plants actually became too big and began to keel over. They were victims of their own success, one of my favorite catchphrases.

The growing population of Rome stressed the government for more services. The military was expensive to maintain and costs kept escalating. The empire needed to be guarded and maintained but with no new lands to plunder, money was in short supply. Government officials became corrupt and there was instability in government as Rome went back and forth between a Republic and a Dictatorship. There was also a loss of traditional values. Like Greece, Rome was a pagan culture believing in polytheism and the Romans had a similar hierarchy of Gods. However, Christianity was taking root in Rome, and their belief in monotheism (one God) challenged the traditions of polytheism. Government officials saw the threat of Christianity, so they staged spectacles in the colosseum to distract and entertain a growing and restless population by feeding Christians to the lions or having untrained Christians fight trained gladiators, which led to the slaughter of thousands. This plan backfired as more of the population rebelled against Christian genocide and became converts themselves. A good portion of Rome became lazy and paid off others to do their dirty work, and unfortunately this attitude seeped into the government and the military that were supposed to be watching out for the welfare of Rome.

One of the most important dates in world history is 476 AD, as the entire advance in civilization came to a grinding halt. Attila the Hun had threatened Rome for many years. Known as the Scourge of God by the Catholic church, he died before the fall of Rome. However, combined Teutonic (German) armies under the leadership of Odoacer were able to take control of the Roman legions in that fateful year. The Romans had tried to negotiate for control of some of their territories but were unsuccessful, thus the curtain came down on the Roman Empire. The Fall of Rome heralded the beginning of the Middle or Dark Ages, where civilization took a large step backwards. As George Harrison of The Beatles sang on his eponymous solo album "All things must pass."

Before I leave the Roman Empire behind, I want to describe some contributions outside of architecture and engineering.

While on the battlefield, Roman surgeons were the first to use antiseptics (hot water) and surgical tools to prevent injuries that would have led to death. The Romans invented the twelve-month Julian calendar, then the Gregorian calendar that included the leap year. Roman numerals were their numbering system, still used throughout the world today and a basis for our numeric system. The Romans were the first to employ the large dissemination of written material in newspapers. There are many newspapers that use the word tribune in their title. In Rome, the tribune was a public official elected by the common classes (plebeians) to look out for their interests.

During the Republic years, Roman law was codified into the Twelve Tables. These were mostly civil laws that protected the citizens and gave them certain rights. Our Bill of Rights owes some of its formation to Roman law as does the concept of a Republican form of government. In a Republic, there are branches that keep each other in check and prevent democracy from becoming totalitarian. The Roman Senate consisted of the lawgivers but also chose the consuls who were the executives in charge of enforcing the laws, similar to our president and vice president. Like Greece before it, Rome has a lot more to its history, contributions, and influence, but again my goal is to connect the dots leading to the formation of the U.S. and its history, which will be the main focus of this undertaking.

The Calendar

I would be remiss if I did not include the fact that the names of the months in our calendar are all derived from Latin. Latin was the language of ancient Rome and is the basis of much of the English language today.

January is named for the Roman God Janus, protector of Gates and doorways. Janus is depicted with two faces, one looking into the past, the other into the future. In our society, if a person is called two-faced he/she is not to be trusted to tell the truth.

February comes from the Latin word februa, which means"to cleanse." The month was named after the Roman Februalia, which was a month-long festival of purification and atonement.

March was named for the Roman god of war, Mars. This was the time of the year to resume military campaigns that had been interrupted by winter.

April derives from the Latin word Aperio means "to open (buds)," because plants begin to grow during this month.

May is named for the Roman goddess Maia, who oversaw the growth of the plants. May also derives from the Latin word maiores, "Elders," who were celebrated during this month.

June is named for the Roman goddess Juno, patroness of marriage and the well-being of women. June also derives from the Latin word juvenis, "young people." Perhaps this is why June is a very popular month for weddings.

July is named to honor Roman dictator Julius Caesar (100 BC - 44 BC). In 46 BC, Caesar made one of his greatest contributions to history, with the help of Sosigenes. He developed the Julian calendar, the precursor of the Gregorian calendar that we use today.

August is named to honor the first Roman Emperor Augustus Caesar. He was the grandnephew of Julius Caesar. He was born in 63 BC and died in 14 AD. The birth of Jesus Christ occurred during his reign.

September is derived from the Latin word septem, "seven." It had been the seventh month of the early Roman Calendar.

October derives from the Latin word octo, "eight," because this had been the eighth month of the early Roman calendar.

November derives from the Latin novem, "9," because this had been the ninth month of the early Roman Calendar.

December derives from the Latin decem, "10," because this had been the 10th month of the early Roman Calendar.

CHAPTER 5

The Medieval Ages

(500 AD - 1400 AD)

THE MEDIEVAL AGES ARE ALSO KNOWN as the Middle Ages and in the early years the Dark Ages. As the barbarians overran Rome and the entire European continent, the civilized people had to devise a system that would allow them to survive the barbarian hordes, who were only interested in domination, plunder, and murder. The system they designed to survive the barbarians and eventually thrive was called feudalism.

Feudalism had its roots in the old Roman manorial system, where the wealthy Roman landowners gave protection to lower class workers in return for their labor in the manner that often involved lots of agricultural work and in early Gaul (France), where Kings gave land to others in return for their loyalty and service.

The Feudal social system was very structured. The following is a hierarchy of the typical manor.

1. King
2. Lords
3. Vassals
4. Serfs

The King would decree orders to his lords, who in turn would instruct the vassal class, and who in turn would grant most of the work to the serfs, who were "bound to the soil" and had no chance to move up in social class. Lords and vassals could move up in class and the lords sometimes assassinated the king to take control. However, they in turn were subject to the same plots, so many of the kingships were short-lived. European history shows the instability of the various European kingdoms, which were constantly plotting against each other looking to accrue more land and power. These European wars would consume both Europe and the Americas up to and including the World Wars of the 20th century.

If a king did survive to old age and had sons, the oldest son became the next king. This is called primogeniture.

Manorial life was set up in a similar way throughout Europe. The castle was the centerpiece of the manor, often built with high walls to repel attacks. Surrounding the castle was a moat filled with water and a drawbridge across the moat. The drawbridge was pulled up when attack was imminent so the moat provided an extra layer of safety. I remember early cartoons on TV in the 1960's showing alligators in the moat. Of course, the European climate was much too cold for alligators to survive. Outside the manor was the village where tools and other products were created. Later on, as times got safer the villages became cities that would trade with one another. Beyond the village were the fields where the serfs did all the farming. There were scouts in the woods who would warn of invaders, at which time everyone would rush into the castle and the drawbridge would be cranked up. The knights of the vassal classes were the actual fighters and adhered to a code of chivalry looking after anyone in distress. Continued bravery could lead a knight into nobility of lord class. Think of the legendary King Arthur of Britain and the knights of the Round Table. They sat at a round table to denote equality of all the knights who served King Arthur.

Along with Feudalism, the power of the Catholic Church helped the people of Europe to survive the Dark Ages. People needed a reason to live and that was provided by their faith in God, who promised them heaven if they led a good God-fearing life. The alternate was going to Hell, which was portrayed as an eternal torture chamber of damnation. If you get the chance, view the old cartoons that show the underworld as a glowing-red cave with sinners there being prodded by a pointy-eared devil with a tail and his pitchfork. They did not have cartoons in the middle ages, but sermons by preachers painted a similar scenario.

The Church did its best to unify Europe with the pope technically having the final authority over any king despite the size of his kingdom. The Church amassed a great amount of land, money, and power throughout Europe. Until clearly defined countries emerged and began to move away from church rule, theocracy (government control by one religion) was the law of Europe. The Catholic Church became harsh and corrupt. Heretics (non-believers) were chased out of Europe or sometimes put to death. Excommunication (removal) from the church was the fate of non-complying kings as well as the other subjects.

Hell was your destiny if you were booted out of the Church. But later as the church expanded, it needed money so indulgences were sold where sinners could buy their way into heaven. That the culture of Greece and Rome was saved was because of the monks in the church. For many monks, it was their sole purpose on earth to translate the knowledge saved from Greece and Rome into the native languages of each country in Europe. It was a painstaking process writing in quill pen ink day after day and night after night by candlelight. Much of their work became organized into what was known as the <u>Illuminated Manuscripts</u>, written text supplemented by forms of adornment along the borders of the paper. Had it not been for the monastic scribes, most of the literature and knowledge of the Greco-Roman Empires would have been lost forever. We are forever in their debt!

The union that prevented Europe from falling into the hands of the barbarians was the formation of the Holy Roman Empire around the year 800 AD under King Charlemagne (Charles the Great). With the blessing of the pope, Charlemagne formed alliances with many manors throughout western Europe, and together they were able to keep the barbarians at bay. Under his reign, the survival of Christianity was assured and he became known to many as the "Father of Europe." As an esteemed leader of the people and military expert, he later became an inspiration for two dictators who had dreams of conquering and unifying Europe—Napoleon and Hitler.

The Crusades (1095 - 1291) were a series of Holy Wars fought for control of the Holy Land in the Middle East, located near the country of Israel today. The wars were fought between the European Christians and the forces of Islam. The Holy Land is the birthplace of three major religions—Islam, Judaism, and Christianity—and has been fought over for 5,000 years, and the conflict continues today. The Pope had gotten reports that Christians on pilgrimage to the shrine of Jesus had been attacked and killed by Muslims who wanted the land for themselves and not to be shared with the Christian infidels (non-believers). The Pope ordered a crusade to the Holy Land to wrest control away from the Moslems. By the way, the term crusades derive from the Latin "crux," which is why the Crusaders had the red cross on their shields. There was no winner in these wars, and the Pope began to give up after the Children's Crusade, where boys were being sent to battle. In the year 1291, the Crusades were history.

There was a positive result of the Crusades—cultural diffusion and knowledge of a new world beyond Europe. The Crusaders returned with wine, olive, oil, silk textiles, and citrus fruits. Oranges and limes would later be used in the Age of Exploration to prevent diseases, such as scurvy, on long ocean expeditions. In regards to sailing, new techniques of shipbuilding returned with the Crusaders along with the astrolabe, a device that allowed sailing at night by using the stars and constellations.

One of the biggest game-changers in the course of history had to be the early explorations of Marco Polo (1254 - 1324). Polo was an Italian from Venice who journeyed on foot across the deserts of the Middle East all the way to Cathay (China). Wanting to learn about the Occidental (Eastern) world, he lived in the court of Kublai Khan, king of the Mongols. The Mongols were feared throughout Europe over the ages. The Mongolian hordes used horses to over-run and plunder civilizations all the way from Poland to China. Polo was a curiosity to Khan, who ordinarily would have beheaded a European with a Cossack sword. Instead, the two bonded and learned of each other's cultures with the result of Polo living in China for seventeen years.

When Polo returned to Italy, it was by sea. In his book, The Description of the World, Polo drew the first map between China and the Far East and plotted the first sea route between China and Europe. Other items Polo took back to Italy included the first noodles which the Italians converted to pasta, coal for fuel, glass lenses, silk, spices, and the concept of paper money that made commerce between people, companies, and nations a lot easier. Is it any wonder that Polo inspired Columbus and the entire Age of Exploration?

The Crusades and the exploits of Marco Polo were the springboard for upcoming changes throughout Europe. People began to get curious about life beyond the manor and the treasures of other worlds. Polo's influence could also be seen in the first trading alliance in Europe called the Hanseatic League centered in Germany and consisting of Western Europe nations who did not want the Italians to have all the wealth of trade from the Middle East and beyond.

Europe was on the brink of once again advancing civilization, but they had to escape one peril that threatened their very existence—the Bubonic Plague (Black Death) 1347-1350 AD. Most likely transferred to rats from fleas on the merchant ships coming into Europe, it was estimated to have killed 30% of the continent's population, 20,00,000 or more. Throughout Eurasia, many millions more succumbed, and it took nearly 200 years to replenish the population of that part of the world. Eurasia is an archaic term but generally refers to the lands of Eastern and Northern Europe that border Russia. The plague was exacerbated by two additional factors of health and hygiene. Europeans did not bathe routinely, which led to a pervading stench of castle life and transfer of body lice and other pathogens. Secondly, sanitation systems were not yet set up, so in growing cities like London the Bubonic Plague was spread by raw sewage in the streets that stunk and infected the groundwater. Eventually, the plague ran its course. I also worry that the end of life as we know it will be because of some microbiological pathogen much like what killed the Martians in the two famous TV movies "The War of the Worlds."

CHAPTER 6

The Renaissance

(1300 -1600 AD)

RENAISSANCE IS A WORD OF FRENCH ORIGIN meaning the rebirth of learning. It is often thought of as the time period bridging the gap between the middle ages and modern-day civilization. During the seeking of and application of knowledge, both classical (Greek and Roman) and newer knowledge gained from the Crusaders guided the growth of Europe through these ages and influenced world development to this very day. There are hundreds of books to be read about this time period, but again my focus will be to highlight some of the accomplishments joining the past with what will be the future of human endeavor.

The Renaissance had its historical and philosophical roots in the country of Italy. There became a movement known as Humanism, which meant embracing the achievements of humanity both past and present in the fields of education, artwork, literature, and science. However, a cultural civil war was brewing between the Humanists, who believed in the supremacy of man and his accomplishments, versus the traditionalists, who believed in a sacred world where theocracy and church dogma should be in control.

Humanism had its roots in Italy, the country closest to Asia and the first to develop an advanced culture due to closer proximity to Asian trade. The stored knowledge of Antiquity mostly resided in Rome, now to be utilized again. The Medici Dynasty—generations of wealthy bankers from Florence, Italy were the financiers of the Renaissance movement and wielded great power, persuading the Catholic Church to nominate a series of Popes who would maintain the Medici dominance in Italy.

One of the great inventions that helped to spread the sides of both traditional (sacred) culture and secular (everyday) culture was the invention of the printing press that used movable type by Johann Gutenberg in 1450. The Bible was a method for those in the Church to maintain control, while the dissemination of information from newspapers was of use to the Humanists. The Catholic Church did not take well to any opposition to its authority and set up the Roman Inquisition—the enforcement arm of the Church. Heretics (non - believers) like the Jews were often put to death, leading to their migration to the Middle East. Fortunately for Gutenberg, he resided in Germany and was also beyond the jurisdiction of the Roman Inquisition.

Germany, a loose association of many small states and not unified as a country until much later, nevertheless was the birthplace of the Protestant Reformation, one of the great social changes of the Renaissance. The old Teutonic barbarian tribes had become more civilized and had embraced the concept of one God (monotheism). They were through war and tradition opposed to the Roman Catholic Church yet they believed in the teachings of Jesus.

Martin Luther began a protest movement in the German states and wrote up a series of religious complaints against the church. He posted these on the door of the Wittenberg Church in the province of Saxony, and they became famous in history as the Ninety-Five Theses, which listed the abuses of the Catholic Church. Luther did not believe in the idea of indulgences—buying one's way into heaven—nor did he believe in the tithe, which was a ten percent tax of your wealth that was to be mandated to pay to the Church. He also had negative feelings about the primacy of the Pope and the complicated and unnecessary bureaucratic structure of the Church with any number of Saints who could be prayed to in times of need, similar to the polytheism of Greek and Roman times.

Luther thought that people should and could pray directly to God, as the Bible said it should be. Needless to say, Luther and all his followers were excommunicated from the Church. Today there are many Protestants denominations around the world that do not utilize one central leader. The good news is both Catholics and Protestants believe in Christ and Christianity, but the Catholic Church has more strictures to follow with the resulting long-time sanction of Catholic Guilt if they get too far out of line. There is no collective guilt throughout the world of Protestantism and the strictures and ceremonies are simpler. The bad news is that this bifurcation of the Christians in the 1500s led to many religious wars throughout Europe and had a direct influence on the development of the United States.

I want to spend time talking about the great minds of the Renaissance, who changed the world forever with their inventions, discoveries, and creativity. Again this will be a short, albeit important list.

Perhaps the greatest mind of all time belonged to a man who had more original thoughts in more fields than anyone: the original Renaissance Man, Leonardo Da Vinci. The only other person of such genius from a more recent time that I can compare him to is

Thomas Edison, who was granted over 1,000 patents for original inventions. Da Vinci is most closely associated with the world of art and his Mona Lisa still is the gold standard for artwork. His Last Supper is almost as famous yet he has no more than about a dozen more paintings. Da Vinci is also known as the Father of Paleontology—the study of fossilization of ancient species. I have utilized some Paleontology as you might have noticed in the writing of this book. Da Vinci was a man of few words. Fortunately, most of his ideas were drawn up, so we have a record of what he devised. Da Vinci had renderings of the first bicycle, helicopter, and airplane, which he devised based on the physiology and flying ability of the common bat. His ideas on movable type no doubt were the inspiration for Gutenberg's printing press. His original drawings also included an adding machine. He was the first to devise a double hull for ships and mused about the use of solar power as an energy source. It would take hundreds of years for the creation of the list delineated, but his genius was the inspiration.

Another genius of the period was the artist and sculptor Michelangelo, also from Italy. His greatest achievement was the upside-down painting of the Sistine Chapel in Rome depicting the creation of Adam and the Earth in a series of events. He also sculpted the statue of David, the biblical hero who slew Goliath along with the Pieta, which shows the slain body of Jesus lying in the lap of the Mother Mary. The church applauded the creations of both Da Vinci and Michelangelo, as these accomplishments allowed the church to help maintain its power against a rising tide of secularism. The church especially liked the publication of Dante's "Inferno" that described in great detail the nine levels of hell that sinners would encounter if they were not allowed entry to heaven. For example, at the ninth or worst level was Judas, who betrayed Jesus. His punishment? His head in the mouth of Satan for eternity being shredded along with his back being torn to pieces by the claws of Satan. No doubt this fear kept a lot of people in line and prolonged the reign of the church as the main power broker in some parts of Europe.

If Bob Dylan, poet laureate of our modern culture, was alive at that time, he might have noted as he did in an early album "the times they are a-changin." Nicholas Copernicus, in all likelihood independently of Aristarchus from ancient Greece, posited that the sun was the center of the universe and not the earth. Because he lived in Poland and was out of reach of the Roman Inquisition, he and his heliocentric theory were not quashed. However Galileo, an Italian often referred to as the Father of modern science, was not that fortunate. He is credited with the invention of the telescope although the first patent was issued to a Dutch inventor in 1608 a year before Galileo actually built the first working telescope. His observations refuted the geocentric theory espoused by the church that the Earth was the center of the universe. For all his fame and notoriety—inventing the first thermometer and providing the scientific method—he was condemned as a heretic against the church, but his great fame spared him death and he was put under house arrest for the rest of his life, where he continued to write scientific journals until his demise.

The Age of Exploration had its roots in the scientific revolution of Da Vinci, Copernicus and Galileo along with contributions from Asian cultures.

CHAPTER 7

The Age of Exploration

THE AGE OF EXPLORATION WAS ALSO an outgrowth of the Crusades and would lead to the discovery of all the continents, plus a myriad of wars both in continental Europe and the two World Wars of the twentieth century. There were many European nations that had eyes on possessing land overseas. These countries included Italy, Spain, Portugal, The Netherlands, and most importantly, the two biggest rivals, England and France. To begin with, what were the motivations for exploration? There are many but most of them involve curiosity, adventure, fame, wealth, and power. Most of the Europeans had an inkling that there was new wealth to be had from the Orient (China, India and Japan). Obviously, whoever got to these places first would accumulate wealth and power before the arrival of other competitors. I think the best way to discuss this phase of the Renaissance is to create a list of the most important explorers and their contributions.

Name	Year	Country	Land Claimed / Contribution
Leif Erikson	1000	Scandinavia	Newfoundland (Vinland)
Marco Polo	1300	Italy	Discovered Chinese Culture
Prince Henry	1400's	Portugal	Ship Captain's School
Columbus	1492	Spain	New World Discoverer
Vasco da Gama	1492	Portugal	The first all-water route to india
John Cabot	1497	England	Claims North America (East Coast)
Amerigo Vespucci	1501	Italy	First cartographer of New World
Ponce de Leon	1513	Spain	Florida
Vasco de Balboa	1513	Spain	Pacific Ocean
Cortes	1519	Spain	Conquers Mexico
Magellan	1519-1522	Portugal	Circumnavigates world
Verrazzano	1524	France	Florida to Canada
Pizarro	1533	Spain	Conquers Peru
Cartier	1535	France	St. Lawrence River

De Soto	1542	Spain	First to cross the Mississippi River
Coronado	1542	Spain	Claims SW U.S for Spain including the Grand Canyon
Cabrillo	1542	Spain	California
Hudson	1608	Netherlands	Eastern Canada, Hudson Bay, Hudson River
Champlain	1608	France	Father of New France, Great Lakes, Montreal, and Quebec
Marquette & Joliet	1673	France	Mississippi River to the Gulf of Mexico
LaSalle	1682	France	All lands west of the Mississippi River

As you can see from the chart, the first explorations occurred in the Middle Ages. The Vikings, a very warlike and polytheistic culture, led by Erik the Red plundered lands in the British Isles and set up kingdoms that would last for a couple of centuries. Being killed in battle was an honor, so the tradition of a Viking funeral was born. Slain warriors were laid out on wooden rafts and put to sea with candles surrounding the raft guiding the slain to their Valhalla (heaven). The Vikings referred to the North Sea and the Atlantic Ocean as the "Sea of Darkness." The North Sea separates Scandinavia from England and is the stormiest body of water in the world. The Vikings feared no man but feared the legendary sea serpents that would overturn ships, much like Melville's great white whale immortalized in <u>Moby Dick.</u> The son of Erik the Red, Lief Erickson eventually surmounted his fear and led the first successful voyage to the New World. He called it Vinland (Newfoundland, Canada). Archaeology tells us that the Vikings left behind artifacts (physical remains) of their life but no settlements. The fact that they were probably outnumbered by hostile natives gave them no permanence in North America, but they were the first of many European voyages to ensue.

Motivation, myth, and a lack of technology would account for the almost 500-year gap until Columbus next set foot in the New World. First of all, the curiosity about new worlds was outweighed by mythology. The world was seen as flat and the ocean full of monsters waiting to swallow up unsuspecting ships. If you ventured beyond the horizon, you simply would cease to exist.

Aided by new advances in navigation and shipbuilding technology, the way became a little clearer for Columbus and his contemporaries. Prince Henry the Navigator of Portugal was an early Portuguese explorer and opened up an academy to tutor future ship captains. Borrowing from Arabic nautical culture, Henry employed lateen (triangular) sails on caravel-type ships that could handle two of these sails at a time. Later on, bigger ships were added with three masts. These lateen sails allowed ships to sail into the wind and to continue by tacking, moving the sails left and right. This technology quickly spread throughout Europe.

Men needed physical strength as well as courage to sail the high seas in the time of Prince Henry the Navigator. The small ships had no cabins or bunks for the crew. When a sailor was not on duty, he snatched a few hours of sleep wherever he could. Without changing his clothes, he curled up on a coil of rope or in an out-of-the-way corner of the deck. In cold or rainy weather, he crawled under a bit of canvas.

One hot meal a day was about all the man could hope for. All cooking was done on deck over an open fire. The men built the fire on a bed of sand or earth. In stormy weather, with rain falling and the vessel rolling and pitching, a fire was out of the question. Then the men ate dry biscuit, a bit of cheese, or a piece of salt fish, and called it a meal.

Columbus was born in Genoa, Italy and was inspired by the journals of his idol Marco Polo, who was also Italian. Columbus felt the world was round but could not offer 100% proof, as no one had ever undertaken such an expedition. His home country was already wealthy from its proximity to the Mediterranean Sea and its trade with the Middle East and China. Still, Columbus felt you could get to China quicker by going west if you could find such a route. To make a long story short, Columbus finally persuaded King Ferdinand and Queen Isabella of Spain to finance three ships to go west across the Atlantic Ocean in 1492. Spain was eager to compete for wealth with the nations of Portugal—whose people have a similar ancestry—and Italy, then the top trading (commercial) nation of Europe. In fact, to avoid war, Spain and Portugal agreed to the 1494 Treaty of Tordesillas that set up a line of demarcation. For example, in South America, the Eastern half would be Portuguese with the result that the Brazilians are of Portuguese descent while western countries like Peru and Chile are of Spanish descent. Both cultures intermarried with native tribes, a topic which will be covered later.

The colonization and Columbian Exchange were the two biggest feats of Columbus' four voyages to the Caribbean Sea until 1503. There has been much controversy as to Columbus' treatment of the natives, who he named Indios (Spanish for Indian) because Columbus thought he was in India based on the color of their skin. Based on my sources, Columbus was not genocidal, despite the revisionist history that seems to be inaccurately in vogue today. Yes, there was exploitation. There always is when colonies are being created, but not to the extent claimed by revisionists. After the voyages of Columbus, there was no appreciable decline in native populations on the Caribbean Islands! The other long-term feat besides the establishment of the first permanent colonies was the Columbian Exchange. The lists of plants and animals both moved between Europe and the West Indies are staggering. The negative is that European diseases killed more natives than gunfire. Natural immunities were eventually built by the native populations. In short, this was the birth of Global Culture. New Spain (North, Central, and South America) grew very quickly because the Spanish Conquistadors (conquerors) employed brutal means to establish and maintain colonies. Why the brutality? The Spanish had been well-versed in the ways of the Prince.

During the Italian Renaissance, writer Machiavelli wrote a very influential but fictional book titled <u>The Prince</u>. The Prince ruled over a mythical country similar to the way a dictator would by employing absolute power and "by employing any means necessary," which would be a guiding idea behind the founding, use, and exploration of colonies. Spain rationalized the brutality based on their goal of absolute power and conquest. When I taught exploration in class I used a phrase I was taught in class decades ago. The phrase was the "Three G's of exploration—for gold, for God, and for glory." Columbus noted that the Indios could be subdued easily by force if necessary and that they would be excellent candidates for conversion to the Roman Catholic Church. Other countries used God both as a reason and an excuse to colonize and "convert the natives." In fact, there were many priests and ministers who were noble, but the speculators used religion as a cover to loot and plunder. The third G, Glory, would be the power and strength of a country based on how much gold and other resources it could accumulate. Adam Smith wrote in <u>The Wealth of Nations</u> that colonies only exist to serve the mother country, so Machiavellian techniques of conquest and control were widely embraced.

The Spanish explorers found plenty of gold in Mexico and Peru but were still not satisfied. There was an American Indian legend of the Cibola—seven cities of Gold—supposedly ready for plunder in today's state of New Mexico. The reality was that the Cibolla turned out to be adobe "apartment" houses occupied by the Pueblo Indians that glowed like gold in the desert sun. Another myth, the El Dorado, a South American area of golden wealth, also proved to be false. Though not successful in finding these areas, the Spanish did create, in terms of area, the largest colonial empire.

The origin of the medical condition known as "Montezuma's Revenge" originated from the exploits of conquistador Cortes, who enslaved the Aztec tribe that had inhabited Mexico in the 1500s. Cortes set fire to his own ships to quell a mutiny and force his 600 soldiers along with fifteen horses and fifteen cannons into Mexico in order to take over Mexico. At first, the Aztecs were in awe of the Spanish as they thought man and horse were one "God" sent to them to replace their leader Montezuma as legend had predicted. One night that myth was dispelled as a native's arrow pierced the armor of a Spanish soldier, who began to bleed. Quickly war broke out between the two cultures. The actual war was short-lived, as Spanish war technology of guns and cannons quickly brought about the death of Montezuma and his ministers. The Aztec Nation was enslaved as gold-miners. Much gold was shipped out of the mines and loaded onto large Spanish Galleons that had arrived to take cargo (gold, etc) back to Spain. Cortes was reassigned elsewhere, but the Spanish maintained control of Mexico. Today when foreigners visit Mexico they are advised to avoid drinking tap water lest they contract diarrhea, "Montezuma's Revenge."

Other conquistadors who lived by the sword also died by it. Pizarro, who conquered the Incan Empire in Peru, was offered a room full of gold by the Incan chief Atahualpa if Pizarro would make some concessions on total control by the Spanish. As Tom Cruise said in the movie Jerry Maguire "show me the money." Atahualpa showed Pizarro the vault then shortly thereafter was summarily killed and the Incas enslaved then forced to become miners. Alas, Pizarro was killed by a rival Spaniard who had his eyes on the gold. In Florida, "Land of Flowers," Ponce de Leon killed many of the natives in his attempt to find the legendary Fountain of Youth. Ironically his life also came to a premature end as he was killed by a native Indian in Florida. It seems there is a God after all!

New Spain was the envy of the colonial world. Spain had claimed a large amount of land in the Americas but there was action aplenty elsewhere. Vasco de Gama, a graduate of Henry's ship captain's school, was the first to establish an all-water sea route to India, setting up an early form of multicultural international trade.

Perhaps the most heroic exploration of all time was that of Magellan, who launched a three-year voyage around the world that proved the Columbian theory that the world was not flat. Another graduate of Prince Henry's school, Magellan sailed west across the Atlantic Ocean with five ships and 270 men in 1519. Eventually, they found a water route at the tip of South America (the strait of Magellan) that could get them across Ocean Pacifico, so named by Balboa. One ship that mutinied and turned back was lost forever at sea. Magellan stopped in the Philippine Islands for supplies but was attacked by the natives, and according to some accounts cannibalized and his ship set on fire then sunk. Two more ships were deemed unseaworthy, so eventually one ship with about nineteen survivors returned to Portugal in 1522, the first expedition to circle the globe. Even though Magellan did not return alive, his name is credited as he was the captain. (In February 1960, the gray hull of the Triton, the largest and most powerful submarine every built, disappeared under the waters of the South Atlantic. Driven by two nuclear engines, she could travel perhaps two to three years without refueling. After eighty four days and 41,500 under-sea miles, she resurfaced having followed the exact route of Magellan's ship Victoria on her historic voyage of 1519.) The nation of Portugal became a seafaring commercial empire but not large enough to set up bigger empires like Spain, France, and England. A similar situation was the case of the Dutch from The Netherlands, who were also seafaring traders but not strong enough to defend large colonies.

Moving away from the friendly rivals of the Iberian Peninsula (Spain and Portugal) let's look at the unfriendly rivalry between England and France, who would ultimately slug it out for control of North America. There is a thousand-year history of good and bad feelings between the two coastal countries separated by the twenty-mile wide English Channel. (Today the two countries are connected by an underwater tunnel called the Chunnel.) The negative relations between the rival nations began in 1066 just before The First Crusade. William the Conqueror from Normandy, France sailed across the English Channel and defeated the Anglo-Saxon King Harald at the Battle of Hastings. It was the only successful land invasion of England and the British never forgot that fact even though they became allies with France in World War I and II.

There were Indian legends of a northwest passage—a shortcut by water across North America to the Far East. Henry Hudson was so sure he found it that he sacrificed his own life and those of his two sons when the crew of his ship, the Half Moon, mutinied and cast them into a small dory as Canada's Hudson Bay was turning to ice around the Half Moon. The crew returned to The Netherlands and did not face charges as it was decided Hudson was not rational and had lost his mind. French explorer Verrazzano, also seeking the Northwest Passage, explored the Hudson River in the area of NY Harbor where the bridge that honors him was built. I read a copy of his ship's log, and it noted a two-hour landing near Staten Island in NY Harbor. No sooner had Verrazzano planted the French flag then the Algonquin Indians came charging out of the woodlands and the French barely escaped! France claimed a larger interior empire in North America than the British, and many of the names in the midwest area are of French origin: St. Louis, Detroit, Chicago, along with the St. Lawrence River that borders Canada.

The one conclusion to be drawn from the chart of explorers was that war would be inevitable. With conflicting claims to the same lands and young nations flexing their muscles, the world was about to get a lot more turbulent. But who would dominate and why? The answer involves one of the great explorers of all time, and though he also circumnavigated the world he never claimed any land. Yet his adventures triggered a naval battle that would shift the balance of power in the geopolitical world.

Sir Francis Drake had a charmed life. A skillful, flamboyant, and self-assured captain, he caught the eye of Queen Elizabeth of England. Or was it the other way around? The Queen was very aware that Spain was the envy of all the other emerging European nations. She also had her eyes on the golden wealth Spain had been accumulating. Spain transported its booty back from The New World on galleons that were big, slow-moving container ships. Seeing that Drake had a good combination of daring and skill, she commissioned him to be an English sea dog (paid pirate) whose mission was to loot as many galleons as he could. The English were already making smaller mobile warships for just such a purpose. Drake gladly accepted his position and for a three-year period, 1587-1590, and robbed the Spanish fleet blind! As you might imagine, King Philip II of Spain was a little less than pleased. Besides losing gold, he saw a chance to unseat the Queen, who now led a Protestant country that opposed and resented the Catholic Church of Spain. The action taken by Phillip II will be a game-changer that equals the Fall of Rome. I did not ask my students to remember too many dates, but this one was special —1588.

Spain sent most of its fleet (armada) to exact revenge for the plunder of gold and put an end to the Protestant movement rising in England. Many factors caused this invasion to be a disaster for Spain. First of all, the late summer and early fall on both sides of the Atlantic is hurricane season. The Spanish Armada of 130 ships lost a good percentage of those ships to hurricane-like storms. Rather than retreat, Spain foolishly pressed the attack. The smaller British warships could outrun and outgun the Spanish galleons.

The result was thirty-five galleons sunk in addition to what the hurricanes destroyed.

The Spanish army never got to land for a long period of time, and when they did their heavy, clunky armor was no match for the enraged Brits charging out of the hills with axes, clubs, and bows and arrows. The result was 20,000 Spanish deaths and 6,000 British deaths. What was left of the Armada limped back to Spain. The wave of Protestantism would sweep through Europe.

It did not happen overnight, but in the next several decades the entire course of history would be changed, just like the Fall of Rome. Queen Elizabeth and her minions had discovered one gigantic truth. Control the seas, rule the world. England increased its navy and commercial shipping, which resulted in the creation of the British Empire, far out-pacing the ancient Roman Empire and birthing a phrase that would apply only to the British. "The sun never sets on the British Empire." England would explore the entire known world and forever leave its imprint on world culture. Spain would slowly lose its empire, and the Spanish American War (1898) was the official end of Spanish imperialism (colonization) in the world. In short, England becomes the big dog though they would first have to fend off France.

(According to British legend, Sir Francis Drake was involved in a game of lawn bowling near his home in England when worried officials warned him the Spanish fleet was approaching with the intent of conquering England. Showing complete disdain for the Spanish threat, he replied, "We have time to finish the game and beat the Spaniards, too," as he turned his back and sent the ball rolling down the green.)

Summing up the three-hundred-year period of the Renaissance, it is safe to conclude that the world came out of its shell. The growing civilized societies in Europe began to outnumber and neutralize the barbarian forces. Europe began to develop nation-states, and their secular power began to replace the grip of the Catholic Church over Europe. The Church's influence was also eroded by the rising tide of Protestantism as manifested by England usurping Spain as the major power in Europe. The roots of continental wars in Europe and later international conflicts can be seen in the conflicting claims over land in the New World. The "New World" terminology was sired by Amerigo Vespucci of Italy, who drew the first maps of all the land between Brazil and the West Indies and disproved the Columbian belief that Spain was at the outskirts of Asia. His map illustrated a new continent that was named in his honor, "Amerigo's Land" (America).

Two old adages apply to the Age of Exploration. One is still well-known today, the other probably not even taught any longer as it would be seen as racist by the revisionists. Before the advent of shipping, caravans traveled on foot across the Middle East, where banditry became too frequent with the murder a distinct possibility. Similarly, small ships crossing the Mediterranean Sea were subject to piracy, often by raiders based in Tripoli. This lawlessness necessitated a change, hence the adage, "necessity is the mother of invention," where larger caravel ships were constructed with lateen sails that were able to open up ocean trade routes and avoid disruption of trade on land and in smaller seas. The other adage has to do with the 3 G's of exploration - gold, glory, and God. Inherent in the latter was a rationale for colonization known as the "white man's burden." This concerned the conversion of polytheistic people to a more modern system of monotheism, the belief in the Christian God. Some argue it was a racist idea as most of those that were colonized tended to have darker skin and were bullied into submission by European invaders. Others argue that this conversion offered the advances of modern science and technology to indigenous people. I will let you decide for yourself, but the bottom line is that European culture was spread throughout the world but especially to America and its native peoples.

Who were the First Americans?

CHAPTER 8

The First Americans

PALEONTOLOGY AND ARCHAEOLOGY SUGGEST that the first people in North America probably arrived here between 15-30,000 years ago. They migrated to what we call Alaska across an extant structure known as the Bering Strait land bridge. Named for explorer Vitas Bering, the Bering Strait is a fifty-mile wide body of water separating Russia from Alaska. During the ice ages, Beringia was a frozen bridge that connected Siberia to Alaska and about 12,000 years ago as the climate warmed—global warming alert—the ocean levels rose and the bridge vanished underwater. {Take note, all you climate change alarmists. This pattern is not new and has occurred many times through the course of geologic history.} Editorial comment aside, the earliest Americans were nomadic hunters following their main food source, the caribou (reindeer), across Beringia into Alaska and eventually much further south as the caribou herds could sense a warmer climate quicker than their human pursuers. Over thousands of years, the hunters migrated south, followed by their ancestors who spread eastwards across the lower forty-eight states. Recent research shows that along the east coast near Delaware and Virginia the earliest Americans may have arrived by sea across the Atlantic as the exact same artifacts of fishing and warfare were found in the south of France and Spain as in Delaware and Virginia. Anthropologists note the similar physical traits between Asians and Alaskans. Both groups have the same skin color along with straight black hair and high cheekbones. Archaeologists point out that the artifacts found on both sides of the Pacific Ocean are mirror images of each other. Paleontologists note that caribou fossil remains also litter both sides of the Pacific. So how do we know which side is older? Radiocarbon dating provides the answer.

Scientists discovered that the element carbon exists in the bones of all living creatures and is virtually indestructible, not unlike today's plastic. Carbon decomposes at an exceedingly slow rate over the millennia and it decomposes at the same rate in bones. The conclusion was that the less carbon found in bones, the older they were compared to other newer bones that retained more carbon. In all cases, fossilization showed that the bones in Asia had less carbon than the same bones found in America, so the Beringia Theory was proven to scientists. Indians were the first Americans and eventually found themselves in North, Central, and South America. Let's see what some of the Native American cultures added to western civilization.

The Mayans of Central America at one time were the most populous of the Indian tribes. Extended droughts may have killed many Mayans, who were also enslaved by the Aztec Tribe of adjacent Mexico. They were a very advanced culture that built pyramids that rivaled those of Giza in Egypt and in both cases without modern machinery. They developed a calendar similar to the Gregorian Calendar in Rome that accounted for a leap year. They were the first ones to produce chocolate and discover and develop rubber. They molded it into a bouncy ball and played a primitive game of tennis or basketball, but being a primitive culture the losers of such games were often put to death!

Before their conquest by the Spanish, the Aztec tribe of Mexico flourished up until the 1500s. This was a very warlike and aggressive culture that scoured the area of Central America for slaves to be used for human sacrifices. Ra was their sun God and, according to the Aztec priests, kept the rains coming for agriculture as long as fresh blood was put into the earth. They were fearful of solar and lunar eclipses so there was much sacrifice assuring Ra would reappear. Watch the movie Apocalypto (2006) to get a good history lesson about the Aztecs and their Mayan captives. One cultural achievement of the Aztecs was hydroponics, where plants could grow without soil for a while exposing the roots to a liquid nutrient then transplanting them into the soil.

Before their enslavement by the Spanish, the Incas dominated western South America. Too far away to be targets of the Aztecs, the Incas built the largest culture in terms of square miles in South America. The center of the empire was located in Peru, and like the Aztecs and Mayans they were also polytheistic. The Incas were mostly farmers who thrived in a warm environment. Their only problem was that much of their area was mountainous, so they had to create a system of agriculture that worked. They did, and it was called terrace (steppe) farming. The Incas dug a series of steps or flat surfaces into the mountainside with the largest, flattest step at the bottom and upward steps smaller. Different crops were planted on each step. Irrigation was no issue as gravity took the rain downhill. Brilliant!

These three tribes are our neighbors to the south. Their ancestors who were the first Americans more than likely had their roots in Asia and as we saw earlier probably originated in the Chinese cradle of civilization near the Yellow (mother) River in China.

These first eight chapters highlighted the advances of ancient cultures and the Old World that led to the development of the New World that included North, Central and South America. It's time now to examine the origin and history of the United States.

CHAPTER 9

Colonial Life in America

IT IS MY OPINION THAT THIS IS THE MOST crucial chapter in this book, and this time period perhaps the most important in the short history of the United States of America. Educational psychologists certify that seventy percent of human intelligence is accumulated in the first four years of human existence. That same percentage or possibly move can apply to the social, economic, and political foundations of this nation that we call our home. My focus will be on the origin of the thirteen British colonies with some attention to colonies created by the French, Dutch, and Spanish.

There were four major reasons for the British colonization of America. The first reason was the fear that the large Spanish Empire (New Spain) would get larger and lead to world domination. The defeat of the Spanish Armada led to the first permanent British colony, Jamestown, Virginia (1607) followed by Plymouth, Massachusetts (1620). The second reason for the British coming to the New World was that England had the world's first over-population issue in the 1500s. There was a lack of farmland for a fast-growing population, so people were looking to move elsewhere.

The Netherlands was the first option, but the Dutch would not allow the British to practice their customs in the Netherlands. America became the next option. The third reason had to do with the issue of religious freedom. The Anglican Church of England had replaced the Catholic Church as the "official" church of England. Though a Protestant Church, it was much like the replaced Catholic Church with a rigid set of rules that many worshipers did not embrace, so they were more or less forced out of the Anglican Church. There was no ex-communication process. The final reason for colonization became the most important as the colonies expanded—a motherload of natural resources needed to fuel the growth of the expanding British Empire around the globe.

There is so much to discuss about the impact of the thirteen colonies and especially New England that the best way to do it is again by presenting a chart of the thirteen colonies, then extrapolating from that chart significant events, people, and the building blocks of our country that derived from the precedents set up by the founders and power brokers of the thirteen colonies.

Thirteen Colonies

Designations	Importance
New England	
Massachusetts	Protestant work Ethic Mayflower Compact Self-sufficiency
Rhode Island	Separation of church and state Right of self-government
Connecticut	Right of the people to elect their chief executive

New Hampshire	Emigrants from Massachusetts
Middle Colonies	"Melting pot of America"
New York	Many nationalities of people Commercial center
New Jersey	Extension of NY
Pennsylvania	Peaceful acceptance of all Faiths including Quakers
Delaware	Emigrants from Pennsylvania
Southern Colonies	
Maryland	A home for both Protestants and Catholics
Virginia	House of Burgesses Plantation Economy
North Carolina	Separated into two colonies
South Carolina	Largest plantations
Georgia	Began as a colony populated by British debtors

New England

Four hundred years ago, the Pilgrims departed Plymouth, England heading to an already established Jamestown, Virginia. However, Atlantic storms and lack of GPS technology resulted in their arrival in an unsettled area that they designated Plymouth Rock in honor of their home port. Their ship, the Mayflower, was about 110 feet long and no more than twenty-five feet wide consisting of four decks that included about 100 settlers and thirty crew members. Before the settlers got off the ship they had already created a document that would be one of the first building blocks of American democracy, the Mayflower Compact, the first set of written laws in America. Captain Miles Standish knew that the people needed guidelines for building a permanent colony in the face of the unknown, so he helped to author the rules that would become the guidelines of the Plymouth Colony.

The Pilgrims leaned heavily on aid from the Wampanoag tribe, especially a man named Squanto, who taught them how to plant corn to survive. Plymouth survived the first harsh winter and gave thanks to their Indian friends—our first Thanksgiving. Unfortunately, relations between the two groups would devolve rather quickly due to in large measure conflicting views of the land. Native Americans were willing to share the land that they viewed as communal, but the Europeans believed in private ownership of land so once the early fences were erected it would not take long for the sparks to fly, hence Indian wars in both Virginia and Massachusetts. We all know how this turned out.

The settlers of Plymouth and other colonies had to be self-sufficient, as there were no industries or shops set up yet to purchase any kind of merchandise. Following is a list of items a family of six was allowed to take on the Mayflower and the other ships to Virginia—one iron pot, one kettle, one frying pan, one gridiron, two skillets, one roasting spit, wood spoons, platters, and dishes—for a family of six! The term "Yankee Ingenuity" described the inventiveness of the early settlers to develop industries and inventions to service their needs, again necessity being the mother of invention. The term "Yankee" originally applied to New Englanders and was expanded in the Civil War to describe everyone residing north of the Mason-Dixon Line, to be explained soon. Because of the harsh climate, diets were restricted to local vegetables and corn. Food had to be stockpiled in the fall. New England did give birth to manufacturing and the energy that powered the early mills. The energy that powered the early mills came from water power. Whale oil, used for heating, made whaling a thriving business before coal was found in the ground.

This self-reliance was shared by all members of the family. Men built homes, tools, and weapons and defended in warfare when necessary. Much of the farming was left to the women and children, who milked cows, planted and harvested crops, and fended off wild animals with guns that they learned to use at a young age. Young children were not indulged and pampered the way they are today by helicopter parents and safe spaces. Children were up at dawn, worked till sunset, were fed last, and not expected to speak lest they were spoken to first. Recalcitrant children could be tortured or in some cases put to death for petty crimes. Life was about survival and knowing your place, lessons that we seem to have lost as we "modernized" our culture. The only day of rest was Sunday when families spent the entire day in church asking God to repent their sins and give them the strength to complete the next week's work.

For my money, the most important building block of American history was the development of what was called the Protestant or Puritan work ethic. I began to describe it in the last paragraph. I bet that some of you reading this book have never heard the term, no doubt because revisionist history is working hard to erase this from the history books. Where did it originate? The two major tribes of England were the Angles and the Saxons. People of this ancestry are called WASPS (White Anglo-Saxon Protestants). This used to be the largest racial-type group in America, but the new demographics have pushed them to the back of the line. Along with help from other groups, they were the ones that gave America an identity. This work ethic emphasizes hard work, discipline, and frugality. People of this persuasion believe in God's salvation for a life well-lived and to pass on to others things you don't require. This work ethic is what gave root to capitalism, the private ownership of business, and the greatness of America but with compassion for the poor. Part of this ethic is charity, and America leads the world in charitable donations. It burns me when some people broad brush many of us with the term "white privilege," when by and large we earned what we received. As an editorial comment, capitalism is not going anywhere so embrace it. Socialist countries have proven to be historical failures. One final thought. If everyone hates America and its free enterprise system, why are so many immigrants busting down the door to get into this country?

So, who were these Puritans that gave America its strong work ethic? The Puritans came to America in 1630, ten years after the Pilgrims. The Puritans wanted to purify or make perfect the church of England. The Pilgrims were separatists, people who wanted to worship God in their own way and thereby left the Church of England. The Puritans with their vast numerical superiority were able to overwhelm the Pilgrim colony and absorb it into what they called the Massachusetts Bay Colony, ruled by unyielding governor John Winthrop. Though very religious, their way was brutal and monolithic. If you did not conform to the church strictures, you were cast out or in some cases put to death. Religion was serious business. If you missed a Sunday session, you were put in a stock (public lockup) to be ridiculed by the citizens. If you fell asleep at a Sunday sermon, a man would tickle your chin with a feather on a long pole to wake you up, or if you were an unruly child you were prodded with the other end of the pole. Women were viewed as weaker than men and their souls more likely to be influenced by the devil, so women were accused of witchcraft and some were burned at the stake. Women had no say in the government, so in effect the Puritan Church ran the colony as a theocracy which could not happen today. Today's Woke Culture is a scary echo of the monolithic Puritan way of life, where if you did not conform you were cast out or canceled to use a current word of erasure from a society.

On the lighter side, an anecdotal story about Puritanical sexual relations. The Puritans were guided by the biblical exhortation to "be fruitful and multiply," but there was a myth that they were not allowed to enjoy sex. So what did they do? They put a cut-out sheet between the two partners in bed so the area of contact was all that was seen, not the joy on the faces of the partners who were not allowed to enjoy it! The fact that Puritannical families routinely numbered ten or more tells me that the sheet between them was just for appearances. They loved it! The other three New England colonies were birthed from emigrants from the Puritan colony of Massachusetts.

The Puritan philosophy of "my way or the highway" didn't appeal much to famous ex-Puritans Anne Hutchinson and Roger Williams. Anne Hutchinson believed that one could practice faith at home, nor did you need the approval of the church clergy to pray. This resulted in a one-way ticket out of Massachusetts for her and her followers. Ultimately she was killed in an Indian attack. Her ideas were not lost on Roger Williams, the founder of Rhode Island and the city of Providence. His contribution to American growth was two-fold—the belief in the self-government of the people and the constitutional principle of separation of church and state inherent in his belief of religious freedom. Williams believed that the church was not meant to be a lawmaking institution and deduced from that the people should be the lawmakers, not the church. He too was literally chased out of Massachusetts, where he hid out in the woods and was rescued by Indians. Eventually, he and his followers set up the Rhode Island colony that received a legal charter to operate from the Church of England and the king, no fan of the Puritans.

Another ex-Puritan set up shop in what is today called Connecticut. His name was Thomas Hooker and his contribution to democracy was that the people in his colony should have the right to elect the chief executive, known as the governor. The people who began the New Hampshire colony were former Puritans looking for more land, as Massachusetts was getting overpopulated. For those of you keeping score at home, Vermont was affixed to New York as was Maine to Massachusetts.

To summarize, I believe that the American identity was born in the region of New England. The Mayflower colonists already had written a document that would begin the American tradition of self-government. This principle was reinforced and somewhat expanded in the colonies of Rhode Island and Connecticut. The business of survival gave rise to the work ethic that translated self-sufficiency into the earliest businesses and the building of industry in New England that became the backbone of their economy and the basis of free enterprise capitalism in America. Yankee ingenuity gave rise to the Industrial Revolution that occurred later and is defined as the change from hand made goods to machine made goods. New England was the first section of America to ban slavery circa 1800. That was six decades before the Civil War was fought. The early culture was one of inventive, god-fearing inhabitants willing to work hard to improve their lives and look to set up a government that would include all and work for all.

Middle Colonies

Whereas New England tended to be somewhat of a restricted society based on conformity, the middle colonies were more tolerant of alternate viewpoints, hence the term "melting pot," which means many nationalities living together harmoniously contributing to a common way of life. While New England started out as mainly Protestants from England, the middle colonies were welcoming people from England, Scotland, Ireland, Wales, Germany, and eastern countries of Europe, especially Poland.

New York, named for the Duke of York, a brother to the king of England, was originally named New Amsterdam in honor of the Dutch capital city of Amsterdam. Henry Hudson viewed the great expanse of open land at the mouth of the river that would hear his name and noticed the connection of the harbor to the Atlantic Ocean. Hudson envisioned a large port city that would help to expand the Dutch trade throughout the world. Later Peter Minuit, the governor of the New Netherlands colony of New Amsterdam, purchased Manhattan from the Indians for twenty-four dollars. Minuit would also set up Fort Christina, the first Dutch colony in Delaware. A Dutch governor, Peter Stuyvesant oversaw the growth of New Amsterdam until 1664. Unfortunately, the British had their eyes on the growing city and simply sailed into NY Harbor and wrested control of the entire area from the Dutch without a fight.

However, the Dutch left a lasting imprint on New York and U.S. culture forever. Three of the five boroughs of NY City have Dutch names. Brooklyn means broken land (islands), the Broncs (Bronx), and Staten Island. Staten means state in Dutch. From the Dutch patroon (wealthy landowners) class came a famous family of presidents—Theodore and Franklin Roosevelt along with an earlier president, Martin Van Buren. Albany, the capital of NY State was originated and built by the Dutch. New York City would be the first of eight capital cities of America. I will leave it up to you to discover the remaining seven.

New York City would transform from a cow pasture to a small city under the new administration of the British. It was only the third-largest city in colonial America, trailing Philadelphia and Boston in total population. It would grow into a major port city and home to a very diverse population both now and then. The fact that the United Nations building was built on the East River in the middle of Manhattan should come as no surprise.

New Jersey was a tract of land given to another relative of the king of England. One of the most iconic battles of the Revolutionary War, The Battle of Trenton was fought in this state. Emigrants from New York populated New Jersey in search of good farmland that is still available today in the western part of the state near the Delaware River.

Speaking of Delaware, it originally was part of the Pennsylvania Colony. Eventually, Swedish farmers were able to get control of the land peacefully and named it Delaware, in honor of the Delaware tribe of Indians who helped them settle the land.

Pennsylvania is an interesting story. William Penn's father was in the military service of the king of England, and the king was indebted to him for his service to the crown. At the same time in England, an anti-war, anti-colonial religious group called the Society of Friends (Quakers) was causing grief for the king, who still wanted to expand the British Empire. The king made a deal with William Penn. Penn was offered a gigantic tract of land to which he would be the proprietor (owner) so long as Penn agreed to take the Quakers with him and of course out of the hair of the king. Penn agreed, and the philosophy of his colony could be seen in the creation of Philadelphia, the city of brotherly love, though many may snicker at that moniker today.

In any event, Pennsylvania, "Penn's Woodlands," became the largest of the melting pot middle colonies. Having attended college there, I can report that in terms of land layout thankfully not much has changed in this beautiful state. Pennsylvania's other big city, Pittsburgh, is named after William Pitt, a British statesman who aided the British to victory over France in the Seven Years War with his pro-war speeches. Called the French and Indian War in America, it would lead directly to the Revolutionary War. The British victory solidified their dominance over France, which would ultimately give control of North America to England.

Before I discuss the southern colonies, I want to explain the story of the Mason-Dixon line that was set up to delineate the border between Maryland and Pennsylvania. This could have become a religious conflict between the Catholics, under George Calvin i.e Lord Baltimore who held sway over Maryland, and a Protestant-based but peaceful colony under William Penn. The two leaders spent about 500,000 dollars to hire an expert British team, astronomer Charles Mason and surveyor Jeremiah Dixon, to draw up a compromise line that would make both sides happy. Not only did this line divide the two future states but it became a line of demarcation between the South and the North in the Civil War.

Southern Colonies

In response to the cooperation shown by William Penn, Lord Baltimore of Maryland helped to establish another building block of religious freedom in America. The passing of the Toleration Act of

1649 allowed religious freedom for all Christian groups in America. It was a reaffirmation of Roger Williams's ideas of religious freedom in Rhode Island. Though the Toleration Act was later rescinded, ultimately religious freedom for all groups became codified in the First Amendment to the U.S. Constitution. Maryland today fits the profile of its neighbors to the north, that of a melting pot.

Virginia was the most powerful of the southern colonies in terms of political and economic influence. Virginia was pretty much a two-class society. Along the coastline, aka the Tidewater Region, large plantations would dominate the topography that resulted in an aristocratic class of owners known as the Landed Gentry. Plantations required shipping to deliver their goods to the more northern colonies. Southern port cities that grew quickly and thrived were Norfolk, Virginia, Charleston, South Carolina, and Savannah, Georgia to name a few. The western part of the state was composed of a tougher breed of people of Irish and Scottish descent who were the opposite of the educated upper crust that inhabited the coastline. Over time those along the hills of Piedmont would form a new state called West Virginia. Many of the inhabitants would be known as hillbillies and had been indentured servants. An indentured servant could not afford to pay for the boat ride to America so they signed contracts that bound them to one owner for up to nine years. At this point, they were set free to mostly become dirt farmers or outlaws. Obviously, they identified with the true slaves, so West Virginia outlawed slavery and supported the North in the Civil War.

In the political realm, Virginia contributed yet another large building block to American democracy, the House of Burgesses. In 1619 this became the first group of elected lawmakers in what would become the United States of America. The House of

Burgesses withstood many attacks from the governors of Virginia but survived and became the model for Congress, the legislative branch of the government.

The original settlement of Jamestown (1607) mostly perished due to Malaria and the preoccupation of gold seekers in the swamplands. Finally Captain John Smith put his foot down and told the all-male colony "If you don't work, you don't eat." This was said with guns in hand. Smith married Pocahontas and with the help of her tribe more crops were planted. Eventually, ships with women arrived and Jamestown thrived as they finally found their "gold," the planting, harvesting, and sale of tobacco. This secured the prosperity of Jamestown and became the main cash crop for sale in the Virginia colony. The entire shipping industry along the coastline began to service the export of tobacco to the North and across the seas. Today the U.S. Navy has its main east coast base in Norfolk, Virginia while naval recruits train in Annapolis, Maryland. Richmond, Virginia would become the Confederate capital city, a mere ninety miles away from Washington, D.C., the capital of the Union.

The Carolinas began as one area but eventually morphed into North and South Carolina. The warmer climate and longer growing season with large tracts of well-watered land was ideal for the growth of even larger plantations than Virginia. Tobacco plantations on "Tobacco Road" morphed into rice, indigo, silk, and "king cotton" plantations the further south you journeyed. Cotton became the chief export, as it was needed in the New England textile mills for the manufacture of clothing. The point being that a thriving trade began between the North and the South. Later on, sugar cane would be introduced to the plantations from the West Indies. Unfortunately, slave labor—began by the Dutch in 1619—would be necessary for the giant plantations to make a profit as they needed plenty of cheap labor and slavery to turn a profit.

The thirteenth and last of the original colonies, Georgia, was started in 1733. Its founder was an Englishman who was really a humanitarian in a way, looking to solve a social problem in England. King George had prisons full of debtors. How can a person pay off a debt if they are locked up? I never understood that rationale. Anyway, James Oglethorpe had a plan. He knew the Spanish in neighboring Florida had their eyes on the colonial plantations. Oglethorpe asked the king to free the debtors, put them on boats, and send them to this new colony where they could repay their debts by defending the land against soon-to-be Spanish incursions. This saved King George lots of money having to pay for prisoner upkeep as well as financing the British army, so the plan was put into motion. Georgia is not the only former colony with some criminal DNA in its ancestry. More British prisoners were banished across the ocean to Australia, which accounts for a good measure of rugged individualism in today's Australian population.

Much like the primordial soup that created an early identity of mankind, the actions of the thirteen colonies gave birth to an early identity for America. America was not going to be a monolithic, puritanical society where everyone would be forced to live according to the overly strict guidelines of one church. There was a famous or infamous Puritan preacher whose sermon "Sinners in the hands of an angry God" is still discussed today as a tool of repressive control. In his sermon, Jonathan Edwards claimed that Hell was a real place and only God will keep you out of it… Avoid sin and obey the Puritan rules, lest you wind up in eternal hellfire!

Thankfully, Puritan power began to wane after the Salem Witch trials of 1692. The Puritans feared the unknown, which they saw as the province of the devil and witches were put here to do the devil's work. All it took was a rumor to convict you and a person had to withstand physical torture to prove their innocence. For example, if someone fell out of a tree while pruning branches and a passerby witnessed that fall that became witchcraft as the person was "flying through the air"! After 200 arrests and twenty hangings, this hysteria came to an end. As documented, many began to leave the Puritan church and live in a more non-threatened way.

On the positive side, the protestant (Puritan) work ethic kept everyone busy and through inventiveness led to the Industrial Revolution. Before this revolution, women in New England had to design and create clothing for the entire family all done by hand and painstakingly slow. This was known as the Domestic System, where the family made their own handmade goods before the advent of the factory system. When the textile mills opened up, women were now able to do other things. Life got easier.

As opposed to the closed society of the puritanical world, open societies were set up in neighboring cultures. Melting pot colonies such as New York, New Jersey, Pennsylvania, and Delaware welcomed people from many nations. The melting pot culture would eventually spread to the New England colonies as the reign of the Puritans came to an end, though today there are still relics of Puritanism known as Blue Laws. They also are disappearing rapidly. An example would be the banning of alcohol sales on Sundays. If Blue Laws were still in effect, there would be no such thing as Black Friday for shopping and no businesses would be allowed to open on Sunday.

Differences in geography led to different ways of living. New England would become urban and industrial, life revolving around the city and its factories. Small subsistence farms produced local crops and the Puritan imprint led to the early ban of slavery throughout New England. The Bible taught that slavery was an offense in the eyes of God. The middle colonies "Bread Basket" produced dairy products, cereal grains like Quaker Oats, and had animal and horse farms. On the other hand, commerce, trade, and manufacturing grew quickly in Philadelphia, Baltimore, and New York City. The Southern Colonies gave rise to large farms and plantations that required slave labor. In early colonial history, there was not that much contact between the colonies, as interstate highways did not exist. Limited intrastate roads connected villages in a given area. Water transportation was the best way to get around, so that is why most cities were situated near waterways—for trade and transport.

Along with the rise of religious freedom, there was another thread of democracy that ran through all of the thirteen colonies, local government. The old saying that "90% of politics is local" was born during this infant stage of America. Local judges known as magistrates arbitrated local issues. For example, if you view New England art from the colonial period you will notice the fences between homes were made of rock and not wood. First of all, New England had rocky soil and quarrymen opened up rock mines for profit. I read an account of an incident in New England that involved one man's pigs feasting on his neighbor's crops. The pigs would blast through the wooden fences so the local magistrate decided that both parties should hire the quarryman to build a stone fence. From this situation a problem had been resolved and a law created to avoid future disputes of this nature. It became a code law applicable to the local community. Much later, America's most famous citizen, Ben Franklin, observed: "good fences make good neighbors."

Despite the success of the early colonies to survive and begin to thrive, it must be remembered that the colonies were not at all united and in most cases had little contact with each other due to a lack of highways. More importantly, although they began to prosper they were under scrutiny and tight control of England, the mother country. Like a parent protecting their children, safety was guaranteed so long as the colonies were obedient. For example, colonial assemblies were now part of the government in every colony and could pass laws, but the king of England reserved the right to nullify (make void) any or all of their laws. The king did extend one right to the colonists in Virginia that became part of our code of law—the right to a fair trial.

During Bacon's Rebellion (1675) in Virginia, Governor Berkeley tried to dissolve the House of Burgesses and order summary executions without trial. Young Nathaniel Bacon and his protestors were having none of that, so they chased the governor out of his statehouse. Bacon died during the insurrection but the king saw the justness of Bacon's cause and decreed that no man could be sentenced to death without a trial. It was another building block in the American democracy. On the other hand, voting was limited to white males who were property owners.

The British were able to control colonial trade by the twin ideas of mercantilism and the Navigation Acts. Mercantilism states that the colonies only exist to service the mother country. Natural resources were shipped back to England, made into finished products then resold to colonists for a profit. The Navigation Acts made sure that British ships were used so that the colonists would not be tempted to trade with competing European nations. The colonies were allowed to set up Triangular Trade with the British West Indies to sell certain products and get raw materials needed to finish production of goods then returned to England. The British made sure that the skins of animals used to create fur garments made it to the ports of England for final production. England was very aware that next to gold extraction the fur trade was the biggest moneymaker and that their main colonial rival France had a huge fur trade that the British envied.

The following are snapshots of colonial life to be followed by some anecdotal history and lastly a current events rhetorical question. The Dutch were the first to introduce dairy farming to the middle colonies, and the Germans introduced crop rotation that replenish nutrients in the soil. The first mailboxes were empty boots nailed into a pole on the roadside. In order to get stagecoach drivers to regularly stop and deliver mail, owners built water troughs for the horses next to the booted mailboxes.

In 1647, Massachusetts law mandated the establishment of grammar schools, which were really high schools in each community. There were elementary schools taught by women, but the high schools trained boys (aged 14) to attend Ivy League colleges like Harvard, Yale, and Princeton to become church or government officials. In Virginia, the College of William and Mary had the same original purpose.

Back in New England, the settlers preferred snowy roads of the winter to wet roads of the other seasons. Why? Being subsistence farmers (family use only for crops) the other goods they transported were heavier and therefore wagons got stuck in the mud. When it snowed, they used large round rollers pulled behind a wagon to flatten out the snow. This made the ice roads easy to drive over until the spring thaw. In another snapshot, one summer there was a plague of crows and blackbirds that were eating up all the plant seeds and crops on vines and stalks. To solve the problem, every male in the village was required to kill at least eight of the avian terrorists and keep the heads as proof! Failure to do so resulted in a fine from the local magistrate.

Concluding this section, what we have is an emerging American identity. Why? The intermarriage of couples especially in the open societies of the melting pot created a new mindset. No longer were they in their home countries, and this new independence forced people to find answers to questions for the first time without traditional knowledge from their former homelands that eventually became foreign nations. For proof, eyewitness observers in seventeenth-century New Amsterdam before the British takeover overheard eighteen languages being spoken in the streets. This was over 400 years ago. The melting pot created a new American identity where most everyone accepted norms and ideas born from an emerging country.

Here is a rhetorical question. Is the concept of a melting pot valid in today's America? Are we all pulling together or are we pulling apart? I hear certain politicians claim that codifying English as a national language is racist. My opinion is that first, anyone playing the race card is probably a racist, and secondly wouldn't a common language bond a country together? It seems to me that the growing gang problem in America is because of a lack of communication that isolates people with only their own kind. Take Japan for example. Because they have a unified culture with common goals and one language, there is little crime as mostly all the citizens are on the same page. A common language to me is where you start if you want a unified and less angry nation.

As I predicted in my first book, it would not surprise me at all to see a second Civil War in this nation. The battle lines are being drawn as we live and breathe.

Freedom of the press was another building block of American democracy born in this time period. Under the First Amendment, the print and today's television media have the right and obligation to criticize the actions of any government official, to speak truth to power. This right grew out of the 1735 trial of John Peter Zenger, who printed stories critical of royal Governor Cosby of New York. Cosby did not much care for the commentary of Zenger, a frequent critic, so he sued Zenger in court for libel, which is not telling the truth and is illegal. It did not take the jury long to decide that criticism is not libel, so Zenger was summarily acquitted and the Zenger Case is celebrated for having given birth to the principle, freedom of the press. Over time, things have changed. What was once a watchdog group over all the government, the Fourth Estate has become for the most part a partisan section of the Democratic Party. Ninety percent of the criticism and lies spoken by the media is in opposition to today's Republican Party that is the more traditional of the two parties. The watchdog has bastardized itself into a cheering section for one side. Censorship is the arch-enemy of democracy.

On a lighter note, do you know why people quickly say God bless you after a sneeze? The Puritans thought that if you did not bless the person that sneezed their soul would leave their body. Those without souls were not allowed to enter heaven and the alternative as we know is unpleasant, to say the least. The German immigrants have an equivalent idiomatic response that some of you know. "Gesundheit!" translates to good health.

One-Room Schoolhouse

The first ones were set up in New England. Made of wood, the windows had no glass, just oiled brown paper and the room had no stove, just an open fireplace. The students were put in charge of gathering firewood. There was an outhouse in the back but detached from the school. Younger children attended school in spring, while the older ones attended in the winter as farm chores waned. Before it became "women's work," an itinerant male teacher would be boarded in a local home. All subjects were taught and most of the males were prepared for the ministry since there were no public schools and children had to bring their own supplies.

Discipline was harsh. Students were routinely rapped on their knuckles by a wooden rod if their eyes wandered. In one Rhode Island school, the whip was employed. One lash for co-ed playing, three lashes for tree climbing during recess, seven for lying, eight for spreading rumors outside of school, nine lashes for swearing, and ten lashes for males sexually harassing females.

Ouch!

New France

With the exception of the thirteen British colonies and Spanish Florida, the French colonial empire included all the land from Eastern Canada as far west as the Mississippi River and as far south as the Gulf of Mexico. In terms of size, it dwarfed the thirteen colonies who were hemmed in by the Appalachian Mountains and the claims of the French that date back to 1608 when they set up their first colony at Quebec, Canada merely one year after the founding of the first English colony at Jamestown, Virginia. Louisiana, named for King Louis XIV of France, was the large swath of land located near the Mississippi River near the Gulf of Mexico. Although much larger in area than the British colonies, the entire population numbered only about 80,000, as compared to the 1,200,000 settlers in the British colonies.

The colonial arrangement in New France was completely different from that of the thirteen colonies. The only major population area was around Quebec and later Montreal, where agriculture became the way of life. There was subsistence farming much like New England. This type of farming is for the family unit with little extra for sale.

The main driver of the French economy was the fur trade, which was very lucrative. This was a very nomadic way of life for the fur trappers who befriended the Algonquin Indian tribes that taught them trapping techniques. This was an example of an updated hunting and gathering society, which was constantly on the move with the result that very few large colonies took root. In lieu of villages, the French operated out of fur-trapping stations where they collected animal skins before taking them by canoe all the way to Montreal. Here they would be sold to fur merchants who used cargo ships to transport the pelts across the Atlantic for processing in the home country. The Ohio Valley became the main center of fur trapping, and this area would be the cause of many skirmishes and bigger wars to follow.

Unlike the government in the thirteen colonies, there was no hint of democracy, as the administration of the government was kept under tight control by the king and his subordinates who lived in New France. France had a long history of monarchs as can be seen by the name Louis. The last King Louis was number sixteen, then France would become a Republic. The point being the people in New France had little to say about control over their own lives.

On the other hand, unlike the British, the French established good relations with the Native Americans. The Algonquin tribes looked forward to meetings with the French Jesuit priests, whom they called the "Black Robes." France was a Catholic country and had evicted a group called the Huguenots (French Protestants) who found safety in the British melting pot colonies and later in New England. The French traded modern weapons and ammunition to the Algonquins in exchange for knowledge about new areas of land where more animals could be found for the fur trade.

New France was a very vast land with many natural resources, but the empire would prove hard to defend. With only 80,000 people in the entire empire, they would have a tough time maintaining their sovereignty should the British, for example, instigate a war. France had an alliance with Spain, another Catholic monarchy, who already despised the British for sinking their armada in 1588. It would not be long for the continental wars of Europe to arrive in the New World.

CHAPTER 10

French and Indian War

(1754 - 1763)

THE CAUSES OF THE WAR AND THE RESULTS had more of an impact on history than the actual fighting of the war itself. This war was an extension of the Seven Years War in Europe that essentially was the entire continent at war with itself. The major cause of the French and Indian War was the rivalry for world domination by the world's two "superpowers," England and France. England never forgot the Norman Invasion of England in 1066 and the two countries had battled each other on and off for centuries. Besides the desire for expanded land empires, the Glorious Revolution (1688) in England deposed the Catholic king, replacing him with a Protestant monarch reinforcing bad religious feelings between Protestant England and Catholic France. In North America, both countries were claiming ownership of the Ohio Valley and its lucrative fur trade. Another cause, often downplayed, was for control of the Grand Banks off the coast of Newfoundland. Growing populations needed other food sources besides agriculture, and this area of the North Atlantic Ocean had the greatest amount of fish to be caught during this time period.

From the onset, England had the advantage. Because they controlled the seas, they were able to get 40,000 troops to America to face off against only 10,000 French troops. France would not commit more troops as the Seven Years War in Europe was an existential threat to their homeland. France had to rely on their Algonquin allies. Thousands of fur-trapping stations were converted into small forts. The British knew the Iroquois Confederacy, six tribes that lived in upstate New York, were sworn enemies of the Algonquin tribes, so the British offered them Algonquin lands if they joined the British in this fight. They became allies of the British for the duration of this war.

Believe it or not, the actions of George Washington actually instigated the war. Washington was an officer in the British Army and along with soldiers in his command, captured a few French soldiers near Fort Duquesne in the upper Ohio Valley. Shortly thereafter, Washington was captured. Because he was not the commanding officer he was freed and forced to return to Virginia. Washington learned that traditional methods of fighting out in the open did not work in wilderness warfare. Washington attempted to warn his superior officers that wearing red and marching single file made them easy targets. The British showed their hubris and demeaned Washington, stating that this is the way our army works and the French and Indians would be neutralized in short order. Not! Washington was correct and would use this knowledge in the not-too-distant future.

The Battle of Quebec in 1759 was the pivotal and last battle of this war. The British Navy sailed up the St. Lawrence River to Quebec, which was a walled city overlooking the river with many cannons available to repel and sink enemy naval ships. England quickly backed away from this walled fortress and debarked its army miles away on land. Eventually the British found an opening and totally surrounded the French with their own artillery and a large army ready for action. With the return of the British navy, the battle was won. After nine years, both sides were tired of the expense of war and were more concerned with their homelands, but England was the clear victor!

The first Treaty of Paris (1763) formalized the end of the French and Indian War. England took control of the entire North American empire of France except for some islands in the Caribbean useful to France for trade. The French government was disbanded, but the French population was allowed to stay so long as they swore allegiance to the king of England and did not take up arms (weapons) against British rule. The French grudgingly agreed to do so. Spanish Florida was taken over by the British too, but Spain remained in control of all lands west of the city of New Orleans. The British seized control of the French fur trade and their naval presence gave them control of the Grand Banks off the coast of Newfoundland.

Canada would become part of the British empire as well but still remains two countries inside of one. Eastern Canada, which extends to the Great Lakes, maintains its French identity. Montreal and Quebec are its major cities and as recently as 1995 almost broke away from Canada to form their own nation, which was going to be called Quebec. By less than one percent of the vote did they agree to not break away. From the capital city of Ottawa to British Columbia on the west coast, the dominant culture is English. There are many cities spread through the provinces - Toronto, Edmonton, Ottawa, Calgary, Winnipeg, and Vancouver—the hockey cities—where the culture is mostly English based. As a matter of fact, Canada has two natural languages, English and French. But as the recent separatist movement in Quebec illustrates, the ancient rivalries are still alive albeit, a little less muted today.

Unfortunately, the Treaty of Paris did not lead to a lasting peace. The joy of triumph by the British was not that well received in the colonies. Bigger changes were afoot, and the French and Indian War was only a catalyst and an omen of larger and more widespread conflicts that would certify England as the world's only superpower—much like the United States today—but its enemies were regrouping and joining together, which would put tremendous pressure on the British Empire especially its thirteen colonies.

CHAPTER 11
Benjamin Franklin

THE AMERICAN EQUIVALENT OF DA VINCI for his enormous amount of contributions to civilization, Franklin was a true
Renaissance Man perhaps only rivaled by Thomas Edison for the
wide range of his contributions to America and the world. During
his long and busy life, he won fame as a publisher of Poor Richard's
Almanac and the Pennsylvania Gazette newspaper, civic leader,
writer, diplomat, scientist, and inventor. Unlike Edison, he refused
patents, as his goal was to help mankind, not make money.

Whenever he saw a need, Franklin tried to find a way to meet
it. He invented America's first practical wood-burning stove, the
lightning rod that prevents buildings from being incinerated by
lightning bolts, efficient street lamps, and bifocal lenses for reading. He organized the first fire department, library, hospital and
police department in Philadelphia. He was the first postmaster in
the United States and arranged for the first paved roads, as well as
mile markers used then and now. In colonial times, the postal rate
was determined by the amount of mileage covered and the receiver
of mail paid the price, not the sender. In 1855 pre-paid mail became
the law of the land as sometimes the receiver of the mail refused
to pay the postage. His groundwork led to the formation of the

first college in Philadelphia, the University of Pennsylvania, an ivy league school. Like Da Vinci, he envisioned warfare in the air. In his thinking, hot air balloons could quietly deploy troops behind enemy lines for surprise attacks. His brainchild was the ancestor of today's paratroopers, a branch of the military.

Franklin's immense talents led him to become one of the Founding Fathers of America. His ideas are in both the Declaration of Independence and the Constitution. Having been to Europe often, he was well-received as "America's most famous citizen" and was appointed ambassador to France under President Thomas Jefferson. Franklin was an epicurean who enjoyed a good time. He mused what life would be without "good eating and good drinking." After the Revolutionary War, Franklin was the main author of the 1783 Treaty of Paris that got America much more land from England than anyone expected.

His experiments with electricity are what originally made him famous in Europe as a scientist. He was the first to prove that a bolt of lightning was a giant electric spark. A myriad of inventions came directly from this experiment and surprisingly said inventions were of American and not of European origin. Samuel Morse's telegraph and its morse code derived from the use of electricity, as did Bell's telephone and the underwater transatlantic cable that linked Europe to America for telephone use. Ultimately Edison's light bulb and record player originated from Franklin's experiments.

Franklin was a student of history and a keen observer of America and what was creating its greatness. He was the first to call for the colonies to unite in the Albany Plan of Union (1754). A famous political cartoon entitled "Join or Die" showed thirteen pieces of a dismembered snake signifying what might happen to the colonies if they did not unite against England was used to promote unification, but half of the colonial legislatures were not ready to give up their autonomy so the plan was rejected. Nine years later after the French and Indian War, Franklin's idea became accepted and actively put into place.

Franklin realized that the growth of the colonies had started with its work ethic and was very aware of the importance of time. He had tremendous faith in the American people and left a good deal of sage advice for future generations in terms of famous quotes. Everyone has heard the phrases such as "honesty is the best policy," "the early bird gets the worm," and "death and taxes are the only two certain things in life." These thoughts are all Franklinesque.

In a more serious vein, I have chosen these quotes to share with you concerning time as both friend and enemy. "Lost time is never found again." "By failing to prepare you are preparing to fail." "You may delay but time will not." "Never leave that till tomorrow which you can do today." "Well done is better than well said." "We are all born ignorant but one must work hard to remain stupid." The last is my favorite, "many people die at twenty-five and aren't buried until they are seventy-five." Time is your most precious commodity. Don't waste it!

An obvious defender of the First Amendment, he would be pilloried by today's safe zone, safe space, and cancel culture crowd.

Other observations were about the politics of his day, but they may be more relevant for many of you today. He said, "it is the first responsibility of every citizen to question authority." The final two quotes I am grouping together and probably are the most relevant in today's secular war over thought control in the United States. "Without freedom of thought, there can be no such thing as wisdom, and no such thing as public liberty without free speech, and those who give up essential liberty to obtain a little temporary safety (safe spaces) deserve neither liberty nor safety." May Franklin's brilliance remain timeless and guide us!

CHAPTER 12
United Kingdom

THE IMPRINT OF THE UNITED KINGDOM, especially England, can be seen in the DNA of the thirteen colonies and throughout much of the seven continents that comprise the world as we know it. Today the U.K. is comprised of the countries of England, Scotland, Whales, and Northern Ireland. They are all independent countries bound together by geography and economic considerations. In colonial times the Republic of Ireland as well as the other four U.K. countries were under tight control by the British. At one time the British Empire covered 26% of the land area in the world and had colonies everywhere except Antarctica. It was by far the largest empire ever controlled by one nation. The British were able to keep this empire together until post WWI, a truly amazing feat. So how did one small group of island countries control most of the known world? An abridged history may provide some clues.

In response to being conquered by the early Romans, followed by the Vikings and finally the French from Normandy, they organized quickly into feudal societies, secure behind their high castle walls, and followed the edicts of the manorial kings who were backed up by their military class of lords and knights with their serfs doing the menial labor. The two dominant tribes became the Angles and the Saxons, both originally from central Europe who were able to eventually rid themselves of the other invading groups.

What spurred their growth was protection by the rough waters that surrounded them. The North Sea and the North Atlantic Ocean are the two stormiest bodies of water on the globe and a bane to conquest by foreigners. The onset of the Crusades got people out of their castles and they got to know each other as they marched to war and back.

The British have a long tradition of ceremony and royalty going back to the Dark Ages and developed a very restrained national personality, a "stiff upper lip," in tough times. The discipline of England could be seen in the class structure, where royalty made the laws that were handed down to the lower classes. Some called the British upper class "proper" or snooty, and there were rules for everything, even warfare. When the English Army invariably won a battle, they demanded that the losing leader hand over his sword to the British leader in charge. This also became an American tradition. In short, isolation by the seas, tradition, and discipline aided the growth of the U.K. The restraint of the British personality would be transferred to the Puritans, who imprinted much of New England with their values of discipline, thrift, and self-sacrifice. A third tribe, the Celts, became the dominant tribe of Ireland and Scotland and often were at odds with the tribes of England.

Two other factors led to the dominance of the U.K. on the world stage. The first factor was the control of the seas by the British navy especially after the defeat of the Spanish Armada. They were the first country to modernize shipping which was key to maintaining an empire. The other factor was the end result of their work ethic, the Industrial Revolution that was born in England. Steam power replaced water power for the manufacturing of all goods, and the first steamboat was invented in England that not need wind power to operate. England knew they had something that no one else had, so in order to keep the Industrial Revolution in England they enacted a law that said inventors and mechanics were not allowed to leave England. Mechanics of course knew the blueprints of new inventions, as they had to know how to repair breakdowns. Of course, this attempt was like trying to prevent a plague from being passed from person to person, so the Industrial Revolution spread quickly, first to America. I did mention that there was tension in the U.K. amongst the nations. This tension was put aside for many years as the exploits of Napoleon posed an existential threat to the entire U.K. With the demise of Napoleon there became a stronger bond between the U.K. countries. This bond would serve them well as they used their new nationalism to triumph in two world wars.

Besides the language of English and a strong no-nonsense work ethic, the UK provided us with some of our democratic traditions. In the year 1215, the Parliament (lawmakers) of England came into being, as Prince John was facing a mutiny of his baron vassals. John had randomly jailed some nobility without evidence (Habeas Corpus), took away their lands, and left them to rot. Threatened by death, John relented, and from his assent came the idea of speedy trials, now including evidence and the nobility having a say over the amount of taxes to be paid to the king.

Prince John's abuses helped to create a bit of English folklore—Robin Hood. Robin Hood had returned from the Crusades and discovered that Prince John had confiscated his lands. When John went to arrest him, he fled into the woods and became the outlaw folk hero who robbed the rich and gave to the poor. Some point out that this may have been the beginning of British socialism as today the British, who are more liberal than America, have a much higher tax rate especially amongst the wealthy—so high that the Beatles in the 1960s renounced their British citizenship to avoid the 70% tax on their income.

The idea of a limited government came from England. In 1688, exactly 100 years after the British defeat of the Spanish Armada, was born the English Bill of Rights, which stated that the king and the Parliament would now rule together, with Parliament having law-making powers. The bill also said the king could tax but only with the consent of Parliament. Lastly, the king could not suspend laws or begin an army without the approval of Parliament.

Today, England's government is a constitutional monarchy. Parliament is similar to our Congress. The upper house is the House of Lords; the lower house is the House of Commons. The upper house seats are passed down from the upper classes to their progeny. They can only review laws. The House of Commons is the lawmaking body, as the people elect them. Their executive leader is the Prime Minister, who is not elected by the people but appointed by the king or queen, whomever is in power at the time. The Royals of England, i.e royal family, have no real lawmaking power but are the figurehead leaders of the U.K. and the most famous and scrutinized royal family on the planet.

This is a brief description of the British Empire that spread its culture to the four corners of the earth. Today the common language of the business world is English, though I am told Mandarin Chinese is also useful to know in the corporate universe. It is from this superpower that thirteen colonies will divest themselves and gain independence. How in the world did they pull it off?

CHAPTER 13

Causes of the Revolutionary War

THE END OF THE FRENCH AND INDIAN WAR in 1763 did not help relations between the U.K. and the thirteen colonies. Many colonists felt no threat from New France. In the same year as the peace treaty was signed, the British Parliament enacted the Proclamation of 1763 stating that the newly claimed lands in the Ohio Valley would not be opened up to colonial settlement. The British claimed that these lands were an Indian preserve and wanted to keep the colonists safe from Indian raids. The reality was that the British intended to heavily tax the colonists to pay off the war debt incurred from nine years of fighting. The British knew that once the colonists settled west of the Appalachian Mountains they would be away from the control of Parliament who could no longer tax them.

The Industrial Revolution had come to America and the colonies were becoming very prosperous and overcrowded which necessitated American western expansion. Inventions such as the power loom and spinning jenny mass-produced clothing, which was traded from New England to the southern and middle colonies. Ben Franklin's infrastructure ideas became the blueprint of hundreds of villages and cities throughout the colonies.

The fact that the colonists were not allowed to expand westward did not sit well with them. The idea of having to pay for a war most of them did not want sent the tension to the next level. England was now seen as a foreign nation with different goals than those of the colonies. They were becoming frenemies but most hoped to avoid an armed conflict. The colonists were very aware that England was looking to expand its empire and the colonies would be the cash cow of finance. They began to protest through their colonial assemblies stating that the actions of the Crown (England) were of no benefit to the colonies. The answer from England was swift. They began to abolish the assemblies of some of the colonies.

Road to Revolution

What is a revolutionary war? The short answer involves a rapid change in government in a short period of time employing violence and the Machiavellian principle of "by whatever means necessary." Noted historian Richard Hofstadter postulates that wars involving major changes do not begin in ruined nations but rather those where conditions are viewed as good but not likely to get better. Collapsed nations do not have the means to effect change, but prospering countries like the thirteen colonies had the power to bring about change.

Revolution also involves two theories of history, the Great Man Theory and the History from Below Theory. In the former, certain famous men in history are seen as natural-born leaders with the power to shape events. They can both be good and evil leaders such as George Washington, Attila the Hun, Napoleon, and Hitler.

In the latter theory, an overwhelming wave of small events causes great changes to occur. In short, do great men inspire events or are they inspired by events? Every revolution is different. In my view, our revolution was a series of events—soon to be detailed—that inspired the rise of George Washington, forever known as the Father of the American Nation.

Before the war is discussed let's look at it from the British point of view and how it is taught in British classrooms. The students in the U.K. and especially England are taught that the empire engaged in a number of wars with their former colonies. Therefore the war with the thirteen colonies was one of many civil wars (wars fought between citizens of the same country) fought by the British Empire.

All wars are fought for money and power. Because England needed more money to pay down war debts and administer its ever-expanding empire, it decided to enforce laws that were already on the books rather than initiate a new series of taxes aimed at looting the economy of a now prosperous set of colonies. The British policy of not enforcing laws was known as Benign Neglect. The colonies quickly realized that the British were trying to stifle the growth of America's "infant industries," as the British would not tolerate any competition in regards to trade. Sir Isaac Newton's third law of motion stated that for every action there is an opposite and equal reaction, cause and effect if you will. However you choose to describe it, things went downhill quickly in regards to the relationship between the British and their thirteen colonies. Frenemies became outright enemies. The following chart best illustrates the actions and reactions of both sides on the road to revolution.

Colonial Opposition to British Actions

British Action	Colonial Resistance
Proclamation of 1763	Violation of terms
Enforcement of Navigation Acts 1764	Smuggling
Stamp Act 1765	Boycott of British goods
Townshend Acts 1767	Nonimportation Agreements
Tea Act 1770	"Tea Parties"
Intolerable Acts 1774	1st Continental Congress
Colonial arms destroyed	Lexington and Concord

The Proclamation Act of 1763 forbade colonial expansion into the Ohio Valley. As discussed, the real reason for this ban was one of taxation. Once the colonists crossed the Appalachian Mountains they were free of British tax collectors. The colonists basically flipped the bird at Parliament and started settlements in today's states of Ohio, Illinois, and Indiana.

The Navigation Acts said that the colonists could only use British ships for trade. This stymied the growth of New England shipbuilding and cut off "black market" trade with other rival nations of England. Black market trade is illegal trade with other nations that avoid taxes. The Acts further stated that raw materials sent to England would be taxed and finished products would be sent back to the colonies sold at a profit. This law essentially attempted to shut down the infant industries of the colonies. The colonial reaction was to increase the black market (illegal) trade with other nations by employing privateer ships. Privateer ships were armed cargo ships. England set up a blockade of the east coast seaports to prevent illegal trade, but the colonists used blockade runners who operated away from the ports and under the cover of darkness to continue trade with enemy nations of England namely Spain, France, and the Dutch. The colonies also started using privateer ships in lieu of a navy, yet to be established. These were like the pirate ship of Sir Francis Drake who pillaged the Spanish Armada, but in this case the British got a dose of their own medicine. Colonial privateer ships with some weapons on board looted then sank British trade ships to the tune of eighteen million dollars—over 300 million dollars by today's standards.

In response, Parliament passed the Stamp Act. This law stated that only British-produced paper could be used in the colonies, and that all paper from playing cards to legal documents had to be affixed with the official seal, a stamp. This act went over like a lead balloon as the colonists immediately organized a Stamp Act Congress, not so much to protest the nuisance tax as to demand that only the colonies should have the right of taxation. From this action came the famous rallying cry of the Revolution, "no taxation without representation." The colonists went further and decided to boycott the import of all British goods. When the first British ships arrived with the stamped papers, the colonists overwhelmed the crews onboard and destroyed all the paper before it could be sold. Because of the economic loss caused by the boycott and the fact that some of Parliament sided with the colonists, the law was immediately repealed, or taken off the books. The colonists rejoiced!

Whatever progress they thought they were making against Parliament was quickly dashed by the next set of laws known as the Townshend Acts that taxed everyday goods such as lead, glass, colonial paper, and tea. When the Virginia House of Burgesses protested these new taxes, King George dissolved it and to add insult to injury also dissolved the New York assembly as well.

The colonial reaction was more heated this time. Radical groups called the Sons of Liberty were formed. The most famous one was led by Samuel Adams and was named the Sons of Liberty. Radicals are not afraid to use Machiavellian methods to bring about change and are often the catalysts of said changes. Throughout the colonies, the hated tax collectors were tarred and feathered and their houses often burnt to the ground thanks to the actions of the Sons of Liberty. Additionally committees of correspondence—letter writers—sprang into being sort of surrogate newspaper of current events. These letters were sent from colony to colony to keep everyone updated. Letters mailed from New England could take up to ten days to arrive in the southern colonies. The Sons of Liberty also made sure that the Tory shop owners—those loyal to the king— were kept in line in terms of maintaining the boycott. Some owners chose to close their shops and return to England, fearful of being either tarred and feathered or worse. A very significant event helped to get rid of most of the Townshend Acts.

In the winter of 1770 outside a Boston tavern, a group of colonists began to harass a group of British soldiers, who they derisively referred to as "Lobsterbacks" for their crimson red uniforms. As the colonists began to throw snowballs or ice balls at the soldiers, the soldiers opened fire and killed five unarmed colonists. Some historians claim this was the spark of the war as blood was spilled by innocents. As a matter of history, a monument was erected to Crispus Attucks, the first Black American to give up his life for the cause of liberty.[The death of Crispus Attucks and many other Black American colonists fighting for independence from England inspired the formation of the antislavery Abolitionist Movement in America that began in the early 1800's. The 1619 Project that is being taught in some American classrooms today spins a totally false narrative that the Revolution was fought to establish slavery in America. Actually quite the opposite is true.] In another twist of fate, John Adams, who would become the second president of the U.S., defended the British soldiers in court. Adams felt what they did was wrong but that everyone deserves a fair trial. Adams pleaded self-defense and the soldiers were set free. Of course, this infuriated the growing Patriot movement in New England and elsewhere. Later on, it was revealed that the judge was a British sympathizer. To quell this near rebellion, Parliament had no choice but to cancel the Townshend Acts except for one item.

The Tea Act effectively banned the production and sale of colonial-made tea. What's the big deal? The drinking of tea in England and the colonies especially New England is and was a huge English tradition. The British consume tea like Americans drink coffee. Shutting down colonial tea shops would generate a lot of money going into British coffers. The colonial reaction resulted in one of American history's most iconic events, the Boston Tea Party in 1773. Led by Samuel Adams and the Sons of Liberty, the colonists donned Indian disguises and snuck aboard British merchant ships docked in the Boston Harbor. They were able to dump over 300 cases of tea into the harbor and by today's measure would be worth between two and three million dollars. The British were not fooled by the rumor of Indian thieves as the Indians were not tea drinkers. The British response would lead directly to war.

The British Parliament quickly enacted the Intolerable (Coercive) Acts of 1774. The Tea Party was the straw that broke the camel's back and with the British response, the war was inevitable. The impact of these laws would be to lock down the city of Boston and place it under complete British control. The details of the acts included blockading the Boston port, dissolving the Massachusetts assembly, bringing criminals to British courts for trials, and imposing the Quartering Act that forced colonists to house and feed soldiers, gaining control over the lives of all citizenry in Boston. In effect, the Quartering Act was yet another form of taxation.

In response, the colonists organized the First Continental Congress. Representatives from every colony except Georgia met in Philadelphia. Most of the delegates did not want to go to war, but they refused to give up their rights such as self-government, taxation, and fair trials. They sent a series of petitions to King George asking him to repeal the Intolerable Acts and grant them their freedoms. Some historians say that the king read the petitions then summarily threw them into his fireplace. Continental Congress also enacted the idea of an Association, where there would be no import or use British products now in all the colonies. John Hancock of Massachusetts was nominated as leader of the First Continental Congress and persuaded the other colonies to expand the letter-writing campaign of the committees of correspondence. Sons of Liberty groups were charged with making sure that British products did not sell in the colonies. The Congress made plans to reconvene if the king rejected their overtures. While future colonial action was still up for debate, Patrick Henry's fiery speeches may have persuaded the colonies to revolt. We will get to him soon.

The use of spies played a pivotal role in the conduct of the Revolutionary War. Washington later acknowledged that without his extensive Setauket (Long Island) Spy Ring the war would have had a much different outcome. Through their spies, the British discovered that the colonists were preparing for war by amassing a large stockpile of weapons near Concord, Massachusetts. American spies in turn warned of the British coming to capture and destroy this stockpile of weapons. They also warned the British were seeking to arrest both Samuel Adams and John Hancock, who were staying near Concord. On the night of April 18, 1775, Paul Revere, William Dawes, and Samuel Prescott rode through towns on horseback announcing that "the British are coming!" Although the quote is attributed to Revere, only Prescott got through to Concord to warn Adams and Hancock away, Dawes and Revere having been arrested.

While we are on the subject, there were a number of famous historical quotes attributed to patriots of the Revolutionary War. Following the list of quotes and speakers of historical importance.

Famous Historical Quotes from the War

- "The British are coming!" Paul Revere and company

- "Don't fire until you see the whites of their eyes" Colonel William Prescott

- "If this be treason, make the most of it" and "Give me liberty or give me death!" Patrick Henry

- "All men are created equal" Thomas Jefferson

- "I regret that I have but one life to lose for my country" Nathan Hale

- "I have not yet begun to fight!" John Paul Jones"

The first quote helped to prevent the arrest and capture of John Adams and John Hancock, who had vital roles in the war and post-history of the war. Not firing upon the British until they were at close range at Bunker Hill suggests one of the colonial weaknesses, a lack of ammunition.

The two quotes by Patrick Henry were inspirational, similar to a half-time speech by a coach trying to rally his team to victory. The second of his quotes "give me liberty…" was stated at the time when the colonies needed that last push to openly rebel against the British.

Jefferson's famous line about the equality of man found its way into the Declaration of Independence. Many consider it to be somewhat hypocritical as an owner of slaves, but he did treat them with respect.

Nathan Hale was a young spy employed by George Washington who was seeking information on British troop movements around the NY City area. Before being hanged, he was rumored to have said, "I would gladly do it again."

John Paul Jones was an early commander aboard one of the first commissioned shops of the nascent US navy. His heroic tale will be covered soon. Similar to Patrick Henry, he was another voice of inspiration.

I am sure there were more, but these were some of the ones I learned as a young student of history. They illustrated the determination and self-sacrifice that was necessary to begin to build this great nation.

Before we tackle the major battles of the war, let's examine the strengths and weaknesses of both sides as they squared off to fight.

Most of the strengths or advantages were on the side of England. They had a much larger and more experienced army backed up by the world's largest navy that controlled the seas. Parliament could raise taxes to fund all the supplies the military would need. In addition, about 20% of the colonists remained loyal to England. The Iroquois Confederacy Indians who helped England defeat the

Algonquin tribes during the French and Indian War also sided with England against the colonists.

The weaknesses for England were that supplies and reinforcements were across the ocean and could take months to arrive. They had to employ mercenary soldiers (soldiers for hire from other countries) to attempt to conquer a very large swath of land, most of North America. As the war lingered there was growing opposition in Parliament.

Every advantage of England was a weakness of the colonies. They had a much smaller and inexperienced army and no navy at the onset. Supplies were hard to get from other nations as the British blockaded the major ports with its navy. Continental Congress had no power to tax so the war effort was financed by voluntary contributions and war bonds to be repaid later.

There were a couple of key advantages for the Americans. They were fighting for a cause they believed in and for their lives and those of their families. Fighting on home turf, they employed Indian techniques of camouflage and quick ambushes hoping to wear down the British. Their biggest advantage was their leader, George Washington, who fits the great man theory of history and was the primary reason for their triumph.

CHAPTER 14

The Revolutionary War

(1775-1783)

IN 1775, A SECOND CONTINENTAL CONGRESS met again in Philadelphia. This session had one delegate from each of the thirteen colonies. All voted for separation from England, and they began to prepare for war. Their first decision was their sagest, hiring George Washington to lead the new Continental Army, which derived its name from the Continental, the money used before the dollar was established as currency by Alexander Hamilton. On July 4th, 1776, the Declaration of Independence was enacted by the Founding Fathers of America. Thomas Jefferson was the main author with much input from Ben Franklin and John Adams. The document is actually a long essay with an introduction, a body, and a conclusion.

The introduction talks about human rights with words for the ages. "We hold these truths to be self-evident: that all men are created equal, that they are endowed by their creator with certain unalienable rights, that among these are life, liberty, and the pursuit of happiness." The introduction also states that the government derives from the consent (approval) of the governed i.e. the people are the lawmakers.

The body of the Declaration lists all the abuses of the king and the attempts of the colonists to peacefully remedy the abuses. The conclusion is that since all peaceful efforts have failed the colonies have no choice but to declare their independence. The Declaration of Independence was signed by the fifty-five Founding Fathers. John Hancock was the president of the Continental Congress and his signature is much larger than all the other signatures. The reason for Hancock's oversized signature is part legend, part truth. King George was myopic (poor vision) and Hancock wanted the king to know, in no uncertain terms, where he stood in terms of the Revolution!

I have to give pamphleteer Thomas Paine his due for his famous document. Paine circulated a pamphlet called Common Sense throughout the colonies urging separation from England. Paine argued that America was no longer British, their goals were different, and as Paine said with passion "The time to separate is now!" His writings certainly made sense to the framers of the Declaration. His pamphlet was also widely read and accepted in England leading to a good deal of opposition to a war with the colonies.

Now that war was inevitable let's examine the strategies that each side employed in order to win the war. The British concentrated on attempting to cut off New England from the rest of the colonies. They correctly perceived that the headquarters of colonial war operations emanated from the area around Boston. The British also wanted to take control of all the port cities on the east coast to cut off supply lines to the colonies.

The colonial strategy was to fight a defensive war that avoided large battles and relied on guerrilla warfare—sneak attacks, small battles, and ambushes—hoping the British would tire of fighting. George Washington would employ his experience from the French and Indian War to carry out this strategy. I chose ten battles to concentrate on from the war.

Battle	Importance
Lexington, Concord (1775)	"Shot heard ' round the world"
Bunker Hill (1775)	Stalemate
Long Island (1776)	Washington Escapes
Trenton (1776)	1st American Victory
Saratoga (1777)	Turning point of war
Monmouth (1778)	British surrounded
Kaskaskia (1778) Vincennes (1779)	Colonies get control of Ohio valley
Yorktown (1781)	Last major battle of the war

There were, of course, many more battles than my top ten, along with other significant events some of which I will detail.

The Battles of Lexington and Concord, Massachusetts were actually small skirmishes fought between the Minutemen and the British, who were attempting to find colonial weapons and arrest Hancock and Adams. The Minutemen were mostly small shop-keepers who kept a musket ready to fight the British at a "minute's notice," hence their nickname. Once these skirmishes ended there were several deaths on both sides and no turning back. Besides Minutemen, each colony had a militia, an unpaid volunteer army not as large as the Continental Army, the salaried army under the command of George Washington.

The "shot heard 'round the world" eventually led to a worldwide rebellion of colonies throughout the world against their mother countries. The American Revolution led to the French Revolution and eventually to colonies of other nations in North America, South America, and other areas around the world who asserted their own independence from the European countries of England, France, and Spain. Eventually, the British and other empires would collapse but not until the 20th century. In short, the American Revolution changed the geopolitical landscape of the world forever. Freedom became the buzz word of the modern world.

The Battle of Bunker Hill was fought for control of nearby Boston and its harbor. The British thought it would be an easy victory, but the colonists fought them to a draw (stalemate) before retreating. The British did not know it, but they were about to be blindsided by one of the most heroic war efforts ever undertaken. Ethan Allen, and his militia the Green Mountain Boys from Vermont, had captured the British Fort Ticonderoga that over-looked the Hudson River in upstate New York. They lugged heavy cannons 150 miles through snow and ice and over the mountains to Dorchester Heights overlooking Boston. The British were stunned! After attempts to dislodge the cannons, the British gave up and sailed out of the city. Boston was free!

Meanwhile, George Washington's Continental Army was in hot water trying to defend NY City from a British takeover. During the Battle of Long Island, trapped on the Brooklyn shoreline across from Manhattan and surrounded by a much larger British force, Washington devised a plan of escape. At night he basically set Brooklyn on fire then quietly moved his troops to a location where his spies had recruited a volunteer navy of small boats to ferry the army across the East River to Manhattan Island under cover of darkness. The British did not fight at night. It was one of their rules of war and Washington used this knowledge to aid his escape. Washington earned the nickname "Old Fox" for his bag of military tricks and tactics he employed. Washington led his army into New Jersey and towards Philadelphia, in order to help "the city of brotherly love" maintain its freedom.

The Continental Army arrived at an area close to Trenton, New Jersey just before Christmas. There was a large mercenary force of Hessian (German) soldiers across the Delaware River. On Christmas night, Washington, listening to the intoxicated Christmas carols being slurred by the Hessians, rallied his troops for a surprise attack. Crossing the Delaware—now memorialized in a famous painting—was no easy task with ice inhibiting the crossing. The "battle" was over quickly as the few guards were overwhelmed and the rest of the Hessians more than likely still drunk. Washington was able to take supplies, shoes, and weapons from the Hessians and actually convinced many to switch sides, which they did. News of this first victory was followed up by another win at Princeton, so the army had something positive to hang onto as the brutal winter set in.

The Battle of Saratoga (NY) was the turning point of the war. A turning point means that one side begins to get the upper hand. England had planned for three separate armies to meet near Saratoga on the Hudson River then unite and march east to retake Boston. One army under General Howe decided to try and capture Washington's army near Philadelphia and a second army was decimated by a combination of colonial and Indian forces near Lake Ontario. General John Burgoyne's army was left there waiting for reinforcements. Meanwhile, patriot troops under the command of Horatio Gates and Benedict Arnold surrounded and defeated Bourgoyne, who was forced to surrender 8,000 soldiers to the Patriots!

Ben Franklin had been in Paris trying to get French support for the war effort. When news reached Paris of the victory at Saratoga by the Americans, the French signed an alliance with the U.S. to send military aid to America. This was one of Franklin's great contributions to the formation of the United States. England was very concerned about this alliance. They changed their strategy and began to think that the South would be easier to conquer, as things had not gone well in the Northeast.

Some mention should be given to the story of Benedict Arnold, whose name today is synonymous with the term "traitor." A brilliant soldier, he is credited with most of the success at the Battle of Saratoga. Unfortunately, he was an egomaniac with an expensive lifestyle. He complained to Continental Congress that he, not Washington, should be the commander in chief of the Continental Army due to his successes. He was reprimanded by Congress, but Washington saw his brilliance and put him in command of an army guarding the fort at West Point, NY, overlooking the Hudson River. Arnold quickly made plans to change sides, so for about 20,000 dollars he initiated a plot to turn over the fort to the British General George Clinton. However, his plans were intercepted en route to the British, yet Arnold was able to escape. He became an officer in the British Army but post-war spent the rest of his life alone in a cheap apartment in London, forever identified as a traitor even by the British who rank honor as one of their core values.

Washington's troops had a very unproductive year in 1778 and found themselves wintering in Valley Forge, PA. It was a miserable winter with his troops forced to live in makeshift huts. Some soldiers deserted and some promised to return in the spring after planting was done on their farms. Washington assigned Baron Von Steuben, a Hessian, to drill the troops in new fighting techniques. This kept the men occupied during the winter. Women in the area also played a pivotal role. They were able to sneak in food and supplies from nearby Philadelphia, which the Continental Army had lost control of. There were a couple of thousand deaths in Valley Forge that winter. Without the support of the women, there would have been considerably more. Today, Valley Forge is a designated national historic site.

Washington's Army came out of Valley Forge ready to fight after a frustrating winter. The patriot forces won a decisive battle at Monmouth, New Jersey just outside of NY City. The importance was that although the British maintained control of the harbor in NY City, they were now surrounded by enemy forces. The long-term effect was that no more battles would be fought in the middle colonies, as all the action now shifted to the West and South.

George Rogers Clark was a militiaman from Virginia who worked outside the realm of the Continental Army. With fellow militiamen from Virginia, Pennsylvania, and North Carolina, he quickly overwhelmed the British outpost at Kaskaskia, Illinois, and in a sneak attack during the winter of 1779 took over the British encampment at Vincennes, Indiana. Surprisingly, the Indian allies of the British did not rally for the British and over time Clark and his militiamen established settlements taking control of the Ohio Valley.

Meanwhile in 1779, Captain John Paul Jones, "the Father of the U.S Navy," was involved in an incident at sea that inspired the ground war in America. Jones had been pirating and sinking British ships off the coast of America and now found himself off the coast of England about to engage in a sea battle with a British ship, the

Serapis. France had lent Jones the ship the Bonhomme Richard to harass British commercial shipping, but taking on a British warship was a more difficult task. The smaller Serapis got the better of the larger Bonhomme Richard, which was about to sink.

According to the rules of war the victorious ship had to give safety to the enemy who were not allowed to drown at sea. The Serapis got too close and when the captain asked Jones to surrender, he replied "I have not yet begun to fight!" Then he was able to hook and pull the Serapis closer. In hand to hand fighting, Jones's crew prevailed and the British were the prisoners. The myth of the invincible British Navy had been broken! People in America rejoiced.

In the South, the British seized control of Charleston, South Carolina, and Savannah, Georgia, the two biggest colonial seaports, but not much else. Credit here must be given to general Nathaniel Greene and Francis Marion, the "Swamp Fox." Although it is not stated, he is the person being portrayed in the movie "The Patriot" starring Mel Gibson.

Like Washington's official army, Marion and the rebels donned colors that blended in with the environment, and as a result they were hard to spot. When the British were forced to use guerrilla warfare, it was just a matter of time before they would surrender. The territory was too big to conquer and hold, especially when you couldn't see the enemy right next to you. The British expected what they called a "gentleman's fight" where you lined up in plain sight of your enemy. The enemy though did not follow the rules of war, and the British could not or would not adapt. The British refused to give up their red coats, which made them easy targets in swampy, guerrilla warfare. Nathaniel Green eventually took back control of the Carolinas, and the British retreated to Yorktown, Virginia waiting for reinforcements from New York to be brought there by their navy.

Although the war technically ended in 1783, the last major battle took place at Yorktown, Virginia in 1781. In the spring, Washington had learned that a large French fleet was headed toward Virginia to cut off the British fleet being sent to aid Lord Cornwallis, the British general, at Yorktown. Cornwallis had been successful in keeping the Marquis de Lafayette, a young French officer sent to help Washington and his army at bay.

Washington saw a chance to end the war. Along with Rochambeau of France and his army, they joined together and quickly marched to Virginia to help Lafayette surround Cornwallis, whose entire army was on a peninsula near the Atlantic Ocean. Cornwallis was able to defend his position though outnumbered by the combined Franco-American forces. Cornwallis kept looking out to sea expecting the British fleet from New York to save him. What he did not know was that the French fleet under Admiral de Grasse had turned back the British fleet. Imagine his shock when he finally saw all the approaching sails—every one of them French! Cornwallis was caught between two overwhelming forces and was forced to surrender. The white flag was the sign of a ceasefire.

The rules of war state that the two generals meet out in the open with the loser handing his sword to the winner. Cornwallis was ashamed and embarrassed. He further humiliated himself by sending out a subordinate officer to give his sword to Washington. The British military band played the song "The World Turned Upside Down." The war would continue with a few more skirmishes, but it was clear who was the winner. Freedom for America! In Philadelphia, they rang the Liberty Bell.

There were many reasons for the defeat of the British. Perhaps the major reason was that after the Battle of Saratoga other nations took up arms and/or poured money into the defeat of England. France, Spain, and the Dutch instigated smaller wars during the course of the Revolution with the result that Parliament may have agreed to peace so they could concentrate their energy defending the homeland from foreign invasion. As it turned out, England maintained its sovereignty as its navy continued to rule the seas.

The Treaty of Paris (1783)

Negotiated largely by Ben Franklin and his protege Thomas Jefferson, the peace treaty was completed in September 1783. Below are the terms of the treaty.

1. Great Britain recognized the United States of America as an independent nation.
2. British troops were to leave the United States "with all convenient speed."
3. The boundaries of the United States would extend north to Canada, west to the Mississippi River, and south to Florida. Florida was returned to Spain.
4. The United States received fishing rights to the Grand Banks off the coast of Newfoundland, Canada.

The Stars and Stripes (1777 flag) flew proudly over NY City as the British sailed out of NY Harbor in 1783. The United States was now a much larger country with a growing population that was ready for westward expansion. The biggest obstacle to the new nation would be the set-up of its government. There were many options to be considered and many compromises ahead before a democratic government would be formally established.

America's First War Submarine

Sergeant Ezra Lee of the Continental Army was probably the first man in history to operate a submarine against an enemy fleet. In the summer of 1776, a powerful British fleet sailed into NY Harbor. The fighting vessels, bristling with guns, anchored just out of range of General Washington's cannons.

Such was the situation when, on a dark night, Sgt. Lee climbed into the submarine, the Turtle. The egg-shaped Turtle was indeed strange looking. It could move on the surface or underwater. The operator propelled it by foot pedals much like those on a modern bicycle.

Attached to the Turtle was a bomb loaded with 120 pounds of gunpowder. A device enabled the operator to attach the bomb to the bottom of a vessel, in this case, British admiral Howe's flagship, the Eagle.

The plan failed as the bomb got loose and bobbed to the surface where it exploded with a loud roar. Lee guided the vessel to shore but future exploits were abandoned. Although America's first war submarine was not really practical, the idea itself was sound.

CHAPTER 15

The Articles of Confederation

(1781-1788)

AFTER 176 YEARS OF COLONIZATION INCLUDING the final eight years of war and negotiation, the thirteen British colonies had been transformed into the United States of America. The first order of business would be to establish a government that could make order out of the residual chaos and destruction leftover from the war. The articles were written by John Dickinson of Pennsylvania and it took nearly four years for all thirteen colonies to ratify (enact into law) these articles.

The fact that it took nearly four years to be passed by Congress indicated the transitional nature of this plan that had many more weaknesses than strengths.

On the plus side, a permanent Congress was set up. Under the Articles, each colony had one representative. Congress was granted the power to declare war, enter into treaties, deal with foreign affairs and operate post offices. The one crowning achievement under the Articles was the passage of the Northwest Ordinance of 1787.

This organized the western lands taken from England in 1783 into what would become the five states of Wisconsin, Michigan, Ohio, Indiana, and Illinois. Once these clearly delineated territories attained a population of 60,000 people, they could apply to Congress for statehood. In these territories, plots of land were all the same size as was the plot of land for the public school system to be set up in each township. Slavery was outlawed in all these territories that stretched from the Great Lakes to the Ohio River. [The 1619 Project overlooks this inconvenient fact in its syllabus.]

The weakness of the Articles were numerous and the Constitution quickly reversed these weaknesses—no executive or judicial branch, no control of trade or power of taxation, no power to coin money or raise an army, and laws could be ignored and, new laws had to be voted for by all thirteen states. The bottom line was that the states retained too much power, having the ability to nullify Congressional laws they did not believe in. The new republic also feared the rise of another monarch.

The Shays Rebellion (1787) showed the weakness of the Congress to deal with a crisis. Daniel Shays, a major war hero, led a rebellion of Massachusetts farmers who were being threatened by Congress for non-payment of debts. Congress was going to seize their farms, so Shays and his rebels armed themselves with government weapons with the intent of killing local officials at the state level if necessary. Fortunately, cooler heads prevailed, but it showed that the government did not have enough money or control over its own population. Change was needed!

CHAPTER 16

Foundations of the Constitution

FUTURE PRESIDENT JAMES MADISON, "The Father of the U.S.Constitution," was the major author and garnered many of his ideas about government from the European Enlightenment of the 17th and 18th century that used reason and individualism instead of traditional ways to establish governments. Madison and the other founding fathers relied heavily on the writings of Rousseau, Locke, and Montesquieu.

Rousseau's *social contract* proposes that individuals give up some of their freedom to an elected leader in return for protection from anarchy that Rousseau defined as too much freedom. John Locke wrote about the protection of *natural rights* - in this case, he advocated for the rights of life, liberty, and property— again with a government elected by the people to ensure that these rights are carried out. Finally, Montesquieu wrote about the separation of power into three equal branches—legislative, executive, and judicial—in his *Spirit of Law*. For nations to avoid the tyranny of a despotic monarch, power should be shared by a number of people each with the ability to curb the power of the others.

The Constitutional Convention

The near takeover of the state of Massachusetts by a group of destitute farmers led by Daniel Shays showed that a new plan of government was needed for the fledgling nation. In the spring of 177 fifty-five delegates from the thirteen states met in Philadelphia in an attempt to establish a workable plan of government for the United States. Of those fifty-five delegates, thirty-nine would eventually sign the document into existence with two Founding Fathers, and future Presidents, not present. Thomas Jefferson was the ambassador to France and John Adams had the same post with England but two future Presidents did sign, George Washington and James Madison.

The conditions for drafting what would become the world's most emulated document were not ideal, to say the least. Meteorologists reported that the spring-summer time span of the convention was the hottest year on record. Independence Hall, where they met, was closely guarded to keep out the unwanted press, plus the windows were kept shut with no ventilation and yet formality dictated that the delegates wear their wool suits! The cobblestone streets were covered with grass to diminish the noise of the constant parade of horse-drawn traffic passing by the building. Debates got testy, to say the least, but under the calming demeanor of the convention president Washington, those representatives kept to the task at hand. When completed in August, the new Constitution was quickly ratified by the states, with the agreement that a Bill of Rights would be attached later.

By 1789, the Constitution became the law of the land and the envy of the political world. Although written hundreds of years ago scholars marvel at the flexibility of the document to coincide with changing times, hence the moniker "a living breathing document." It is beyond the scope of this book to thoroughly detail the entirety of the Constitution, though in terms of total verbiage it is the shortest one in the world, as well as the oldest. I will attempt to outline the structure of the Constitution—again like the Declaration of Independence—a long essay, separated into articles. Next, I will show how the Constitution solved many of the issues left over from the Articles of Confederation and how it dealt with a myriad of other issues both now and then. The simple fact that there have only been twenty-seven changes (amendments) to the Constitution shows that the Founding Fathers created a document that would address any issue that could arise. It was as if they had a crystal ball.

After a number of compromises agreed upon by the Founding Fathers, the Republic of the United States was officially born with something for everybody. One agreement was the establishment of a federal form of government, where power is shared between the state governments and the national government, headquartered in Washington, D.C. The founders were very aware of states' rights and the fear of another monarch, so they agreed that power should be limited by dividing the power between state governments and a national government. This is known as federalism. Many people still prioritized their state loyalties first and a national identity second. As you will see the whole issue of states' rights will be a major cause of the Civil War in the 1860s.

The Great Compromise worked out the question of who should have more power, the smaller populated states or the states with more people? The New Jersey Plan said that Congress should remain as it was with each state having one representative. On the other hand, the Virginia Plan said that the larger states should get more representatives. The compromise agreed upon was the formation of a bicameral (two-house legislature) with the lower House of Representatives favoring the big states as the bigger the population the more representatives it received. The upper house of the Senate favored the smaller states as each state would receive two senators.

The next compromise was the Three-Fifths Compromise having to do with slavery. Southern culture referred to slaves as property, but when the Constitution was being written those slaves were now "people" to be counted for representatives to congress. Northerners objected, arguing that you can't have it both ways. The compromise was that sixty percent of the slaves were counted as a population. Even as the Constitution was being fashioned already there are two underlying causes of a civil war, slavery and states rights, that could threaten all the good work of the founders.

Compromises aside, Congress needed help governing America so two more branches of government were added—the executive and judicial branches. This is called the separation of powers where each branch has its own job. Congress (legislative branch) are still the lawmakers while the executive branch led by the President carries out or enforces laws leaving the Judicial Branch to interpret laws and hand out punishment for breaking laws. In today's world, the branches are supposed to have separate but equal power, though some think the executive branch may be too strong, while others feel the courts are crossing the line and becoming activist lawmakers.

The Founders also set up a system of checks and balances to make sure one branch did not accrue too much power. Some simple examples to start. The president can veto (reject) bills from becoming laws. The Congress can, as you well know, impeach the President and remove him if both houses of Congress agree. The Supreme Court has the power of judicial review, nullifying old laws passed by Congress or the states or rejecting previous rulings by the

Court itself. Judges may be impeached by Congress and legislators (Congressmen and Senators), can be removed by the Supreme Court.

Let's examine how some of the problems left over from the Articles of Confederation were solved by the new U.S Republic. By granting Congress the power to tax, the size of the army could be increased as well as the expansion of the navy. Congress now had the power to coin money and abolished all the state currencies that had hindered trade between states. An anecdotal story to explain how trade was or was not accomplished under the Articles. Each state had its own money and did not trust the value of the money from other states. The other problem with trade was that every time a merchant crossed a state line his products were taxed before he could sell them. Intrastate trade (within a state) was good, but inter-state trade (between states) not so good. In those days, roads were wooden and when a wagon went to cross a state line a gatekeeper with a large wooden pike would put the pike through the wheels of the wagon until the tax was paid hence the birth of a turnpike (toll road). Many of you have traveled along well-known turnpikes such as the Florida or New Jersey Turnpike. Congress abolished many of the barriers to trade between the states. Tolls today are used in theory for road maintenance and construction. With the use of the dollar, trade was encouraged and flourished.

In summary, the Great Compromise (1787) established a two-house Congress with full legislative powers. After this hurdle, the executive and judicial branches were added with a system of separation of powers and checks and balances. The U.S. had set up a federal system of government with shared powers ultimately to be determined by the voting will of the populace.

CHAPTER 17

Structure of the Constitution

- Preamble (Introduction)
- Article 1 Legislative Department
- Article 2 Executive Department
- Article 3 Judicial Department
- Article 4 Relation of States to each other
- Article 5 Amending the Constitution
- Article 6 General Provisions
- Article 7 Ratification
- Bill of Rights: First Ten Amendments
- The other seventeen Amendments

THE BEST-KNOWN WORDS IN THE CONSTITUTION are the opening words of the Preamble. "We the people..." this famous phrase showed clearly that the Founders believed in a government that derived from the consent of the governed. When the convention completed the Constitution, the document was given to the people for approval. Only when the people had given their consent did the new government of the United States begin to exist.

Let us look at the qualifications one must meet to run for the House of Representatives and the Senate plus the responsibilities beyond lawmaking.

To run for the House you must be twenty-five years old, have been a resident of the U.S. for seven years, and reside in the state you represent. There is only a two-year term of office but no limit to the number of terms you can serve. Because there is little job security, many look to move up to the Senate. To be a Senator you must be thirty-five years old, a citizen of the U.S. for nine years, and reside in the state that elects you. The term of office is six years and there is no limit to the number of terms you can serve. The leader of the House is called the Speaker of the House and becomes president without being elected if a catastrophe kills the president and vice president. If you have been following the news, you already know that the House can impeach (charge) a president with a crime and the Senate conducts the trial, if there is one. Only three presidents have been impeached—Andrew Johnson, Bill Clinton, and Donald Trump—but none have ever been removed from office. Richard Nixon would have surely been impeached and removed for instigating the Watergate Scandal but chose to resign, citing health reasons.

Most bills (proposed laws) have to be ratified by both the House then the Senate. These bills go next to the desk of the president who can sign them into law or veto them. If both houses of Congress feel strongly for the passage of the bill they can override (repass) the bill by a two-thirds vote of both houses. The president cannot veto twice as the people have spoken, so the bill becomes law. One way Congress controls the president is by having the power of the purse. If the president or other government agencies support a law, the

House of Representatives can choose not to pay for that law, again giving them the final say in the lawmaking process.

Perhaps the greatest power of Congress is the so-called "elastic clause" that stretches the power of the Constitution to deal with future events. For example, in WWI the elastic clause was used to create the USAF. [The USAF became an official branch of the military in 1947] Germany had the Luftwaffe (Air Force) and the U.S. saw the threat it posed to world security so Congress authorized the money for the technology, creation, and training of the Air Force personnel necessary to combat and defeat Germany. The elastic clause was the crystal ball gift of the future provided by the founders and is perhaps the main reason that the U.S Constitution is referred to as a "living, breathing document." Congress has the right to declare martial law in times of emergency where the military takes control of the government until the crisis has passed and citizens temporarily lose their rights. When the crisis is over, the rights of citizens are restored. During the Revolutionary War, the British issued writs of assistance, which were search warrants issued without habeas corpus (a body of evidence). Congress no longer has that right.

Taken collectively, powers granted to Congress are called *delegated* powers. Powers not granted to Congress are called *reserved* powers and are given to the states. Examples of state powers include laws setting up the school systems and setting speed limits on local roadways. *Concurrent* powers are those shared by the state and federal government, such as taxation and road building. The federal government can tax you on your income, while the state can enact excise or sales taxes. Many states are witnessing population growth at the expense of other states, as their taxes are lower and/ or non-existent.

Let's look at the qualifications one must have to run for the office of president and some of the responsibilities and perks a president will receive as the leader of the nation. Rightly so, the Constitution limits the presidency to natural-born citizens. This applies to the vice president as well. People who become U.S. citizens can aspire to any governmental office outside of the presidency. The idea of dual executives is an ancestor of the Roman Republic, where two top executives were co-consuls with equal power.

You must be at least thirty-five years of age to run for president, and if you have been out of the country, perhaps serving in the military, you have to be a U.S. resident for fourteen consecutive years. The twenty-second amendment of 1951 limits the president to two terms of office. Only president Franklin D. Roosevelt served more than two terms during the Great Depression years in the 1930s. The president is the commander-in-chief of all the military branches. War and peace strategies of the Pentagon (the generals) must get the approval of the president before they are implemented. The president can propose laws and grant pardons (releases) to certain types of criminals. The president is in charge of foreign policy and can write treaties with other nations with Senate approval. Every year, the president gives a State of the Union presentation on television. The opposing political party can rebut that message after the president is done with his presentation. Besides enforcing laws, the president is the leader of his political party and is acknowledged as the leader of the free world, so he has a lot of power, to say the least. The president can also take executive actions known as executive orders, often leading to rancor from the political party not in power. Ex-President Obama used to brag "I have a pen and a phone" when the Republican-led Congress would not work with him.

Perks of being president are lifetime FBI security for himself and his family, free-living in the White House with all food shopping, etc. done for him and at taxpayer cost. The president also has a private, armed jet, Air Force One, to take him wherever he wants to go. To avoid a calamity, the vice president uses Air Force Two. The President and his family also get free lifetime healthcare. An old term applies here RHIP—rank has its privilege. If the president can not function in the capacity as president, the vice president assumes his position. Since this is an emergency there is no provision to elect another vice president, so a prominent member of the party in power will become vice president.

Unlike the first two branches, there are no elections in the Supreme Court of America—the highest court—but there are elections in the lower courts. The Judiciary Act of 1789 allows Congress to create more courts in America as the need arises. To become a justice of the Supreme Court you have to be nominated by the sitting president and approved by a majority of the Senate. There are one hundred U.S. Senators, and if there is a tie vote the vice president, who is the leader of the Senate, casts the final tie-breaking vote. Once you are a Supreme Court judge, it becomes a lifetime appointment unless a judge is impeached by Congress. Currently and for the last several decades, there are nine judges on the Supreme Court. Since they can serve for decades their decision-making has more long-term consequences than those of a president.

The Supreme Court only considers about fifty cases per year. They have the final say on the legality of old laws or old court cases. This is called *judicial review*. If they find a law is unconstitutional from any level, federal, state, or local, that law is stricken from the books. The Supreme Court only considers cases that have national importance, i.e. affordable health care. They are not concerned with smaller issues unless they threaten the integrity of the Constitution. The only criminal case where they originate the action is in the question of treason. These cases begin and end in the Supreme Court. The Supreme Court is an appeals court at the highest level where those convicted look for the last chance. Most times the Supreme Court declines to hear cases of appeal, so the ruling in a lower court is the final verdict.

Article Four of the Constitution describes the procedure for the addition of new states and guarantees the safety of all the states. This article also includes the principle of extradition. Those who commit crimes in one state are not free if they flee to another state. This is the province of the FBI. Once a person is apprehended in another state, he is returned to the state where the original crime occurred. If said criminal commits a crime in the second state then he/she is subject to two trials, one in each state. States utilize "hot pursuit" laws where police vehicles may cross a county line chasing a perpetrator of a crime who they witnessed committing the crime. Counties also extradite criminals back to the county where said crime was perpetrated.

Article Five describes the amendment procedure. Beyond the two-thirds vote of both houses to add an amendment to the Constitution, there is also a second way. Within a set time period if three-quarters of the states—thirty-eight— vote for an amend-ment, it is a done deal. Article six is the Supremacy Clause of the Constitution meaning that the U.S Constitution is the highest law of the land, more powerful than the government that was derived from the Constitution. In matters of law, federal laws supersedes, or at least are supposed to, laws of states.

If you are following current events, one case that is sure to arrive in the Supreme Court one day is the law concerning Sanctuary

Cities. Large cities like Los Angeles and New York City are not complying with federal authorities who have arrest warrants for criminal aliens. The law is very clear that these cities must help round up these criminals. As of now, they are not complying. The last section in this article is the acknowledgment that the new United States owes debts to itself i.e banks and other countries and intends to pay down these debts. Guess what? This has never happened, so the National Debt is a huge number and huge issue that no one wants to deal with. Banks try to get this debt-money repaid to them and their only recourse is to charge you more for borrowing money for home and car buying and credit cards. Without this National Debt, things would be a lot cheaper to buy and you would have more money to spend and save. Those of you who are in the younger generations will have the double whammy of paying down your college loans and helping to pay off the national debt. Any politician promising voters free this or that is lying through their teeth. Former politician Al Smith put it bluntly. "There is no such thing as a free lunch." Someone must pay the bill!

The ratification of the Constitution is covered in the last article. Nine of thirteen states were required to sign for the enactment of these laws. The Constitution was technically in effect in 1789 when George Washington became the first President. Delaware was the first signer of the Constitution in 1787, hence its license plate, The First State. The Bill of Rights was added in 1789 and Rhode Island the last ratifier in 1790.

CHAPTER 18

The Bill of Rights

THE FIRST TEN AMENDMENTS TO THE Constitution are the Bill of Rights and were added immediately to the Constitution as some of the founders were worried that there was no direct language in the Constitution concerning the rights the country fought so hard to achieve, hence this addendum to the Constitution. Some of this material will be dry, but I will attempt to add some color by applying the Bill of Rights to some more recent issues.

Bill of Rights

Amendment 1	Freedom's amendment
Amendment 2	Right to bear arms
Amendment 3	Quartering of soldiers
Amendment 4	Search and seizure; warrants
Amendment 5	Rights of the accused
Amendment 6	Right to a speedy trial
Amendment 7	Jury trial in civil cases

Amendment 8	Excessive bail or punishment
Amendment 9	Powers reserved to the people
Amendment 10	Powers reserved to the states

Freedom of religion in America has been a controversial issue in our country from colonial times to the present. All of the Founding Fathers believed in a creator that blessed the birth of our country and many felt that Christianity should be the affirmed national religion. The dissenters pointed out that this would create a theocracy and other religions would be excluded. God was very important in the writing of the Constitution, though ironically James Madison, the major author of the Constitution, was an atheist along with several other presidents. The compromise stated that so long as a religion did not condone violence it should be allowed to exist. There are constant disputes today about prayer in public places as well as the placement of religious symbols, especially around Christmas time. Then there are the Atheists, members of the emerging cancel culture, who want to abolish religion and God altogether. I am glad they get their day in court. I am doubly glad that they lose about ninety-five percent of their cases.

We do have freedom of speech guaranteed by the Constitution. This allows people to criticize their government and to freely express how they feel about any number of subjects. They are even allowed to burn the American flag in protest. This dates back to the 1960s, as many Americans protested the Vietnam War and helped to bring about the war's demise. In the 1970s, Iran's Revolution took down the Shah (leader) and replaced his government with an Islamic Theocracy. They took American hostages and burned our flags, blaming America for the rule of the Shah who they claimed was put in place by the oil interests and the U.S. government. I have never been a fan of flag-burning. It is an insult to our great nation, but it has been legalized by court cases. The one disclaimer in regard to this freedom is that although you can verbally criticize and parody public officials, you may not threaten them with violence or retribution. All you trolls on the internet take heed.

From the Zenger Case, previously discussed, was born freedom of the press—and today's TV and Internet media—to criticize government officials. Often called the Fourth Estate, the role of the press has unfortunately changed over the last several decades. The press used to be an impartial watchdog, ready to growl at any or all politicians that seemed to be corrupt. This was a great tool of social control by the people. However, in today's highly politicized world about ninety-five percent of the written and television media are positioning themselves as an arm of the Democratic Party. The press used to be a neutral watchdog. That neutrality went out the window with the advent of the Vietnam War in the 1960's and the Watergate Scandal in the early 1970's.

Freedom of assembly allows citizens to join together peaceably to discuss issues that affect them. The limit to this freedom is that these meetings are not allowed to morph into angry mobs who destroy property and buildings, etc. There is too much of this happening in America today as we speak, especially the Antifa mobs burning down our cities.

The Second Amendment right of citizens to own guns actually began with the militias of the thirteen colonies and the Minutemen shopkeepers in New England. Many court cases have affirmed the right of gun ownership. Today many argue that because of deaths due to the use of firearms, guns should be made illegal for sale to the general public. The American population of over 300,000,000 is less than the estimated amount of guns presently in our country today. You might as well outlaw breathing as an attempt to get rid of all the weapons in existence. The root cause of gunplay is mental illness. Putting more effort into solving people's issues is the key to some lessening of gun violence and homicides from firearms.

The Third and Fourth Amendments to the Constitution have a common philosophical birth. In British jurisprudence and colonial America, both cultures affirmed the phrase that "a man's home is his castle," meaning there must be strong certifiable evidence of illegal activity present for the authorities to invade one's privacy and enter their home. Under the Bill of Rights, soldiers may only be put into the homes of citizens during times of martial law, where all rights are temporarily suspended. No longer can writs of assistance—warrants without Habeas Corpus (evidence) be permitted. Search warrants have to be specifically written by the authorities and signed by a judge. The right to privacy and the prevention of random police searches have been addressed, especially by the Fourth Amendment.

The Fifth, Sixth, Seventh, and Eighth Amendments are collectively known as "the bill of rights of the accused." These amendments protect the rights of persons who have gotten into trouble with the law.

The Fifth and Sixth Amendments describe the due process of law. A person has to be indicted (accused) of a crime by a grand jury then given a written statement of charges against him/her. A person has to be proven guilty and does not have to testify against themselves in a court of law, known as "pleading the fifth (amendment)." There is also no double jeopardy allowed. This means you cannot be tried twice for the same crime. Once charged with a crime, a person is entitled to a speedy trial of his peers and is entitled to a lawyer for defense, and if the accused can not afford a lawyer the court will provide one. The defending attorney can cross-examine witnesses testifying against the accused.

Under terms of the Eighth Amendment, torture may not be used in pre-trial interrogations or post-verdict if the person is found guilty and put in jail. In some cases, bail is posted to allow certain low-level offenders to remain free until their trial begins. This bail amount has to be affordable. In higher profile cases, where there is doubt about the return of an accused for his trial, bail is not allowed as the accused is considered a flight risk, possibly escaping to another country. By the way, not all countries have extradition agreements with each other. The issue of bail is becoming a flash-point in our changing society. There is a big push from the Left to eliminate bail. That would have the effect of emptying most of the jails in America. No wonder legal guns are getting difficult to purchase. People are scared of the many thousands of criminals being let out of jail.

Two additional legal concepts originated with the Fifth Amendment. The first concept is known as eminent domain. If the government decides it needs to confiscate private property for a public need, they are allowed to so long as they compensate the person losing their property. This occurs with roadbuilding for example, where homes or businesses may be in the way. Once the government demolishes the property they must relocate you nearby and pay you equal or more compensation for your relocation. The second legal concept concerns so-called Miranda Rights, originated from the Supreme Court Case of Miranda vs Arizona (1966). Ernesto Miranda was accused by the Phoenix police department of kidnapping and raping an eighteen-year-old girl. After two hours,

Miranda confessed and signed a written confession. It was later revealed that at the onset of the trial that there was no attorney present, nor were his rights read to him at the time of the arrest. The case was suspended on a technicality. In the retrial, he was found guilty but served only five years of a much longer sentence, getting parole for the remainder. Again fate intervened. Whether you believe in God or cosmic payback, Miranda was knifed to death outside a bar in 1976.

Police procedures changed. Officers were told to tape the Miranda Rights to the sleeves of their shirts as a reminder to read potential criminals their rights at the time of arrest.

Amendments Nine and Ten add no new rights to the Constitution. They simply affirmed two principles—that the federal government of Washington, D.C is only allowed to do certain things and that any powers not given to the national government are retained by the people and the states.

This is a very cursory summary of the Bill of Rights. There have been books written about the laws and the cases that have amounted from squabbles over the interpretation of the laws. It is important to remember that "facts" can be subject to interpretation, like two sides to every story. A legal idea implicit in the Bill of Rights is the statute of limitations. This is a law that sets the maximum amount of time that parties involved in a dispute have to initiate legal proceedings from the date of an alleged offense, whether civil or criminal. After a certain amount of time, certain crimes can no longer be prosecuted, so people can literally "get away with murder."

The Electoral College

A final creation of the Constitutional Convention was the establishment of an electoral college that had nothing to do with any institution of higher learning. There are a total 538 votes amongst the fifty states. To win the Presidency, one must get 270 or more electoral votes—more than half the total—to be certified the winner. This means two things. One, you have to win the popular vote, the vote of the people, and two, every electoral vote is important to reach 270. This ensures that the smaller populated states are not ignored. In theory, a candidate can win the nine most populated states and have more than the needed 270 electoral votes while the loser could win the other 41 states and lose in the electoral college. If we had a direct democracy, the big states and cities would get all the attention and have more than their share of power. However, the U.S is set up as a Republic, via the Great Compromise, so all parts of America get a say in the government.

After the popular votes have been totaled and the winner determined, a couple of days later the 538 electors chosen from the winner's political party meet in the Capitol Building to cast their votes. Almost 100% of the time they are loyal and vote for the victor of the election.

Birth of Political Parties

From the Constitutional Convention debates arose the first two political parties in America, the Federalist Party and the Anti Federalist Party, aka Democratic-Republican Party. The Federalist Party favored a strong central government with business and industrial leaders taking the lead in directing government policies. Famous Federalists included James Madison, Alexander Hamilton,

John Adams, and two future Supreme Court Chief Justices, John Jay and John Marshall. Opposed to the Federalists were the Anti-Federalists, led by Thomas Jefferson, favoring a weaker central government, states rights, and a Bill of Rights, all of which would prevent another monarch from taking control of America. They believed that the middle class of farmers and small business owners and everyday people should be the drivers of policies in America.

George Washington did not believe in political parties, as he believed they created division in society, as seen today. Over the decades, the names of the parties have undergone many changes. Today, the Federalists have become the Republicans while the Anti-Federalists have become the Democratic Party, which is morphing into the Sociocrat Party as there is a generational civil war within today's Democratic Party.

Traditionally, the Democrat Party has been referred to as the "big tent" party as they embrace many different groups of people who want to, in some cases, radically change America. All this diversity could be a strength or perhaps a weakness. Only time will tell.

The Republican Party generally has been the more traditional party, using the lessons of history to guide policy. The Republican Party was the party favoring the wealthy, but recently they have expanded their outreach to others using their success in elections as a recruiting tool. Republicans view incremental change as acceptable and inevitable but feel that too much change leads to upheavals in society. As I stated earlier, a second civil war is foreseeable in this country given the seemingly total disaffection of one side toward the other. With the results of the 2020 presidential election in the books, it seems like the demographics of party membership have flip-flopped. More on this topic to follow near the end of this book.

There are any number of alternative parties to the two major parties. Some examples are the Green Party, Libertarian Party, and, yes, the Communist Party, constitutionally sanctioned.

Millennial History

CHAPTER 19

The Early Presidents

WITH A PLAN OF GOVERNMENT IN PLACE, a fragile new nation looked up to its "father" to lead the way. Without opposition, Washington became president of America from 1789-1797.

Washington forever shaped the government of the United States. He and his advisors devised a number of precedents to help the government run smoothly and protect its safety. A precedent is an example to be followed later, a first if you will. I think it best to list the precedents established then explain them.

Precedents

1. Cabinet
2. Two-term presidency (praeses)
3. Establishment of U.S. Army
4. Appointed members of Supreme Court
5. Made Thanksgiving first national holiday
6. First state of the union address and census

7. President may propose laws

8. Only President to free his slaves (posthumously)

9. Established foreign policy of isolationism

The cabinet are advisors that are appointed by the president to help him run the government. Originally there were only four cabinet posts, all led by the secretaries. There was Secretary of State Thomas Jefferson who dealt with foreign affairs, Secretary of the Treasury Alexander Hamilton who dealt with monetary and fiscal (tax) issues, Secretary of War Henry Knox, and Attorney General Edmund Randolph, who dealt with legal issues in the nation. From the inception, there was tension between Jefferson, an antifederalist, and Hamilton, a hard-core Federalist, and Washington had to arbitrate their disputes, but because of their wisdom and experience both were irreplaceable.

Hamilton single-handedly created the financial structure of the U.S. Republic. He eliminated all state currencies and made the dollar bill the common medium of exchange, greatly increasing trade. He understood that business and industry had to grow, so he initiated tariffs—a tax on imported goods—to encourage the growth of America's infant industries.

Hamilton used different methods attempting to pay off the debts of war to other countries and to colonial banks and those who invested in the war effort. First, he proposed selling some of the western lands in the NW Territory to settlers who wanted to move there. Second, he proposed excise or sales taxes on certain goods made within America. Third, he sold government bonds aka savings bonds to individuals. When these bonds matured, the government paid back the investor back plus interest. Lastly he set up a National Bank that collected taxes and coined money. After the war with England, Hamilton remarked that "the price of liberty is debt."

Unfortunately, this debt has never been fully repaid from day one. Hamilton also directed the National Bank to go more into debt by paying off all the money owed to foreign nations. He reasoned that omitting to do this would lead to a lack of foreign trade as the U.S. would not be trusted to pay its debts. He was correct on the first premise, but the national debt continues to pile up and I have already explained the effects on us today—higher taxes and higher costs for many products and higher interest rates for credit card usage.

Outside of Franklin Delano Roosevelt, the precedent of a two-term president has been the norm. Washington felt that any more than two terms could lead to too much power accruing in the executive branch. As historian Richard Brookhiser noted, "Washington's last service to his country was to stop serving." Washington also chose the term president as his title. President originates from the Latin term "praeses," meaning leader.

Washington's Continental Army morphed into the U.S Army over time, Congress saw the need for a navy, marines, coast guard, and air force and eventually they were funded and expanded.

Several early presidents owned slaves, yet he was the only president to set his slaves free. You have to attach an asterisk to this action, as they were not freed until the death of Washington in 1799.

Some of the other precedents are self-explanatory, except for the U.S. foreign policy of isolationism, or non-involvement in world affairs. The next section will show you how and why U.S policy of isolation evolved, as well as how Washington protected the new nation from both internal and foreign invasion.

Protecting America

1. 1793- Neutrality in France - England War
2. 1794- Signing of Jay's Treaty
3. 1794- Battle of Fallen Timbers
4. 1794- Whiskey Rebellion

Washington had to make a tough decision in 1793. France appealed to the U.S. to return the favor of French aid during the Revolutionary War and to now send aid to France to fight England. Our country was too weak and could not engage in another war, so he decided on neutrality (not taking sides). This led to bad feelings with France.

England wanted America to be its main trade partner, so the Jay Treaty was signed in 1794. It avoided war with England, temporarily, but did not solve the issue of impressment—the kidnapping of U.S. sailors by the more powerful British Navy.

The British and their Indian allies were still causing trouble in the Ohio Valley. Washington sent "Mad" Anthony Wayne and his army to the Ohio Valley to quell that disturbance. Wayne had served under Washington in the Revolutionary War and was a ferocious Indian fighter. After Wayne's victory, the British soldiers were removed and the insurrection ended.

We have already discussed the Whiskey Rebellion, where the new government flexed its muscle without much resistance—Washington being there sent the message that the U.S. meant business and the rebellion was ended with the promise of a reduced excise tax on the production and sale of corn whiskey in western Pennsylvania.

As Washington prepared to leave office in 1796, he counseled the nation with his Farewell Address, one of America's great speeches because of its long-term impact. Washington expanded the growth of America by warning the country to "avoid entangling alliances," especially with Europe. Without interference the country could grow quickly, he asserted. Of course, protection by two oceans was of further assistance. America followed his advice and engaged in a policy of isolationism that was in effect up until WWI when our national security was threatened. In this time period, America grew to be the world's unchallenged superpower.

Most historians rank him as the second most famous president to Lincoln. I see it the other way around, for without Washington there is no Lincoln. It's also personal as Washington is in my family tree. Before my parents died, they gave me written papers from my father's grandmother, and upon doing the math I deduced that I am a fourth-generation great-nephew of Washington, who had no children. He was too busy fathering America!

John Adams (1797-1801)

John Adams became the second president, defeating political rival Thomas Jefferson in a close election. Though Adams was a Federalist and Jefferson an Anti-Federalist, Jefferson became the vice president as he received the second-most votes for president. It wasn't until the latter 1800s that candidates formed a "ticket" where would-be executives were of the same political party. Could you imagine the chaotic government we would have today if Donald Trump was president and Joe Biden vice president? Anyway, Adams was only a one-term president for reasons to be discussed soon. Historians agree that Adams's greatest accomplishment was keeping the U.S. out of a war with France. Here are three historical actions that occurred under the Adams Administration, followed by some explanation.

Events

1. XYZ Affair (1797-1798)
2. Alien and Sedition Acts (1798)
3. Nullification Theory (1798-1799)

Adams sent three American ambassadors to France to attempt to end the bad feelings between the two nations over the issue of U.S. aid that France needed to fight England. Three French agents, infamously called XY and Z, demanded a $250,000 bribe *before* negotiations began. The outrage was immediate. Two of our delegates returned to America as Congress and the general population called for war against France. Those in Congress who were pro-war were called—and still are today—war hawks. Those who opposed the war then and now are called "doves." For historical context, look at the 1960s-1970s protests of the Vietnam War and the peaceniks at Woodstock. The use of the symbol was omnipresent.

The furor of Congress during the XYZ affair led to the great expansion of the U.S. army and navy. U.S. naval ships attacked and sunk French ships at sea, but Adams did not want a general war, though he was in the minority. Cooler heads did prevail but this was one strike against Adams. (Historians today agree that Adams did the right thing at the time preventing war with France)

The advocacy of the Alien and Sedition Acts by John Adams was another reason for his one-term tenure in office. Passed by Congress as a result of xenophobia, these acts were unconstitutional but the Supreme Court, the "weak sister," of the three branches did not nullify these laws. The Alien Act gave power to the president and Congress to evict any person seen as an alien enemy toward the U.S. especially Frenchmen, who were feared as spies. This of course violates the 5th Amendment procedure of due process. The Sedition Act took away the freedom of speech and freedom of the press as newspapers were not allowed to criticize the government during this troubling time.

In response, Vice President Jefferson actually led the opposition to these acts. He influenced lawmakers in Virginia and Kentucky to use *states' rights* to oppose these laws. States' rights say that states can choose not to obey federal laws by nullifying them, similar to the days our country was governed under the Articles of Confederation. *Nullification* meant those laws no longer apply in the states of Virginia and Kentucky. These principles became a direct cause of the Civil War and are used by sanctuary cities today as a rationale for not enforcing laws in regards to illegal aliens. Anyway, France had to focus on its European wars, so the XYZ Affair came to a negotiated end. Two other factors may have caused Adams to be only a one-term president. People had not forgotten that Adams had defended the British soldiers at the Boston Massacre trial. Many did not care for his personal demeanor. He was viewed as somewhat snooty and his Puritanical background was in opposition to the new melting pot identity of America. But he must be given credit for maintaining the independence of America, avoiding war with both France and England.

Thomas Jefferson (1801-1809)

A protege of Benjamin Franklin, he became the first Anti-Federalist President of America. A true Renaissance Man—author, diplomat, writer, governor, and inventor (the dumbwaiter and swivel chair)—he had great faith in the farmers and the commoners of America, given an education, to rise to leadership positions in America. He was probably the first and last president to reduce the size of government and National Debt. He eliminated the whiskey tax and other excise taxes and reduced the size of the military after the threat of war with France had passed. Conversely, he added more land to the U.S. than any other President and at a marginal cost. A lot happened during his two terms of office including the following:

Jeffersonian Contributions

1. Major author of the Declaration of Independence (1776)
2. Established the USMA (1801)
3. Marbury vs. Madison (1803)
4. Napoleon and the Louisiana Purchase (1803)
5. Lewis & Clark Expedition with Sacagawea (1804)
6. Perhaps the largest family tree of any president
7. Died on the same day as rival John Adams (1826)

Though his most famous words, "all men are created equal…" are the cornerstone of our democracy, some critics wonder if those words are hollow since he was a large owner of slaves like many of the Founders, who collectively had a tough time rationalizing the existence of slavery in a democracy. I'll let you decide. Jefferson saw the need for a professional army in a hostile world. He immediately secured funding from Congress to establish the USMA (United States Military Academy) at West Point, NY. To become a cadet today you must be nominated by a local politician and have excellent grades and behavior.

The Supreme Court case of Marbury vs. Madison established two precedents for the court and eliminated the moniker "weak sister" as this branch had been inferior in power to the other two branches. Chief Justice John Marshall—a Federalist and enemy of Jefferson—along with his other associate justices, through a series of rulings established supremacy of the court and judicial review. To make a long story short, Marshall's court ruled that in all cases, without exception, federal law supersedes any and all state laws. He further stated that the court could review any law or previous court case and find them to be unconstitutional and taken off the books. Because Marshall powered up the Supreme Court, he is known as "the Father of the Supreme Court."

The growth of the United States was aided immensely by the rise of the dictator Napoleon Bonaparte in France. He was a great man of history, if for all the wrong reasons. His conquests are legendary and had brought most of Europe to its knees except England, which was protected by its powerful navy.

Napoleon needed money for his wars of conquest and made Jefferson an offer he, and Congress, could not refuse. If the U.S. paid him fifteen million dollars they could possess the entire Louisiana Territory that today makes up parts of thirteen states and was the single largest land deal in U.S. history. Even arch-enemy John Marshall had no objections. For a few cents per acre the

U.S. was able to eliminate both England and France from the new western lands.

This new expanse of land had to be explored and mapped, so Jefferson hired Lewis and Clark to do the job. They in turn hired Sacajawea, an Indian maiden, to join them. They would help her find her brother along the way. Her calm demeanor and Indian heritage prevented any hostilities to occur between the two cultures. That would occur soon enough. The expedition left from St. Louis in 1804 and journeyed northwest to the Pacific Ocean. They returned by 1806 with journals replete with descriptions of the land, animals, natural resources, and the many Indian tribes they encountered. Of course, this led to a great push of westward expansion once people read about the rich new world of the west. Sacajawea became a national treasure. Though she died young, Clark raised her two children. She is in the Women's Hall of Fame and to honor her a commemorative coin was minted with her visage on it in the year 2000.

Jefferson sponsored other expeditions into Colorado and Texas. "The expedition into the area of Colorado was led by Zebulon Pike, for whom the famous Pike's Peak is named. F.J Turner, in his *Frontier Thesis*, states that the Lewis and Clark expedition was the most "formative event in U.S. history." The Louisiana purchase added 827,987 square miles of land, doubling the size of the United States.

The one blunder of the Jeffersonian administration occurred late in the second term of his presidency. The Napoleonic Wars created severe shortages of supplies for both England and France. American merchant ships made a profit when they were able to get to England or France. England seized the cargo of ships heading to France and continued to impress (kidnap) sailors who they claimed were Englishmen. Some were and some were not. The American Navy was not strong enough to deal with the problem, so Jefferson forced Congress to issue an embargo that stopped trade with all countries. American business ground to a halt. England and France found new trade partners in South America. The Embargo Act of 1807 was a fiasco and was terminated in 1809.

Jefferson may have the biggest ancestral family tree of any president. His wife Martha bore him six children, but only two lived long lives, while Martha herself died at a young age. Jefferson never married again but began a long relationship with Sally Hemings, a half-sister slave of his wife, who was three-quarters white. She may have given Jefferson up to six children. He took her to Paris several times but did not leave much-written information about their relationship. I have seen aerial photos of a Jefferson family reunion. There are thousands of people in those photos, quite amazing.

It is also true that Jefferson and Adams died on the same day and year, appropriate for both of them. They both died July 4, 1826, fifty years to the day of the signing of the Declaration of Independence! Jefferson passed first and Adams's last words, a few hours later, questioned if Jefferson was still alive.

James Madison (1809-1817)

Jefferson's huge success as president allowed Madison, who was Jefferson's Secretary of State, to succeed him as president, the third Virginian to become president. Though short in stature, standing just five feet and four inches tall, Madison had a profound influence on America, being the major author of the Constitution. Some people and events that brought notoriety to the Madison administration are as follows:

1. War of 1812 (1812-1814)
2. Star-Spangled Banner (1814)
3. Military generals who became presidents
4. First protective tariff (1816)

Often called the Second War for Independence, the three main causes of the war were the three I's—Impressment, Interruption of trade, and Indian conflicts. New England business leaders sarcastically referred to this avoidable war as "Mr. Madison's War," as the war set back the economy and as noted could have been avoided.

It was clear that the U.S was unprepared to fight this war, as the British Navy torched the city of Detroit on the Great Lakes and more importantly were able to torch our capital city of Washington, D.C. According to journal accounts, the president and his wife, socialite Dolley, were hosting a dinner at the White House as the British were approaching Pennsylvania Ave. They barely escaped capture as the British contemplated eating the still warm dinner left behind.

Fortunately, things improved for the U.S. as the British were repulsed at Baltimore and New York City. Meanwhile, on Lake Erie the U.S Navy defeated the British fleet and U.S troops led by future president William Henry Harrison defeated a combined British and Indian force led by Tecumseh and his Confederacy of tribes. Upon the death of Tecumseh and the defeat of his tribes along with the defeat of the British Navy, the entire Northwest Territory was forever under control of the U.S. government. [Harrison's victory at the Battle of Tippecanoe became part of his successful campaign for president in 1840. "Tippecanoe and Tyler too!] In Europe, Napoleon had somehow escaped exile and was amassing a large army threatening the British mainland. The navy was recalled to England ending the impressment of U.S. sailors and allowing trade to get back to normal. The Treaty of Ghent was signed in 1814 in theory ending the war, yet the biggest battle, the Battle of New Orleans, was fought in 1815 as the news of the treaty had not yet reached the southern United States. This is where general Andrew Jackson solidified his fame by completely routing a much larger British army and allowing him, like Harrison, to become a future president.

Jackson's fame was achieved at the Battle of New Orleans. The British made a major blunder in the long battle at New Orleans by attempting to cross an open beach only to be cut to ribbons by Jackson's smaller army hiding behind a retaining wall. The British lost over 2,000 men to about 100 for the Americans. Jackson became a folk hero. Perhaps only Yorktown in the Revolutionary War was a more complete American military victory over the British.

Francis Scott Key was aboard an American ship in the Baltimore Harbor on the night that the British were shelling Ft. McHenry that guarded the harbor. The shelling raged into the night yet the U.S. flag stood strong, with bombs bursting in air. Key wrote down the words that would be our national anthem, The Star-Spangled Banner. It wasn't until 1931 that Congress designated it as the National Anthem. The runner-up was the melody America the Beautiful.

After the war, Madison saw that our new industries needed to grow more to compete in the world marketplace. In 1816 with the approval of Congress, the first protective tariff was passed. This tariff made foreign goods more expensive, protecting America's fledgling industries. In today's world tariffs have been used against us. This has caused a lot of stress, especially between the U.S. and

China, who clearly want to eclipse our economy as number one in the world.

With the War of 1812 in the rearview mirror, the U.S. was in a good place. European powers were preoccupied with Napoleon. Our country had doubled in size and following Washington's ideas on isolationism along with the protection of two oceans the U.S was poised for a rapid westward expansion.

James Monroe (1817-1825)

He was the last of the Virginia Dynasty of presidents. He took control of a much more stable country with only one pressing problem, slavery. I would have to say that the only other period in our history similar to this one was post World War II America under President Eisenhower, where there was widespread tranquility across America.

Most of the accomplishments under Monroe's administration have to do with land management in the U.S. and for the first time beyond its borders. To wit:

1. The Era of Good Feelings (1817-1825)
2. Adams- Onis Treaty (1817-1825)
3. Missouri Compromise (1820)
4. Monroe Doctrine (1823)

The "Era of Good Feelings" coincided with the demise of the old Federalist Party. The old guard of Washington, Adams, and Hamilton, who was killed in a famous gun duel with Aaron Burr had come to an end. The party would rebrand itself in the future but during this quiet time, people were fairly happy under one big apolitical tent. The one issue left unsolved was that of slavery. Most of the previous presidents who lived in this democracy were willing slave owners.

Monroe saw a chance to add to Jefferson's land acquisition legacy by getting Congress to agree to sign the Adams-Onis Treaty (1819) with Spain. Spain needed money, so they sold little-used Florida to the U.S for 5,000,000 dollars. The U.S. now had total control of the East Coast and of all the land to the Mississippi River.

There was an equal number of slave states and free states before 1820. This changed as Missouri applied for statehood as a slave state. The Northern Congress was fearful of becoming a minority in terms of power, but fortunately Maine applied for statehood as a free state after having broken away from the control of Massachusetts, thereby maintaining the balance of free states and slave states in Congress. Looking at the issue of westward expansion and slavery, Congress drew an imaginary line at the latitude line of 36* 30*, the southern border of Missouri. Going forward, all land north of that line would still be free but popular sovereignty (a vote of the people) who determine slavery, or no slavery, in new states south of that line. The Missouri Compromise issue proved to be a band-aid solution to the continuing issue of slavery in an expanding America.

Monroe's notoriety is forever associated with his Monroe Doctrine (1823). This statement of foreign policy was a corollary to the Washington policy of Isolationism. Monroe told the world to stay out of North *and* South America. New colonies were no longer allowed and conversely, the U.S. would not interfere with the European world outside of trade.

The new countries of South America applauded this policy, as did all of North America.

The only problem was there was no way to defend two continents from interference. This policy was a "paper tiger," but it was effective because of the new respect accorded America, having defeated England twice in warfare. The Europeans had defeated Napoleon but were very depleted from years of war and needed a break from future turmoil, so the Americas began to grow as independent nations. Remember the shot heard 'round the world? It was taking effect. By the way, James Monroe became the third president to pass away on July 4th. His last year was 1831.

CHAPTER 20

Henry Clay

(1777-1852)

THOUGHT OF AS THE GREATEST AMERICAN never to be elected president, Clay contributed so much to the growth of America. Involved in politics for over forty years, he was known as one of America's great public speakers. He was Secretary of State and Speaker of the House as well as a senator from Kentucky. He lost three presidential elections to two war heroes—William Henry Harrison, Andrew Jackson, and James Polk, the greatest non-Virginian pre-Civil War president, who was responsible for getting Texas into the United States. Though Kentucky was seen as a south-leaning state, Clay advocated for the growth of America vis-a-vis its industrial base.

Two of Clay's lasting contributions were the following:

1. The American System (1816-1828)
2. The Great Compromiser (1820-1850)

Clay's American System incorporated three elements. The first was the 1816 tariff that protected the small but growing U.S. industries and manufacturers. The second element was the maintenance of a national bank to finance the growth of the business world. The third element was the expansion, financed by the government, of the American infrastructure of highways and canals to facilitate trade, travel, and homesteading.

His greatest achievement in road building was the 600 mile Cumberland Road that connected Washington D.C. on the Potomac River to the land leading to the Ohio River. This was the second macadam (paved) road in America with thousands more to follow. He had a vision of the entire East and Midwest being linked by one waterway, so he pushed for the completion of the Erie Canal in upstate New York. This was the last link of a waterway that connected New York City to the Great Lakes and continued down the Mississippi River to the port of New Orleans. Trade was possible now from the Atlantic Ocean to the Gulf of Mexico. A series of locks had to be built between lakes and rivers to equalize the water height so ships could safely sail through.

Clay also earned the moniker the Great Compromiser for working out treaties that diffused sectional crises. Though a slave owner himself, he did what he could to prevent his nation from going to war over the issue of slavery. Clay earned his experience in negotiation by getting the British to sign the Treaty of Ghent (1814) ending the War of 1812, costing his country next to nothing. President Madison then asked him to negotiate the Compromise of 1820, just discussed, which appeased both sides and kept the stress of the slavery issue to a minimum. Thirty years later, president Millard Fillmore asked Senator Clay to work with Senator Stephen Douglas to work out the Compromise of 1850 having to do with the spread of slavery further west. Details to be revealed later, but again Clay was successful in keeping his country from going to war over a single issue.

CHAPTER 21
Sectionalism

THOUGH WESTWARD EXPANSION WAS GROWING the two major power regions of America were still the North and the South. Both had very different lifestyles, much of which owed to their geography. Sectionalism is defined as loyalty to one's region (section) of the country rather than the country as a whole. The Mason-Dixon Line was originally drawn to avoid a conflict between the bordering states of Maryland and Pennsylvania. This line took on a new meaning in 1780 when Pennsylvania abolished slavery. Over time, all of the states north of this line also abolished slavery. Now this line was the demarcation border between free states and slave states. Let's look at how the two sections were totally opposite.

North	South
Urban-Industrial	Rural-Agrarian
Fast-paced life	Slow-paced farmers
Outlawed slavery	Slavery- economic tool
Pro- tariff	Anti- tariff
Strong central government	States rights and nullification

The three largest cities in the U.S. were Boston, Philadelphia, and New York City. Many suburbs were offshoots of these urban areas. Both areas are very crowded and competitive with a faster pace of life. The Northeast is the home of business and industry, though there was subsistence agriculture in New England and the Bread Basket was located in the middle states, where large commercial farms were located but not as expansive as Southern plantations and with the shorter growing season.

In the South, the climate is much warmer and there are long distances between plantations and farms. Their villages are few and far between with the cities located near rivers or the ocean for shipping and receiving goods. Agriculture is time intensive, so the pace of life is slower and revolves around the farm or plantation.

The Puritans and the Quakers were the first to outlaw slavery, the Puritans near Boston and the Quakers near Philadelphia. Both groups took guidance from the Bible that said it was immoral to keep others in bondage. Although Christianity was just as strong in the Baptist South, slavery was seen as a necessary evil, an economic tool needed for survival.

Northerners favored the protective tariffs as it made imported goods more expensive and allowed the new northern industries to flourish. Southerners disliked tariffs, because they were forced to buy goods from the North now as European goods became too costly. The South would not really industrialize until the onset of the Civil War when they were forced to do so.

Lastly, the North favored a united and strong central government that kept everyone safe and on the same page. The national government seemed to favor policies beneficial to *the North*. The South was ingrained with a history of state's rights and nullification. These methods would be employed as the efforts at compromise slowly began to fall apart.

CHAPTER 22

Westward to the Mississippi

WITH THE STABILITY CREATED BY THE EARLY presidents culminating in the Era of Good Feelings, America was at a good jumping-off point to begin to explore and settle the new lands of our country south of west of the Appalachian Mountains to the Mississippi River.

In the Southeast, the worn-out spoil of the Tobacco Road States, together with a growing population led to a migration of people to the deep south- Alabama, Mississippi, and Louisiana—to start even bigger plantations with cotton becoming the main cash crop, hence its nickname "King Cotton." The South did not need Clay's American system, as it already had an extensive system of connecting waterways for transportation that was a natural occurrence.

North of the Mason-Dixon line, it was a different story. Clay's American System along with the Industrial Revolution would provide the means and modes of transportation necessary to tame the wilderness and turn it into habitable land.

The term frontier began to enter the American lexicon in the early 1800s. The Frontier can be thought of as the boundary between the known and the unknown. There were four modes of transportation created in the first three decades of the nineteenth century that would transform the Frontier into rural, agrarian, and subsequently urban industrial areas:

1. Improved roads
2. Canals
3. Steamboat
4. Railroad and Telegraph

Macadam roads, created by Scottish inventor John McAdam, replaced the wooden and dirt roads in the early 1800s. Like today's roads, they were flat and slightly tilted to allow water to run off to the side. These roads allowed the heavy stagecoaches and Conestoga (covered) wagons to smoothly transport the great distances of this new America. The canvas-covered Conestoga wagon was created in 1750 in Conestoga, Pennsylvania, and could transport entire families and all their belongings. The term "wagon train" originated from the procession of many wagons following each other on their way west. They were also a means of protection from Indian attacks.

The Big Ditch (Erie Canal) was completed in upstate New York in 1825. This canal served two purposes. The booming New England population used it as a conduit to the new areas around the Great Lakes for settlements which quickly became states. As noted, the Erie Barge Canal was the last link of transportation from New York Harbor to the Gulf of Mexico. The growth of new businesses and industries as well as all the new cities around the Great Lakes owe their birth to the completion of the Erie Canal.

The first barges and boats on the Erie Canal were pulled by horses at about two to three miles per hour. The invention of the steamboat by another Scotsman, Robert Fulton, quickly made the old system obsolete. His ship, the Clermont, could go upstream with little water resistance, so trade and travel time were greatly reduced. Soon there were steamboats up and down the Hudson River and more so on the Mississippi River. Before his acclaim as one of America's greatest writers, Samuel Clemens aka Mark Twain was a steamboat captain on the Mississippi River. This was his inspiration for his characters Huck Finn and Tom Sawyer.

The period of canal transportation did not last too long. In 1827, only two years after completion of the Erie Canal, a charter was given to the Baltimore and Ohio Company to build a railroad between the two cities of Baltimore Maryland, and Wheeling West Virginia. Engineer Peter Cooper from New York invented the steam-powered Tom Thumb, the engine that pulled the rest of the train. Within forty years, the entire United States from New York to Los Angeles and San Francisco was linked up by a series of railroads known as transcontinentals.

Railroad management realized they had to keep track of the railroads in case there was a breakdown or attack by thieves or Indians. Necessity being the mother of invention, Samuel Morse invented the telegraph using his Morse Code that transmitted words across overhead wiring. The first words telegraphed by Morse were suggested by his friend Ann Ellsworth. "What hath God wrought?" Was she happy or anxious about the future?

All along the Mississippi, cities developed at a remarkable rate as new industries and farm crops were planted. On the west side of the river, prairie lands were the main geographic formations. There was a shortage of trees and soil was tough to break up until the invention of the steel plow. This led to the growth of large corn and wheat fields, some used for food and some used to raise livestock. The city of Chicago, non-existent in 1800 was the largest city between the Appalachian and Rocky Mountains in 1860 and became the center of the slaughterhouses of animals processed for food. Other cities that grew rapidly were St. Louis, Cincinnati, Milwaukee, and New Orleans.

A number of items of American in the old Northwest Territory, slices of life if you will, I found interesting:

1. Cumberland Road
2. 1788 "Mayflower"
3. Clapboard "Shoes"
4. Defending Indian attacks
5. Horse and Locomotive Race
6. Low bridges

Around the time of the Revolutionary War, Daniel Boone led a group of settlers through the forests and established the village of Boonesborough, Kentucky. They had to clear a path by hacking down forestlands that led to the creation of a miles-long road. It became so well-traveled and designated as the Cumberland Road, America's first national road.

Before there were steamboats for transport, flatboats, propelled by oars and a huge rudder were first used on the Ohio River in 1788. The first flatboat carrying forty-eight colonists were named the Mayflower, honoring the Pilgrims. Shoes were hard to make, so people carried clapboards with them in the cold months. Worn out shoes and feet don't mix well with ice and snow on the ground, so if you had to be outdoors you *ran* and stopped often and put your feet on the wood you were carrying to warm up and avoid frostbite.

Unlike the solid-state construction of housing today, frontier housing was made of wood with slats between each board. It made for colder indoor conditions but you could see through the slats to make sure Indians were not lurking outside your home ready to strike. When the covered wagons stopped traveling they always formed a circle to prevent Indian attacks. This is the origin of the phrase "circling the wagons" in times of danger.

Peter Cooper's Tom Thumb was challenged to a mile race by a horse and buggy. Both contestants lined up on railroad tracks. The horse and buggy took a big lead but once the engine got going it surpassed the horse and buggy until a mechanical failure shut it down just short of the finish line. Although it lost the race, the future was put into motion, no pun intended.

Passengers used to pay good money to take river cruises on the Erie Canal. The Below deck was so overcrowded that getting to the top deck was a priority. There was only one problem. The bridges spanning the canal were so low that all the passengers had to lie flat on their back every time they went under a bridge. Thank God those riverboats were not steam-powered yet!

In less than twenty-five years all of the new land south and west of the Appalachian Mountains to the Mississippi had been explored. By 1848 all the land from the Atlantic Ocean to the Mississippi River had been organized into states, approved by Congress.

CHAPTER 23
Andrew Jackson
(1829-1837)

ANDREW JACKSON BROKE THE MOLD of the six previous presidents upon taking over the White House in 1829. (The term White House came into being during the War of 1812, as the British had burned it and was repainted white). Having defeated John Quincy Adams, the son of John Adams, Jackson, and his followers initiated the birth of the Democratic Party in America. Adams had been a member of the short-lived Whig party, much like the Federalist Party of his father. Jackson, because of his upbringing, was a disciple of Thomas Jefferson and had empathy for farmers and the common man. They in turn loved him, but his enemies both feared and loathed him. Donald Trump is often described as a modern-day Jackson, who was a doer, and if you opposed him, became a bulldozer.

Born of Irish heritage in rural South Carolina, he was already an orphan at age fourteen. His combative personality also stemmed from an incident that occurred in the Revolutionary War one year prior. A British officer ordered him to clean off his boot, and when Jackson refused the officer slashed him across the forehead with the blunt end of his sword. Jackson's only response was a look of hate that drove the officer away.

In his military career, he was shot several times, bending but never breaking, hence the nickname "Old Hickory" after a type of tree with a good deal of elasticity. The Battle of New Orleans made him a national hero and for removing the Seminole Indian menace from Florida, he became its first territorial governor. He also was a self-schooled local attorney then a member of the House of Representatives and senator from the State of Tennessee.

He received the moniker "cowboy president" for the near-riot he incited on his inauguration day at the White House as president. After the red carpet was rolled out and all the dignitaries in place, Jackson invited *all* of his minions in the streets to come up the stairs and join the party. The establishment politicians were aghast as his cowboy friends proceeded to wipe the horse dung off their spurs onto the carpet and walls of the White House. It surely made people temporarily forget about the burning of the White House by the British in 1812. That day the press corps described Jackson as the "mob president."

I used to assign an essay question to my students about Jackson. The question was, "Was he a good president, bad president, or both?" You can decide after we examine the following topics:

1. Jacksonian Democracy
2. Spoils system
3. Trail of Tears
4. Secession
5. King Andrew

There have been books written about democracy under the Jackson administration. His major contribution to democracy was that because of his enormous popularity among the majority of the populace and the fear he engendered in the elite classes, he was able to influence all of the state legislatures to allow the common man the right to vote. Before Jackson, the right to vote had been limited to wealthy property owners who were white males. The new states of the South—Tennessee, Kentucky, Alabama, Louisiana, and Mississippi—quickly got on board the Jackson train. In the northern states, legislators rewrote constitutions that expanded the right to vote. Other minority groups would have to wait, but it was the first step and essence of Jacksonian Democracy.

His extension of the spoils system was another area that illustrated the spread of democracy. These are jobs given to loyal campaign workers and friends who help a candidate get elected. They are appointed advisors to the president and though qualifications should count they are not necessary.

Washington's cabinet was the original example of executive spoils position in America. Jackson's cabinet was larger than the original four of Washington and was called the kitchen cabinet as his advisors often met in the kitchen of the White House to discuss and make policy—again much to the chagrin of the so-called establishment. Modern cabinets have hundreds of workers helping the president, none of them elected.

A major negative of the Jackson administration was his dealing with minorities. His plantation (The Hermitage) employed slaves, though mostly Jackson was a benign despot in his dealings with his slaves. The Indians were a different story. Because many of his army corps lost their lives in battle with Native Americans, Jackson was downright cruel in his dealings with them. As noted, he was able to get Florida settled as a state by forcefully removing or killing any of the Seminole Tribe that opposed him.

In 1830, he persuaded Congress to pass the Indian Removal Act. Indians were a nuisance to American settlement, so they had to go. Tribes from Georgia and other states including the Creek and Choctaw numbering up to 60,000 were forced to march across the Mississippi River all the way to the Oklahoma Territory. They were "guided" by the U.S. Army and along the way up to 4,000 died from this forced march. There were no burials and the trek became known as the "Trail of Tears," certainly a lower watermark for our country's history.

A series of protective tariffs were causing a lot of grief, mostly in the Southern states that were most affected. These tariffs forced Southerners to buy goods from the hated "Yankee" businesses of the North at a much higher price than preferred and cheaper British goods. Jackson had to walk the tightrope as he was a Southerner and did not like the fact that the North was profiting from the South, but he was also the president sworn to uphold the laws of the Constitution.

This tariff issue in the 1830s led to a whispered campaign of secession (breaking away from a country). John C Calhoun from South Carolina was Jackson's vice president and hated the tariff, so he wanted to nullify (disobey) it. If Jackson allowed Calhoun to get his way, nullification would lead to secession. This entire crisis came to a head at a cocktail party at the White House honoring Jefferson. One politician raised a glass to popular sovereignty (a vote of the people) and federalism, two opposite philosophies. Jackson jumped out of his seat, raised a glass, and giving the death stare to Calhoun said "our Federal Union, it must be preserved." Calhoun sat down and with a shaking hand replied meekly "the Union, next to our liberty, most dear." Jackson won the power struggle. Though he was a states' rights advocate and a Southerner, you must credit him for putting the country first.

Jackson's Whig Party opponents began to refer to him as "King Andrew." There is a famous political cartoon of Jackson with a royal scepter in one hand, a veto in the other hand, wearing a crown and stepping on the Constitution. Here are two good examples showing the regal power that Jackson brought to the office.

Chief Justice John Marshall, hated by Jefferson and Jackson, ruled that the State of Georgia could not trespass on the grounds granted to the Indians. This invalidated the Indian Removal Act. Jackson sniffed "Marshall has made a ruling… let him enforce it." Enforcement is the job of the executive but with Congressional support, his hatred of the Indians carried the day. The Indians were removed and Congress did not impeach Jackson.

In the second case, Jackson made it no secret that he hated the National Bank. It was half-owned by Northern businessmen and half-owned by the government. Northern businesses always got business loans but not enough capital was left for southern farmers and plantation owners who wanted to expand. Jackson could not wait until 1836, the year the bank's charter (license to operate) expired.

Jackson refused to recharter the Bank, claiming it was not mentioned in the Constitution, so it was unconstitutional. Opponents argued, and correctly so, that Hamilton had used the elastic clause to charter the bank. They were correct. They lost! Jackson got rid of the bank and took the bank's assets and put them into state banks, "pet banks" closer to home. Southerners were pleased; the Whigs cried foul. At the end, "King" Andrew had triumphed again.

The Jackson Presidency was an omen to what would be the gathering storm of the Civil War. The South had increased political power now with the right to vote extended to the common man. Though Jackson was a strong president, there was a suspicion that he was quietly favoring his Southern upbringing. Although Jackson quelled the secession movement initiated by his own vice president, there was growing concern that sectional differences might not be able to be handled in a peaceful manner. Many people like Henry Clay were working hard to keep the nation united. Would they be successful?

One of Jackson's unfulfilled goals was the addition of a large swath of land that would include what would become Texas. Jackson was able to enlist one of his young surrogates whom he mentored in the army—Sam Houston—to obtain his goal. They had a symbiotic relationship. Houston was the son Jackson never birthed and Jackson was the father figure missing in Houston's young life. Both survived multiple wounds from gunshots, knives, and swords that would have killed lesser men. They became part of what may be referred to as Frontier Founding Fathers. Their rugged individualism and contributions to the growth of America were prime examples of F.J Turner's "Frontier Thesis."

CHAPTER 24

The Reform Movement

DESPITE THE RAPID GROWTH AND SUCCESS of America, there were social problems not being dealt with that gave rise to the Reform Movement in America in the 1800s. Influential writers of the time such as Ralph Waldo Emerson and Henry David Thoreau called for more introspection, fearing that the individual was losing control of himself, caught up in the pursuit of the material world created by the Industrial Revolution. Sound familiar?

Thoreau framed the conflict thus—the Individual versus the Industrial Revolution. Emerson was interested in building meaningful communities. "Always remember the divine spark in your neighbor's heart. Help your neighbor, if he needs your help; but above all, never use your neighbor for your own selfish purposes." [I just finished reading the late Alex Trebek's book entitled *The Answer Is* and he shares a similar sentiment worth repeating. Trebek said, "A good education and a kind heart will serve you well throughout your life." This was a pathway to developing an understanding for others by becoming more knowledgeable.] Their writings were a driving force behind the following reform movements:

1. Prison Reform
2. Women's Rights
3. Anti Slavery movement)Abolitionism)

Prior to the 1800s, people with mental illness were incarcerated in the local prison, where they spent the rest of their lives being both neglected and tortured. People who spoke out irrationally were thought to be possessed by the devil. This belief stemmed from the old and outdated ethos of Puritanical times. Chained to walls, jailers literally tried to "beat the devil out" of the inmate, hoping to solve the problem.

In 1841, a Massachusetts woman named Dorothea Dix began a two-year investigation of treatments meted out to mental patients. The resulting study was shocking in its detail of widespread abuse. Her efforts resulted in the construction of new hospitals that offered real treatment in over twenty states.

In the 1840s, the case for women's equality was taken up by Lucretia Mott, Elizabeth Cady Stanton, and Susan B. Anthony. Mott and Stanton garnered enough support to hold a convention at Seneca Falls, N.Y. (1848). They issued a Declaration of Sentiments (modeled after the Declaration of Independence), which began: We hold these truths to be self-evident: that all men *and* women are created equal…" Stanton would later collaborate with Susan B. Anthony to write up a proposed law that would grant women the right to vote. It was handed to Congress in 1878 but was not made law until 1920 with the passage of the Nineteenth Amendment, aka the Susan B. Anthony Amendment. In 1979, Congress honored her as the first female citizen to be used in coinage with the issuance of the Susan B. Anthony metal dollar coin. [Wyoming was the first state to grant the right to vote to women. Western men viewed their women as co-equals when it came time to tame the environment popularly referred to as the "Wild West."]

The antislavery movement in America had many champions in the 1800s. The three most famous abolitionists, at the beginning of the movement were William Lloyd Garrison, Frederick Douglass, and Harriet Tubman, the latter two former slaves. Garrison, a New Englander, began a newspaper called *The Liberator* whose sole content was stories about abolitionism. Like the committees of correspondence during the Revolutionary War, the newspaper kept people informed about the cruelty of slavery in America.

Garrison and Douglass went on extended tours of the Northern states, rock stars of their time period. Garrison, a powerful speaker, would always speak first, but Douglass was the main attraction. A powerful speaker in his own regard, he was a big man with something to show the crowds that came to see him. An escaped slave from Maryland, first he described the evils of slavery, then took off his shirt, turned around, and revealed the whip scars that ran up and down his back. People were shocked! This was the visual evidence of abuse. The movement began to grow.

Harriet Tubman, also an escaped slave, was known as the "Black Moses" of her people, having led over 300 slaves to freedom. She made nineteen separate trips using the "underground railroad" and was never captured. The "underground railroad" was a series of farmhouses and other hiding places that stretched from Alabama to Canada. These houses belonged to abolitionists in the South as well as poor farmers who identified with the runaways in the states north of the Mason-Dixon Line. They traveled by night using the North Star in the Big Dipper to guide them north to safety. The leaders like Tubman were called "conductors" of the "railroad."

Originally getting to free states like Pennsylvania was the goal, but harsher fugitive slave laws and ruthless bounty hunters extended the "stations" all the way to Canada, where they were truly safe. It is estimated that the underground railroad may have liberated between 60,000-100,000 slaves. The antislavery movement did not solve the issue of slavery in America. Unfortunately, it would take a war, but it was a step in the right direction.

CHAPTER 25

Timeline of Slavery

1619 First Slaves in America

1700 Escalation of slavery

1780 Slaves fight in the Revolutionary War

1793 Invention of the cotton gin

1831 Nat Turner Rebellion

1840s Escalation of Antislavery movement

1852 Uncle Tom's Cabin

1863 Slaves in the Union Army

1865 13th Amendment

THE DUTCH BROUGHT THE FIRST SLAVES back from the African Atlantic Coast country of Angola in 1619 aboard a British privateer ship named the White Lion. As Virginia colony governor George Yeardley noted, "twenty and odd negroes" were brought to Point Comfort near Jamestown, Virginia for sale to those who could afford them.

The capture of African slaves was a dirty business. The Dutch, followed later by English slave ships, would become friends with the coastal Africans offering them guns and ammunition to keep in return for trekking inland and rounding up their enemies to be brought to the coast and enslaved aboard the ships. The Europeans did not have to do the dirty work and paid a small price for such precious cargo.

Once in America, families were broken up never to see each other again. Because the new plantations were small at first the amount of slavery was negligible until around 1700. As plantations grew, demand for cheap labor also increased quickly so by 1760 there were about 150,000 slaves and by 1810 that number doubled. It is estimated that during the Revolutionary War about 5000 slaves fought as soldiers and sailors against the British. Ironically, England was opposed to slavery.

There were several slave rebellions of note, with the Nat Turner Rebellion (1831) in Virginia being the most famous. Turner, a slave, organized seventy-five other slaves into a small army and over a two-day period murdered sixty whites. It took the Virginia militia to end the insurrection and Turner was hung for his misdeeds. Turner's death inspired the rapid growth of the antislavery movement in the 1840s, which we just examined.

There is an old saying that I learned in high school that said "there is nothing more powerful than an idea whose time has come," obviously about dramatic change. In 1793 Eli Whitney invented the cotton gin. It was a machine that separates the sharp seed from the soft fiber. Slaves often bloodied their hands by separating the seed from fiber until this tool of the Industrial Revolution came along. Immediately plantations got much larger with cotton fields now stretching across the Mississippi to Texas, without a doubt making the Civil War inevitable.

In the same vein, the book Uncle Tom's Cabin (1852) by Harriet Beecher Stowe, an Abolitionist, had a major impact, helping to initiate the Civil War. In the novel, Uncle Tom was a slave who was obedient but when his first master died, evil Simon Legree became his new master and beat him constantly. Tom refuses to disclose the whereabouts of runaway slaves, so Legree beats him to death. Tom is portrayed as a Christ-like figure with regards to his good deeds and character and as a martyr when he is put to death.

This book sold an unheard of 300,000 copies at the time. It was a major driver of the Civil War. However, the book did present a stereotype that was not true. In reality, beating slaves was a tool of last resort. How could the plantations be successful if the slaves were getting beat up? Yes, there were examples to be made. Simon Legree, who was a fictional character, might have publicly hung one of his slaves then thrown the dead body into the slaves sleeping quarters at night. The message was clear: if you try to run this is what will happen. The vast majority of slaves were well kept and since they did not know about a free life some fought with their masters against the North whom they saw as invaders. It is true that 186,000 black soldiers joined the Union Army but some were freemen from above the Mason Dixon Line.

Slave owners also had a hierarchy of slaves to lower the risk of rebellion. At the top were house servants who were educated in the real world and home-schooled the children and ran the day-to-day operation of the main plantation mansion. Slaves also became skilled artisans who could build and repair physical structures that needed to be added or repaired. They also knew about the outside world. These two social groups were kept away from the great numbers of field workers who did not know about the outside world, and the plantation owners wanted to keep it that way, otherwise, rebellions would have been much more pervasive. Of the nine million people living in the southern states, one third were slaves!

It is sad to note that up until 1850 our nation's capital, Washington, D.C. was a center of slave auctions in America. Imagine what foreign diplomats thought about this sad irony that in the capital city of democracy slave trade was being conducted steps from the White House and the Capitol Building. Embarrassing! Slavery technically ended in America in 1865, the last year of the Civil War, when Congress passed the thirteenth amendment banning slavery in America.

As a postscript to this topic, one of the best Civil War movies ever made is Glory (1989). It examines black-white relations in an all-black army regiment from Massachusetts and is a true story. It stars Denzel Washington and I highly recommend it to one and all.

CHAPTER 26

Manifest Destiny

THIS WAS A NINETEENTH-CENTURY DOCTRINE that stated the expansion of the United States was justifiable and inevitable. The land east of the Mississippi had changed from territorial to statehood for all by 1848. Now it was time to go west of the Mississippi and explore the rest of the Louisiana Purchase and whatever else was out there "from sea to shining sea."

The Industrial Revolution expedited the exploration of western lands with new inventions and sources of power. We spoke about how the cotton gin led to the large expansion of plantation life as far as Texas. A "sister" invention, the reaper by Cyrus McCormick contributed to the growth of wheat farms on both sides of the Mississippi.

Before the mechanical reaper, rows of men had to cut down hundreds of acres of wheat fields with hand scythes. It was slow and labor-intensive. The reaper cut down the wheat fields like a lawnmower would cut grass. Wheat is processed into cereal and is also used to feed livestock so both industries prospered.

Another technological advance was the creation of interchangeable (replacement) parts for contraptions like the reaper and the cotton gin. No longer did the entire machine have to be thrown out.

Replacement parts were created to fix the parts that were broken. These are also known as standardized parts and are a huge component of the car, truck, plane, and railroad industries.

The final advance associated with the Industrial Revolution was the discovery of new power sources to replace the water power of the old steamboats etc. Coal was discovered in Pennsylvania, Ohio, Kentucky, and Alabama. Coal allowed trains to run faster and longer. Iron ore was found in the ground and later processed into steel, which replaced the wooden frames of trains and houses and buildings. Transportation now was more available than ever, but the western lands had to be mapped before the railroads and eventually, cars could make their way there.

The so-called Mountain Men were the ones who did the dirty work of exploring the Rocky Mountains and beyond to the Pacific Ocean. More than any other group, the Mountain Men epitomized the "rugged individualism" of the American explorers of the west. This archetype brought a different form of democracy to the west detailed in Frederick Jackson Turner's "Frontier Thesis." There were many famous mountain men who fearlessly explored the west. I would recommend Bill O'Reilly's book, *Legends and Lies: The Real West* in which he details the exploits of many men who opened up the west to civilization. I chose three of these men who explored and mapped an insane amount of land on foot!

1. Jedediah Smith
2. John Muir
3. John C. Fremont

Smith was not famous until after he passed away. When his maps were recovered and found to be accurate his notoriety was validated. On foot and largely alone, he explored the northwestern Rocky Mountains all the way south to the Santa Fe trail in New Mexico. His maps led to routes that the transcontinental railroads, and other explorers, would follow.

John Muir was known as the "Father of the National Parks" and the founder of the Sierra Club, a powerful lobby group of environmentalists. After hiking in upstate New York along the Great Lakes, he later continued his hike from New Jersey to Florida, making notes about all the flora and fauna he came across. But he wasn't done. He hiked from the Pacific Northwest of California to Alaska a number of times! Yosemite National Park in California was his creation and all the adjoining parks like Yellowstone exist because of his efforts. His diaries and drawings inspired thousands of settlers to go to California and the Oregon Territory. In short, he was a one-man Lewis and Clark Expedition.

John C. Fremont, "The Pathfinder," also covered an amazing amount of land mostly with an assist from Kit Carson, one of the legends in the O'Reilly book. Fremont is credited with expanding the Oregon Trail which stretched from the Missouri River to the Oregon coast. Along the way, he explored the Rocky Mountains and the Great Salt Lake in Utah. Not quite done exploring, he expanded the land claimed by the U.S in the New Mexico Territory. Transcontinentals would one day get to Los Angeles and San Francisco because of his efforts.

Fremont was also a war hero, nearly a U.S. president, and chased the Spanish out of California. He got into trouble as he claimed to be the governor of California but was not elected. When he refused to step down, he was arrested and charged with treason but was let go and went back to exploring until his death.

All the western lands required to complete the manifest destiny of the "lower forty-eight" states were settled by the mid to late nineteenth century with Arizona becoming the last of the lower forty-eight states to attain statehood in 1912. The lower forty-eight states excluded Alaska and Hawaii that became states in 1959.

Dozens of books have been written about the settlements of the west. For purposes of brevity, I want to discuss the following situations that led to the near completion of the United States as we know it today:

1. Annexation of Texas (1845)
2. Oregon Country (1846)
3. Utah Territory (1847)
4. Mexican Cession (1848)
5. California Gold Rush (1849)
6. Gadsden Purchase (1853)
7. Kansas - Nebraska Act (1854)
8. Purchase of Alaska (1867)
9. Annexation of Hawaii (1898)
10. The "Wild West"
11. Pony Express (1860)

Texas (Tejas in Spanish) walked a long road towards becoming a state. In 1821, Mexico gained its independence from Spain and immediately looked for immigrants to grow the country. Around

1830 Stephen Austin, a frontier founding father, led 300 American families into Mexico and was given thousands of acres of land to farm and develop. The land was free but the Texans were not allowed to use slaves and they were supposed to convert to Roman Catholicism from Protestantism. Neither one of these changes was embraced and since there was little enforcement, life went on until Santa Anna became the dictator of Mexico. He began to cancel land contracts with the Texans and sent his police to enforce all the laws that were being ignored. When Austin asked for a peaceful solution he was thrown in jail for two years.

With Austin released from jail in 1835, the Texans united and declared their independence from Mexico. There were several skirmishes between the Texans and the Mexican Army that set the stage for one of the most remembered events in U.S. history—the battle at the Alamo. The Alamo was a Spanish mission that the Texans converted into a fort to defend themselves from the Mexican Army. There were only about 180 defenders inside the mission including Jim Bowie— inventor of the lethal bowie knife—and Davy Crockett, "King of the Wild Frontier," whose legend is often confused with Daniel Boone, the founder of Kentucky. Crockett was from Tennessee.

In March 1836 after the women and children were set free from the Alamo, the battle was on. The 180 defenders, waiting for reinforcements that did not arrive on time, held off thousands of Mexican soldiers for ten days until they were out of bullets and had to fight with knives and bayonets. Santa Anna's army not only killed but slaughtered the defenders. Being gutted like animals aroused a wave of great anger and resentment in Texas and the rest of America.

"Remember the Alamo!"became the rallying cry of Sam Houston, the general of a larger and extremely angry American Army that quickly defeated Santa Anna's army and led to Texan independence in 1836. [In California, the hot winds that blow out of the desert are named for Santa Anna who emerged from the Mexican desert to turn up the heat of war against the Texans in the Alamo] Sam Houston is the only American to be elected governor of two different states in America, first Tennessee then Texas.

Texas became an independent country - The Lone Star Republic - and asked the U.S. to annex it. The term annex means to take over land, usually by force. Initially, Congress did not want to annex Texas, because Texas was a slave state and would give the south an advantage in lawmaking with one extra state. Additionally, Congress did not really want a general war with Mexico. In 1845, the issue came to a head over the disputed southern border of the U.S. which the U.S. claimed was the Rio Grande River but Mexico claimed was the Nueces River further to the north.

The Mexican-American War (1845) was a quick victory for America, resulting in a gigantic area of land being surrendered by Mexico to America. General Zachary Taylor overwhelmed the Mexican Army in Texas and rode his popularity as a successful military hero to the presidency. Winfield Scott took over Mexico City and forced the Mexicans to surrender. Nicknamed "Old Fuss and Feathers" for his attention to military protocol, Winfield Scott was America's longest-serving army general. He served a total of forty-seven years in the war of 1812, the Mexican-American War, and the Civil War where he helped to develop the Anaconda Plan that ultimately defeated the South. Why he was never elected president I'll never know.

Besides the annexation of Texas in 1845, the bigger gain from the Mexican War was the Mexican Cession, finally negotiated in 1848. The U.S. paid fifteen million dollars for California, New Mexico, and the disputed land in Texas. If that wasn't enough, the bigger gain was the land Mexico ceded (gave away) to the U.S. at no cost. The region included the present states of Utah, Nevada, Arizona, Colorado, and parts of Wyoming. Most of the gold, silver, and uranium mined in the U.S. came out of these states. Texas has become a giant oil producer. Irrigation has converted much of that dry land to agriculture.

Oregon Country

This land that would become the states of Oregon, Washington, and some of Idaho was disputed by the U.S. and England. Before the War of 1812, they had agreed to share the land, but the U.S. ceded the land, rich in furs, to England as a result of the War of 1812. Unfortunately for England, the new Oregon Trail brought hundreds of Americans from the midwest to the Pacific coast far outnumbering the British fur-trappers.

England also had to deal with President James Polk, a disciple of the aggressive Andrew Jackson. Polk had just overseen the conquest of Mexico in the Mexican-American War and was interested in reacquiring the Oregon Country.

When peaceful negotiations failed, Polk began to saber rattle. This means to threaten the use of force to obtain an objective. The newspapers backed him up with the headline "54*40* or fight!" The U.S. claimed that Oregon ended at that latitude line. Another war with England was averted by setting the northern boundary at 49*, which was an acceptable compromise for both nations. One of our most effective and underrated presidents, health issues made Polk a one-term president.

By the way, you can still see the deep ruts in the prairie lands that the wagon trains left on their way to Oregon over 150 years ago. Officially now America stretched from sea to shining sea. Manifest destiny had been accomplished but there was more to do.

One Day President

March 1849, on Sunday at noon President Polk's term expired and he did not seek re-election. George Dallas (a city got named for him) was out as vice president when President-elect Zachary Taylor refused to be sworn in on Sunday, the Lord's day, we were without a leader for that day. Third in line was Missouri Senator David Atchison. Folklore holds that Atchison succeeded to the presidency for this day, but who's to say for sure.

Earlier in this decade, there were three presidents who governed in the same year. The eighth president Martin Van Buren completed his term on March 3, 1841. William Henry Harrison was inaugurated as the ninth president the next day but died of pneumonia soon after on April 4th. Vice President John Tyler was then sworn in as the nation's tenth president.

The California Gold Rush of 1849 did more than any other event to spur the growth of the west. In a tributary near the Sacramento River, at a place called Sutter's Mill, was the first discovery of gold flakes on the shoreline and in the stream itself. The nearby city of San Francisco became a virtual ghost town as people dropped what they were doing to come there to dig for gold. Hustlers charged as much as a thousand dollars for a spade (shovel) used for gold-digging. One wagon train crossed America with a total of 459 wagons.

On the sides of the wagon was the popular slogan "California or Bust!" People took ships to Mexico then came overland while others booked passage through the Isthmus of Panama then sailed up the Pacific Coast. Only a handful of miners got wealthy. They were the ones that dug deep mines. Claim jumping became a problem of law and order. You had to stake your claim and guard it lest someone "jump" you before the claim was certified on paper.

One person who did get wealthy was Levi Strauss. He was the first to manufacture blue jeans made of denim that would not rip while mining. Today the name Levi is synonymous with blue jeans. The real "gold" lay in the nearby San Fernando Valley with its rich soil and other natural resources. Today it is the largest dollar-producing agricultural region in America. The rapid growth of the population led by the 49'ers led to a quick admission of California as a state in 1850.

Thousands of settlers bypassed the Utah territory on their way west but one religious group made it their home, the Mormons. This Christian sect was founded in upstate New York by Joseph Smith in 1830 but was forced to move several times because of their belief in polygamy. Polygamy is the belief of multiple spouses for men and women and was not accepted by mainstream Christian America. Smith was murdered by townspeople at Nauvoo, Illinois and his clan forced to leave.

Now led by Brigham Young, they settled in Missouri but were quickly evicted as they were anti slavery while Missouri was a pro-slavery state. Eventually, they found their way to the area of Salt Lake City, Utah which became their creation. Far away from everyone else, they irrigated the desert and became prosperous in farming and business.

The Supreme Court outlawed polygamy in America, but the Mormons get around this by having common-law marriages i.e. marriages without a ceremony. Once in a while, a case of polygamy makes the news if child abuse becomes an issue. Since the Mormon culture dominates the state government and social life in Utah, they are generally not taken to task by the federal government.

Gadsden Purchase

There was another border dispute between the U.S. and Mexico, but this one was solved peacefully. The southern border of the two countries in the states of Arizona and New Mexico was not drawn clearly. U.S. diplomat James Gadsen was authorized by Congress to offer the Mexican government ten million dollars for a relatively narrow strip of land that would link California to Texas. Mexico agreed to the offer and the new land was earmarked for the route of a new transcontinental railroad that would ultimately link the east coast to the west coast of America. Antislavery forces opposed the purchase as they thought it would lead to slavery coming to the southwestern region of America.

Kansas-Nebraska Act

Illinois Senator Stephen Douglas (The Little Giant) had his eyes on the White House. Douglas pushed for the organization of the Nebraska Territory to be divided into two states, Kansas and Nebraska. Once they became states another transcontinental railroad could be funded by Congress and he (Douglas) would get the credit for initiating the project. The bill became law as two states were created. Douglas became the frontrunner for president.

However, the issue of slavery was further exacerbated by the passage of this act. More details to follow.

Purchase of Alaska (1867)

The Russian nation had not experienced the Industrial Revolution, so they were a poor nation led by a czar (king) who was looking for income. The Americans and the Russians were actually friends in those days. When Secretary of State William Seward offered a little over seven million dollars for Alaska, the Russians accepted. Congress authorized the money, but by only one vote, otherwise, Russia would be in our backyard today. The American press and most of the people mocked this purchase, referring to it as "Seward's Icebox" or "Seward's Folly." They stopped laughing in 1896 when the Klondike Gold Rush began—as big as the California Gold Rush of 1849. They really stopped laughing when the biggest reserve of oil in America was discovered under Alaska in the twentieth century. Alaska is twice the size of Texas, the next largest state. The cost of this land purchase was about seven cents per acre!

Annexation of Hawaii

Hawaii was an independent nation ruled as a monarchy for hundreds of years. In the 1800s many American missionaries and planters came to Hawaii. The planters started sugar cane farms that turned into small plantations. The American sugar planters became more powerful and forced Queen Liliuokalani to abdicate her throne. They set up a republic under president Sanford Dole (Dole Pineapple). The U.S. government annexed the islands under a storm of native protest but when the U.S. Navy arrived the rebellion was quieted. To this day, some Caucasians are referred to as "haoles," a derogatory description of white people.

The "Wild West"

The Wild West evokes images of lawlessness, gunfights, Indian and animal attacks, amidst the backdrop of a rugged and unpredictable environment. Pioneers initially traveled alone with their families in Conestoga Wagons, but later large wagon trains were more prevalent because of the safety in-numbers factor. Settlers not motivated by the gold rush were encouraged by the Homestead Act of 1862. This act gave settlers 160 acres west of the Mississippi at no cost so long as they agreed to remain there for five years to develop the land. One example of this act that showed both the good and lawless aspect of such a land give away occurred in the Oklahoma Territory.

To encourage land settlement thousands of acres of unassigned land were to be given on a first-come, first-served basis on April 22, 1889, at noon. However, a large contingent of settlers came to the land sooner. In short, they cheated. Because there was no local government, there were no punishments meted out. Later on, some of that land made room for the University of Oklahoma whose nickname is the Sooners—named for those infamous land grabbers.

Because of the vast size and rugged topography of the west, settlements were few and far between. Farming was not a popular way of life as the climate was dry. Many settlements were often temporary as they sprung up quickly due to the wealth found in mines. Once the mine ran out of its ore, towns were quickly abandoned and became "ghost towns," many of which still stand and the only occupants now are tumbleweeds that blow through the deserted streets.

Similar to California, there was widespread claim-jumping near the mines that often resulted in murder in the areas of Nevada, Colorado, Idaho, and Wyoming. In the mining towns, prostitution became rampant and the job as local sheriff was often vacant given the high mortality rate of that position. It was not until these lands became official territories that local courts and jails were set up and federal marshals assisted the local sheriff. The bottom line is that mining towns were transient and resulted in a nomadic way of life for all involved. Once they moved on they were subject to hostile Indian attacks as well as wild animal attacks by bears, mountain lions, snakes, and scorpions. Lacking medical facilities and supplies, the death rate was high during this time period.

To counter the lawlessness of murder, bank robberies, and cattle rustling the settlers resorted to Frontier Justice. This is punishment for alleged crimes without due process. Local residents organized vigilantes to track down criminals and "justice" was swift, often in the form of lynchings (hanging). Gunfights were also used to settle scores between rival groups or the individual "showdown" between two adversaries. Cattle raising became a large industry in Texas and other places. All cattle were branded with the seal of the owner's ranch. You were dead meat if you were caught rustling (stealing) cattle. Stagecoach robberies were a common sight and some robbers actually were able to stop trains and rob them as well.

The Range Wars of the 1800s were the biggest and worst example of lawlessness in the west. Homesteaders had fenced off their 160 acres up and down the length of the Mississippi River. Trouble began when the Texas cattle drives headed north to Chicago where the slaughterhouses were. The herders moved the cattle as quickly as they could. As the cattle stampeded, they ran roughshod over everything in their path including the farms of the ranchers. For years there were shooting wars aplenty as both herders and ranchers were killed along with some of the livestock. Not until the railroads utilized cattle cars did these wars end. The local governments and the federal government refused to get involved.

Pony Express

Before the advent of the telegraph system, the Pony Express was the fastest way to transport important mail halfway across the country. The service began in St. Joseph's Missouri near the Mississippi River and terminated at Sacramento, the capital of California. Delivery time was "reduced" to about ten days and the express was in business for only eighteen months from April of 1860 until October of 1861 when the telegraph came into existence.

The qualifications for this job limited employment. The Express was looking for young male riders, ages fourteen, under 125 pounds, and without a family. The salary was $100-$159 per month and your average route covered seventy-five miles before you handed your satchel to the next rider. There were 184 stations with 120 riders using 400 horses. Riders were given a Bible and they took an oath not to swear, get into fights, or drink, but because of the stress and fear of Indian attacks, most riders were drunk. Remarkably only four were killed by Indians, two froze to death, one was hanged after he got drunk and shot a man, and one died an unrelated death. The average cargo knapsack, the mochila, weighed twenty pounds. Ironically more people were killed by Indians and bandits at the outpost stations that were not well-defended.

Manifest Destiny had become a reality through the infrastructure of modern roads and though the transcontinentals were yet to be completed, the economic future of America seemed to be unlimited. Foreign nations had been removed from our territorial borders and the U.S. had the natural protection of two oceans. Everything seemed rosy, but would it be undone by the issue of slavery, the dark cloud that continued to hover over the American nation?

CHAPTER 27

Abraham Lincoln

(1809-1865)

WIDELY ACKNOWLEDGED AS AMERICA'S greatest president, Lincoln was almost completely a self-made man in terms of education and knowledge. Born in a Kentucky log cabin, Lincoln moved to Illinois at an early age with his father who was a widower but later remarried. The adults in his life were semi-literate at best and Lincoln received only about one year of homeschooling by traveling teachers. Motivated by his mentors, he developed an insatiable thirst for knowledge and would trudge miles to get possession of one book to read. It is said that he never read that many books but the ones he read he retained their lessons forever, especially a book about the life of George Washington. Lincoln so revered Washington that he was able to get a tiny piece of Washington's coffin and made it a part of his ring that had a bust of Washington on its face.

Lincoln was an imposing figure standing 6'4' tall and with his famous stovepipe hat atop his head closer to nearly seven feet. He developed his immense physical stature by becoming a rail-splitter for the local train company, where he surmised the importance of industrialized America. A self-made attorney, he gained local recognition as a barrister. More importantly in those days, attorneys and judges traveled together from town to town for the next case. Lincoln always held court with his peers telling funny stories and passionately sharing a wealth of knowledge in many subjects. He parlayed his passion, knowledge, and self-deprecating humor into four terms as an Illinois state senator.

Lincoln's political profile rose quickly when the new Republican Party nominated him to run for the U.S. Senate in Illinois in 1858. His opponent was the very popular Democrat Stephen Douglas who had succeeded in passing the Kansas-Nebraska Act that set in motion the building of another transcontinental railroad. Before the debates, Lincoln had given the timeless "House Divided" speech to his Republican backers. In the speech Lincoln said, "the country can not endure half-free and half-slave." He continued that, "the Union will endure, be it all free or all slave." Lincoln did not like slavery but was not an abolitionist. Like Andrew Jackson before him, in his mind the Union must be preserved by whatever means necessary. These words would echo again in the Gettysburg Address. The actual debates, though serious, had a comical appearance. On one side stood a nearly seven-foot Lincoln with a high-pitched squeaky voice and on the other side Stephen Douglas, a foot shorter but with a booming voice hence his nickname the "Little Giant." Douglas, who was well-dressed, unlike Lincoln, whose old clothes sagged off of him, was the winner of the election but his views on slavery would cost him in 1860. Douglas felt that popular sovereignty, a vote of the people, should determine the issue of slavery. Many northern voters, who were the majority, feared that slavery would dominate the new western territories and states. In effect, Lincoln had lost the battle but won the war.

CHAPTER 28

Pre-Civil War Events

FOR MANY DECADES, THE U.S ATTEMPTED to prevent the onset of a civil war. Henry Clay had drawn up two compromises, the Compromise of 1820 and the Compromise of 1850, in order to prevent the country from disintegrating. Andrew Jackson had ended the threat of secession by staring down his own vice president and promising to use force against any state that wanted to secede. Since he was a Southerner, a man of the people, and feared, there was no rebellion of the South under his watch. The phenomenon of manifest destiny, especially the Gold Rush, galvanized the attention of the public for a great number of years.

Yet there were two Americas inside of one. Northern America was crowded and industrial. With an advantage in the House of Representatives that allowed for the passage of tariffs to protect new industries from foreign competition, they were able to grow their companies. Southern America was agricultural with a slower pace of life. The tariffs were resented by the South, forcing them to buy "Yankee" goods that they could have gotten cheaper from Europe. The South had an economic imperative for the use of slavery, while the North viewed slavery as morally reprehensible and outlawed it.

Working against efforts to keep the country united was the invention of the cotton gin and the publishing of Uncle Tom's Cabin—the cotton gin greatly expanded the acreage of plantations and the need for more slaves, while Uncle Tom's Cabin created a stereotype of cruel treatment of all the slaves by all the plantation owners. It would take a series of events, mostly in the 1850s to trigger our nation's largest internal catastrophe. Let's look at the following:

1. Compromise of 1850
2. Bleeding Kansas (1854-1861)
3. Dred Scott Case (1857)
4. John Brown's Raid (1859)
5. Election of Lincoln (1860)
6. Ft. Sumter (1861)

In retrospect, the Compromise of 1850 was the last peaceful attempt to save the country from splintering. California sought entry to America as a free state. This would give the north an advantage of one state over the South. California needed a strong state government in order to keep law and order in and around all the mining sites. To balance the entry of California as a free state, Henry Clay advocated for popular sovereignty in regards to slavery in the rest of the Mexican Cession. Both North and South were concerned because of the many potential states that could be created from the Cession. The North agreed to a Fugitive Slave

Law, which stated that runaway slaves had to be returned to their owners and everyone had to comply with this act. In return, the South agreed that no longer would slave auctions be conducted in the nation's capital city. No one was thrilled with this compromise, but it did postpone the war for another ten years.

You recall that the Kansas-Nebraska act did result in the creation of two new states. Kansas applied for statehood first, followed by Nebraska. Popular sovereignty was going to decide if these states would be free or proslavery.

Trouble began in Kansas in 1854. The Abolitionists, led by the fanatical John Brown, set up a legislature in Kansas. At the same time, a rival legislature was set up by proslavery forces. Brown was from Massachusetts but came to Kansas to stop the spread of slavery. One night John Bown and his posse murdered a group of proslavery advocates in the middle of the night. Brown allegedly carried a Bible in one hand and a shotgun in the other as he played the role of God's avenging angel, killing those who would enslave. Brown and his followers fled Kansas when an arrest warrant was issued. "Bleeding Kansas," however, remained in a civil war for a number of years. Eventually, Kansas became a free state as the proslavery forces were driven out, but the bloodletting was an omen of things to come.

Though Southern interests had been dashed in Kansas, they won a big victory in the Dred Scott Case of 1857 that was appealed to the Supreme Court. Dred Scott, a slave, had been taken by his master from the slave state of Missouri to the free state of Minnesota. Returning to Missouri, Scott sued in the court system for freedom since he had moved to Minnesota. Chief Justice Roger Taney, a Southerner and an Andrew Jackson appointee, ruled against Scott.

The Court ruled that Scott was not a U.S. citizen and was "property," and "property" can not sue in the courts.

Taney also ruled that masters could take their slaves anywhere in the country and they still would be considered slaves. This ruling emboldened the South and petrified the North. All the new western lands could become slave states. This case raised animosity to the highest level between the two major sections of this nation.

Events do not occur in a vacuum, so while the South rejoiced in its legal victory, John Brown had other plans. With twenty-two followers, he hatched a plan to organize all the slaves into an army and overthrow the aristocratic plantation owners of the South. On the night of October 16, 1859, John Brown and his tiny gang seized a federal arsenal (weapons storehouse) at Harper's Ferry, Virginia. The word spread to the local plantations but not one slave showed up to fight. An attachment of U.S. Marines under the command of the soon-to-be-famous Robert E. Lee made prisoners of Brown and his group.

The trial showed a different side of John Brown. He cut his hair and ceased his crazy behavior and was very courteous in court, admitting his guilt and accepting his fate—death by hanging. This trial further divided and inflamed both North and South. The South feared that an army of fanatics like Brown would descend on the South to overturn their way of life. Many northerners viewed Brown as a martyr, willing to die for a cause the North believed in, the abolition of slavery. The time for compromise had long passed. The unofficial war Brown had started resulted in deaths of people on both sides of the issue of slavery.

Election of Lincoln (1860)

A fractured election of 1860 reflected the state of the Union. The Democrats nominated Stephen Douglas to run against Abraham Lincoln, the Republican Party candidate. Douglas seemed to oppose the Dred Scott decision, as he still advocated for popular sovereignty in re to slavery. Many Southern Democrats turned against Douglas and in a second convention nominated John Breckenridge from Kentucky as another alternative. Because the North had a much larger population Lincoln won the election. President Lincoln pleaded with the southern states to remain in the Union and maintain ownership of slaves. However, the South viewed Lincoln as an Abolitionist and led by South Carolina began to secede (breakaway) from the Union in early 1861. War now was a virtual certainty. It would need one more trigger to make it official.

While we are talking about political parties and philosophies, let's get the truth out in the open. I am not disputing the fact that the caucasian race kept the black man in bondage. However, there is a falsehood propagated by mainstream culture that the roots of racism can be traced back to the formation of the Republican Party and that today's Republicans are systemically racist.

The first Republican candidate for president was John C. Fremont, the founder of California, in 1856. As you are now aware, California entered the Union as a free, non-slave state in 1850 with the guidance of Fremont. In 1860, the second Republican candidate for President, Abraham Lincoln, won the election. He did not like or favor slavery, but if slavery preserved the Union, he would live with it.

Go back several pages in this book to the early presidents of Jefferson, who penned the Declaration of Independence, James

Madison, "the Father of the Constitution" including the Bill of Rights, and Andrew Jackson, the hero of the common man who expanded the right to vote. What did they all have in common? They were white Southerners who owned many slaves and did not emancipate them. What else did they have in common? All of them represented the Democratic Party. If you were never taught this, it would come as no surprise. Granted that the philosophy of the Democratic Party has somewhat changed over the decades, but a fact is a fact! One of my major motivations for writing this book is to set the record straight.

Fort. Sumter (1861)

Many view this as the first battle of the Civil War, but since war was not officially declared I will call this the trigger event that touched off the war.

On an island in the middle of Charleston Harbor lay Fort Sumter, built to protect Charleston from any manner of enemy naval assault. As Southern states seceded, other arsenals had been taken over, but Major Robert Anderson, the Union commander, would not surrender the fort to the Confederacy. Lincoln sent a supply ship to the fort that was now being pounded by Southern artillery fire. Anderson refused to surrender on April 12, 1861, but did so the next day. Lincoln had warned that he would not fire the first shot, but if the South did he would use *all* military forces at his disposal. The darkest chapter in U.S. history was about to begin - and it would last four grueling years.

CHAPTER 29
Civil War
(1861-1865)

THE SECESSION OF THE SOUTHERN STATES in America after the installation of Lincoln as President of the United States resulted in the creation of a new country, the Confederate States of America (CSA), who did not want to go to war with the U.S., hoping for a peaceful break away. Their one and only president was Jefferson Davis, a former U.S. Senator from Mississippi, who had fought in the Mexican-American War.

Monikers used to describe the combatants were Blue vs. Gray and Yankee vs. Rebels. The most painful reminder became father vs. son. As the war progressed, most of the casualties that resulted from divided loyalties within families were from the so-called border states. These states included Maryland, Delaware, West Virginia, Kentucky, and Missouri. All of these states advocated slavery but refused to secede from the Union. Their importance was as a buffer zone—an area of neutrality—between the South and the North. They formed an extended Mason-Dixon line all the way to Missouri. So who had the advantage? Let's take a look:

Resources of War

North	South
Population: 22,000,000	9,000,000
Railroads (miles): 22,000	9,000
Factories: 118,000	20,600
Factory Workers: 1,2000,000	100,000
Industrial Cities: New York Philadelphia Boston Pittsburgh	Atlanta
Bank Money: $421,900,000	$76,000,000
Food Production: 717,000,000 bushels of grain	316,000,000 bushels of grain

Much like the Revolutionary War one side seemed to have all the advantages except for one:

Military Advantages

North	South
Fought far away from home	Fought on home grounds
Had to invade and conquer the entire South	2. Fought a defensive war
Inexperienced soldiers	3. A culture of firearms and superior leaders
Used navy to blockade Southern ports	4. Much smaller navy compared to the North

Although the South was characterized as more agricultural than the North, most of their farming produced inedible products such as cotton, tobacco, indigo, and silk. There were plantations that grew rice, sugar cane, and wheat, however McCormick's reaper was not in use in the South, so hewing the wheat was done painfully slowly by hand, taking men away from military service. Meanwhile, the bread-basket states of the North grew twice as much food and processed it much faster.

The South hoped that England would support them with needed military wares in exchange for raw materials. The North realized this and blockaded the seaports of Charleston, Savannah, and New Orleans as quickly as they could. England also did not approve of slavery and did not recognize the CSA as a new country, so the South was on its own for the most part.

The strategy of the North to win the war was one of divide and conquer. This was called the Anaconda Plan, devised by General Winfield Scott. They wanted to split the Confederacy in half by taking over the Mississippi River thereby not allowing goods to leave Texas, Louisiana, and Arkansas and arrive in the eastern quadrant of the South. The North also wanted to capture Chattanooga, Tennessee, the railroad hub of the South as well as Atlanta, Georgia, the manufacturing center, and Richmond, Virginia, the capital of the CSA and its communications center. In short, the North wanted to fight a war of attrition, wearing out the South and depleting all available resources.

The Southern strategy of fighting a defensive war was actually very simple. Faced with engaging much larger armies, they relied on quick, unanticipated counter-attacks using their superior experience and knowledge of the land. They hoped that an inexperienced Northern Army would eventually tire of the fight and return home. From what I know, both sides underestimated their opponent and neither side believed the war would last four years. Most historians recognize the genius of Robert E. Lee for prolonging the war for the Southern cause as long as he did.

Robert E. Lee was a native Virginian and son of "Light Horse Harry" Lee, who was a cavalry commander in the Revolutionary War and one of George Washington's most able officers. Raised on a plantation just outside of Washington, D.C., Lee had always studied history as a young man and was appointed to West Point for military training and graduated second in his class. He was a war hero of the Mexican American War and was offered command of the Union Army but would never fight against his home state of Virginia.

The Civil War was the first war that had pictures from cameras. What I found so amazing was how the stress of war ages someone, especially if you are a leader. Before the war, Lee was a young man. Four years later he looked like a grandfather. He died in 1870 a mere five years after the end of the war.

Ulysses S. Grant became the Union commander halfway through the war and had a totally opposite profile from Lee. Grant grew up poor and attended school in a one-room schoolhouse in rural Ohio. As a young man, every job he attempted either did not work out or was an outright failure. Somehow he was appointed to West Point, where he graduated fifteen years after Lee but towards the bottom of his class. He was not good looking or well dressed and at first not respected. Small in height, he developed a small man's Napoleonic Complex. In short, "I'll show you what I can do." And boy did he ever! In his journals, Lee spoke of his admiration for Grant as an opponent. He compared him to a bulldog who never gives up even though he seems to be beaten.

There were hundreds of battles fought early on, with the Confederacy winning a large majority of those battles. The first battle of Bull Run (1861) is instructive. On a bright, sunny April day, a Union Army marched out of Washington, D.C. to engage a Confederate Army at Bull Run, which is near Manassas, Virginia. Dressed up politicians and their wives wearing hooped skirts and carrying picnic baskets tagged along to cheer for the Union Army as if they were attending a sporting event.

Sitting in an open green field, they clapped as the Union Army went into the woods to engage the Rebel Army. Gunfire rang out and not too much later a tattered and disorganized Union Army ran out of the woods being pursued by the Confederates. It must have been an amusing sight to watch the politicians in their tuxedos and the women trying to run away in a total panic. The Confederate Army marched up to the green field and stopped, laughing all the way. The lesson was that this war was no joke, as many Union soldiers were killed. The myth of a quick victory for the North was dashed at this first encounter.

If you know the plot from the movie Saving Private Ryan, this anecdotal story will sound familiar. This was an excerpt from a letter written by a war widow from the state of Maine to a friend. She tells of her husband going off to war and later about the enlistment of her five sons. The husband is killed along with three of his sons. A fourth son is discharged with a serious leg wound and dies in a winter storm before he can return home. He was walking at the time of death. The last son survives the battle but is permanently disabled. This is but one of thousands of examples of the horror and devastation brought about by our nation's bloodiest conflict.

The Civil War also witnessed the advent of photography and new weapons of war. Matthew Brady was a roving photographer who took over 3500 photographs of the war, covering both Union and Confederate personnel and scenes of famous battles. The iconic

Brady Collection contains black and white still photos of Lincoln, Lee, and Grant as well as many others. Photography was not an easy job. The clunky camera and its set-up were almost as big as the man carrying it. If this subject interests you, the Brady Collection is a must-see.

New weapons included the mortar, espionage balloons, and Ironclads, the first iron-plated warships. In 1862 off the coast of Virginia, the Monitor, a Northern ironclad, engaged the Merrimac, a Southern ironclad. Cannonballs that used to destroy wooden ships bounced off the sides of both vessels. Though neither side won, new technology was on the horizon. Mortars are bombs launched from a base that are lobbed into the air and explode on enemy lines, killing many at a time. They are still used today, and their killing distance has greatly increased. Today's surveillance drones are an ancestor of hot air balloons that operated silently and allowed observers to chart enemy positions from the air. These were effective until WWI when the new air forces could easily shoot them out of the sky.

I wish to share with you my Top Ten events of the Civil War:

1. Capture of New Orleans (1862)
2. Battle of Antietam (1862)
3. Emancipation Proclamation (1863)
4. Battle of Vicksburg (1863)
5. Battle of Gettysburg (1863)
6. Draft Riots (1863)
7. Battle of Chattanooga (1863)
8. Sherman's March to the Sea (1864)
9. Battle of Richmond (1864)
10. Surrender at Appomattox Courthouse (1865)

As you recall one of the objectives of the Anaconda Plan was the control of the Mississippi River. This would necessitate co-operation between the Union armies and the U.S. Navy, under the direction of Admiral David Farragut, the first commissioned admiral in the U.S. Navy. Farragut had the use of thirteen wooden ships that rather easily defeated the Southern resistance at New Orleans and cut off a large number of weapons, and cotton produced in Texas, that were headed for the rest of the Confederacy. The Army would have to do the rest of the dirty work to take control of upper Mississippi.

Though the ground war was not going well for the Union, they achieved their first, but very costly, victory at the Battle of Antietam (1862). This was the single bloodiest day in U.S. history as 23,000 men died, as did six commanding generals. Lincoln was so dissatisfied with the hesitant tactics of General George McClellan that he was summarily terminated even though he was the winning general.

Lincoln was waiting for a victory so he could finally issue his famous Emancipation Proclamation, which he did on the first day of 1863. The Proclamation stated that all slaves in the states in rebellion against the U.S. are now and forever free. Not only was this act idealistic it was also politically brilliant, as it did not free slaves in the buffer zone of the border states. Lincoln needed these states to be neutral, realizing that the opposing capital cities were only ninety miles apart. By allowing the Border States to keep their slaves he kept the Southern armies at arm's length. The South, of course, paid no attention to this law. The Emancipation Proclamation was the ancestor of the so-called Civil Rights Amendments to the Constitution.

The summer of 1863 witnessed the Northern control of the Mississippi River after the Battle of Vicksburg. General Grant marched his army down the Mississippi and laid siege to the city of Vicksburg, in the state of Mississippi, that lay atop a high hill with guns guarding the river. A siege is a continuous battle with no let-up. Grant attempted numerous uphill ascents with his troops, who were in near rebellion due to repeated failure. But the bulldog in him would not accept defeat, and finally Vicksburg was taken after nearly running out of supplies and numerous assaults. Lincoln had been looking for a man to lead the entire Union Army. Other leaders were timid. Lincoln had finally found the man he wanted.

At the same time Grant was conquering Vicksburg, America's most historic battle was being played out in the fields of Pennsylvania, the Battle of Gettysburg. This was Lee's second attempt to invade the North. His first attempt was the failure at Antietam, Maryland. Lee knew the war was not in his favor now, so he planned a back-door attack on Washington, D.C. If he was successful, he hoped that England would join the South in the war. Lee marched up the Susquehanna River into southwestern Pennsylvania, where he was spotted by Union scouts patrolling the area. Ironically the battle was fought on Independence Day weekend near the now historic village of Lancaster, Pennsylvania.

The objective in any battle is to get the high ground, that nine times out of ten is a big advantage. In this three-day battle, Cemetery Ridge was the high ground that the North obtained on day two of the battle. On the third day, a desperate Lee authorized a suicide mission known as Pickett's Charge to commence. George Pickett and his cavalry led a direct frontal assault on the ridge that had no cover. In hand-to-hand combat, 15,000 men died in fifteen minutes! Only a small atomic bomb could kill quicker. This showed the desperation of the battle, as the South was reduced to bayonet fighting. Pickett retreated, having lost seventy-five percent of his forces. The fighting was so severe and the loss of life and blood so intense there are still bloodstains etched into the rocks 160 years later.

A day later when Pickett did his roll call, a "here" received a sob while silence received a gasp. It was his most painful time. In another poignant moment, a Union officer asked why a young private was digging a grave for a Confederate soldier. The private looked up and said, "he's my brother." In three days more than 50,000 men lost their lives in battle, almost as many as the entire Vietnam War that lasted almost a decade. Gettysburg was the turning point of the War. A defeated Robert E. Lee and his troops retreated to Virginia. The noose was being tightened.

A few weeks later, Lincoln took a train from the nation's capital to Gettysburg. A cemetery was being dedicated there for the Union soldiers slain in the struggle. Lincoln wrote a speech on a notepad on the ride to Gettysburg. He was having trouble finding the right words and feared that the speech would be an abject failure.

The words that Lincoln uttered that day have echoed and reverberated in the minds of Americans since the day of the speech. One of the great reaffirmations of American democracy and strength, the verbiage is equal to that of the Declaration of Independence and the U.S. Constitution. The opening sentence "Four score and seven years ago" dated back to 1776, the birth of America. Lincoln's insecurity is seen in this famous passage. "The world will very little note nor long remember what we say here; but I can never forget what we did here" and the last line most revered "that the government of the people, by the people, and for the people, shall not perish from the earth." When I was in high school, we had to memorize and repeat the entire speech. Lincoln was reminding us that this country was unique and certainly worth dying for. His last line was his message to future generations. Message received!

Because of the large numbers of fatalities, the U.S. Congress passed into law the first conscription act (draft) forcing men to serve in the military. This act was seen as unfair because if you had 300 extra dollars you could buy your way out of the draft. The disclaimer is that by today's standards that would amount to $5800.00, an average salary for the year 1863.

Trouble soon began in New York City, where many new Irish immigrants who came here to survive the Potato Famine, found themselves being drafted into war now that they were citizens. They focused their anger on the local authorities, whom they overwhelmed, and especially free Blacks who were not citizens and could not be drafted. Estimates of up to 500 deaths occurred before army troops that had fought at Gettysburg were called in to end the four-day riots. Many blacks, local police, and abolitionists were the victims, with blacks being hung from the closest lamp post. This certainly did not reflect well on the North, which was supposed to be guaranteeing safety for its black population. Prejudice was alive and well outside of the confines of the Confederacy. The movie *The Gangs of New York* concerns itself with these Civil War draft riots.

Later in 1863, another part of the Anaconda Plan was accomplished at the Battle of Chattanooga. General Grant came to the rescue of Union forces that were surrounded at Chattanooga, Tennessee. Not only did Grant disperse the Confederate Army, he proceeded to destroy the rails that the trains used to exit and enter the city. With the South further divided, supplies were hard to come by and troops could not be transported quickly to new battlefronts. There is an old 1940's song "The Chattanooga Choo-Choo," a jazz song written in homage to the Civil War Battle of Chattanooga.

In 1864, Total Warfare was introduced as a new method of war. Grant knew he had Lee on the run, so he ordered General William Tecumseh Sherman to totally destroy the state of Georgia. Sherman's huge army burned Atlanta to the ground. [The movie Gone with the Wind is about this event.] After Atlanta, the major industrial city of the South was destroyed, Sherman's soldiers spread out for sixty miles and marched southeastward to Savannah, a coastal seaport, robbing, burning, and destroying everything in sight that could not be used by Sherman's Army.

Georgia is a very lush, green state with a great deal of agriculture. If there were satellites in the air in 1864, the images of Georgia would have been all green except for a sixty-mile brown spot in the middle of the state stretching to the sea at Savannah. Grant wanted the war to end quickly. Total Warfare was the method used to achieve that goal. Sherman's name is still despised in the South and especially in Georgia for the utter devastation he inflicted. There is an old song entitled, "The Night They Drove Old Dixie Down" sung by John Baez and redone by The Band. It describes the destruction of Georgia in the march to the sea.

Robert E. Lee had to "circle the wagons" around the capital city of Richmond, Virginia. Most of the Confederate armies were decimated and supply lines were now cut, so all Lee could do was try to defend Richmond and rally his troops. As the combined Union armies forced Lee out of Richmond, Matthew Brady was on the scene with his camera. The first movie camera captured the burning of Richmond. Although the film is grainy, you can see the flames enveloping the buildings. [I used to watch this on A+E TV but I think YouTube might also have the film if you are at all curious.] Richmond was reduced to embers. The battle was lost. The war was lost. Lee's army was weakened and out of supplies. He raised the white flag, calling for a truce.

On April 9, 1865, Lee and Grant met at a small brick building in a village named Appomattox Courthouse in Virginia. Lee handed his sword to Grant, symbolizing the end of fighting. Grant only asked the Confederate soldiers to lay down their weapons. They were allowed to keep their horses, as Grant knew they were needed for farming in the spring. When the two leaders walked outside, the Union soldiers began to clap and cheer. Grant ordered them to immediately silence. He said that the Confederate soldiers are again your countrymen. The two leaders saluted each other for the final time. The war was over.

Depending on the source, as many as 600,000 to 1,000,000 people died in the war that lasted four long years. Lincoln had succeeded in preserving the Union by word and deed despite periods of heavy opposition in the North that was tiring of the war effort.

U.S. Grant would go on to become a two-term president, though he was tired of public life post-war. Grant suffered great bouts of depression while in the White House. He became dependent on alcohol to deal with the nightly horrors of warfare remembered in dreams. As a result, his presidency was unspectacular, but there was one light moment remembered.

Grant liked to drive his horse team fast. One night a police officer in Washington, D.C. pulled over Grant's horse and wagon. The officer began to write him a speeding ticket before he realized it was the president. Grant insisted on paying the twenty-dollar fine.

Lee, as mentioned, would die five years after the war in 1870. The huge plantation that Lee had owned across the Potomac River from Washington, D.C. in Virginia was confiscated and transformed into Arlington National Cemetery, a burial ground for many soldiers as well as two past presidents—William Howard Taft and John F. Kennedy. It is home of the Eternal Flame, commemorating one and all who died in service to America.

CHAPTER 30

Assassination of Lincoln

(1865)

ON THE EVENING OF APRIL 14, 1865, Lincoln was assassinated at Ford's Theatre in Washington, D.C. while watching a play with his wife. During an intermission, the star of the play, John Wilkes Booth, a Southern sympathizer was able to get access to the balcony above the stage where Lincoln and his wife were sitting. There was no Secret Service yet and in a cruel twist of irony, the bill to establish the Secret Services was sitting on Lincoln's desk awaiting his signature. As Booth leaped out of the balcony after shooting Lincoln, he yelled out "sic semper tyrannis" (Thus ever to tyrants), which was the Virginia state motto. On the same night, Secretary of State William Seward and Vice President Andrew Johnson were also targeted for execution, part of a large conspiracy to restart the war. Seward was only wounded and Johnson was never attacked. Booth escaped to a local farmhouse and was tracked down twelve days later. As the marshals set fire to the barn where he was hiding, he refused to come out and was shot by a marshal when he went for his gun. He died soon after and four others were hung as part of the conspiracy and another half dozen received life sentences in jail.

Lincoln died the morning after he was shot behind the ear. A few days later a train draped in black drove slowly toward Springfield, Illinois. Villages emptied to see the train as it passed from town to town. Not until his death did Americans realize how strong a hold this man had on the affections of the people. Lincoln was fifty-six years old at the beginning of his second term as president.

CHAPTER 31

Women of the Wars

LET'S ACKNOWLEDGE THE CONTRIBUTIONS of some famous women in American history who helped to shape and aid the growth of America from the Revolutionary War to the Civil War.

Abigail Adams was the wife of second president John Adams and the mother of John Quincy Adams the sixth president of the United States. Criticized by some for being wealthy and elitist, the reality is that she was one of America's first feminists. She advocated for women's suffrage (the right to vote) and for women's rights in regard to property ownership which had been restricted to white males. Her ideas about the role of government and people's rights earned her the nickname "women's co-founding father," as she was able to write more clearly than her Founding Father husband John. Their ideas about the necessity of a strong federal government led to the framing of the Declaration of Independence and Constitution.

Born in Philadelphia, Betsy Ross was an upholsterer who became a lifetime flag-maker for fifty years. One of her more famous flags was the one she created for the Pennsylvania Navy. Word of her skill led to a meeting with George Washington, who was looking for someone to create the stars and stripes. Although historians disagree, Ross is largely credited with the design of our first flag known as the Betsy Ross Flag.

"Molly Pitcher" became a generic description for a water carrier. The inspiration for this name may have originated from the exploits of Deborah Sampson. Only men were supposed to actually fight in the Revolutionary War. Sampson learned how to use a gun, dirtying up her face and pulling up her hair under a hat, she was able to fight for a period of time. After she was outed, she was allowed to remain in the Continental Army where she fetched water for the soldiers. She inspired other women to volunteer in the same capacity, hence the moniker Molly Pitcher.

In the Civil War, there were many more deaths attributed to infection rather than direct gunfire. Surgery was crude as hand saws were used to amputate limbs oftentimes resulting in gangrene and ultimately death.

Young Clara Barton was determined to help end the suffering. After the Battle of Antietam, she received the nickname "Angel of the Battlefield," as she actively tended to the wounds of fallen soldiers, saving their lives. Later on, Barton became the founder of the American Red Cross and lived to see her organization grow greatly before her death at age ninety. Barton may have been inspired by a contemporary of hers in England, Florence Nightingale. Nightingale tended to fallen British soldiers during the wide-ranging Crimean War in Europe in the 1850s, a few years before the Civil War. Nightingale is credited with being the founder of the modern nursing profession and probably a role model to Clara Barton on the other side of the Atlantic Ocean.

CHAPTER 32

Reconstruction

(1865-1877)

RECONSTRUCTION WAS THE PERIOD when the nation tried to rebuild post-war so that all the sections of the country could successfully co-operate. The key word is tried, as there were some successes but some lingering failures. Had Lincoln not been assassinated, some of the ill will of Reconstruction would surely have been avoided.

There were three objectives that needed to be solved. The first was the physical rebuilding of the Southern farms, cities, schools, and factories destroyed by the war. Because of a hostile Congress controlled by the northern states, federal funding would be limited so the Southern states had to mostly fund the rebuild.

Another task was to look after the Freedmen, the former slaves, who had to make their own way in life. The national government did offer a good deal of help with their plight.

There was also a political question. Under what terms would the former Confederate States be readmitted to the Union?

The national government set up the Freedmen's Bureau to help former slaves. In hundreds of local communities, agents of the

Bureau gave food and clothing to the local inhabitants. They also found jobs for many and public land was given to them to start their own farms. Local schooling was also set up and funded. Where plantations still existed, the Freedmen now became sharecroppers, working for the owners but retaining a portion of the crop to be sold or consumed as food. No one was forced to remain on a plantation if they did not want to.

Lincoln's plan for Reconstruction was the easiest on Southerners. If you swore loyalty to the U.S. you would be able to vote or hold political office, except if you had been in the Confederate government under Jefferson Davis.

When Lincoln died, his vice president took over. Andrew Johnson was from Tennessee and though an honest man was gruff in dealings with people. Northern Republicans did not like him and saw an opportunity to install a Radical Reconstruction Plan. They wanted to punish the south by dividing it into five military districts with an army in each district to carry out harsh rules imposed by the Radical Republicans. They did not want any former Confederacy government officials nor any former Confederate soldier to have the right to vote. In short, all who opposed the Union could not vote.

The only voters allowed were the freedmen, carpetbaggers, and scalawags. Carpetbaggers were Northerners who quickly moved south putting all of their belongings in a 'carpet bag' looking to exploit the South for gains of money and power. Scalawag was a derogatory name given to white Southern sympathizers who abetted the North, traitors to the old Confederacy.

The Radicals were able to impeach Andrew Johnson, but he avoided removal by a single vote in the Senate. He was the wrong man in the wrong place at the wrong time. With Johnson powerless and along with the approaching presidency of U.S. Grant, the

Radicals were able to enact their plan, as they knew they had Grant in their corner. The Radical rule was not all bad as they enacted three amendments to the Constitution, the "Civil War Amendments," numbers thirteen, fourteen, and fifteen.

The thirteenth amendment was drawn up before Lincoln's death in 1865. This amendment abolished slavery in America and was ratified into law in 1865. The major plank of the fourteenth amendment ratified in 1868 granted full citizenship to Black Americans. It also deprived former Confederate soldiers the right to vote. The fifteenth amendment ratified in 1870 said that no citizen could be deprived of the right to vote based on skin color. These amendments were fundamental and necessary. They were also very functional at the time, punishing the Confederacy and allowing the North to control the lives of the Southerners. This was the major lingering failure of this time period.

However, the disenfranchised old guard of the South fought back in several ways. Where they could be instituted, Black Codes, laws that suppressed the rights of blacks, were established. Often known as Jim Crow Laws, these were local laws designed to keep black voters away from voting booths during local elections. Among the many Jim Crow Laws were the following:

1. Poll Tax
2. Literacy Test
3. Grandfather Clause

On election dates, as blacks approached the voting booth some were scared off by whites brandishing heavy sticks in a menacing way. Others who got by the first obstacle were asked for a high sum of money before they could vote. Sharecroppers often were not paid with money, so they were told they could not vote. This practice, of course, was and is totally illegal.

At other polling booths, blacks were asked to read difficult material before voting. For example, if they could not read the language of the Constitution or the Declaration of Independence, they were denied the vote. This was known as a Literacy test.

The grandfather clause was the perfect "Catch 22" for denial of the vote. The voter was asked for proof that their grandfather had voted in some previous election. This was a totally egregious case as the right to vote had just been granted to black Americans.

The fiercest resistance to black Americans and other groups came in the formation of the Ku Klux Klan, a nativist group of White Protestants, angry and frustrated by their loss of power and looking for revenge against anyone not of their bloodline. Surprisingly birthed in the free state of Indiana, the movement drew most of its supporters from the former Confederate States, though today the Klan is alive and well north and south of the Mason-Dixon line. The Klan is a national organization but at its onset operated on a purely local level. "Normal" folks at day donned white sheets and hoods at night, terrorizing blacks with burning crosses and in extreme cases carried out random lynchings. [The term lynch likely originated during the Revolutionary War. It derived from the phrase Lynch Law, a term for a punishment without a trial.] These domestic terrorists have continued to operate with impunity even though Congress quickly passed a law in 1871 banning Klan activity.

In the early 1870s, a new liberal wing of the Republican party began to emerge. They ended Radical Reconstruction and began to work with, not against many in the South who had been disenfranchised. In 1877, President Hayes ended military supervision of the South. Carpetbaggers and scalawags were on the run and the general population was able to vote and regain control of their own state governments. Reconstruction had officially come to an end.

CHAPTER 33
Indian Wars

WITH THE CIVIL WAR AND RECONSTRUCTION largely in the rearview mirror, the focus of America now turned to the semi-developed land west of the Mississippi River and east of the Rocky Mountains stretching from the Dakotas to Oklahoma collectively known as the Great Plains.

Largely skipped over by gold-seekers and other miners, this land became a focus as a result of the completion of the first transcontinental railroad at Promontory, Utah (1869). Homesteaders were now close to railroad lines that could provide building and other supplies that they needed such as barbed wire to fence off their land. Unfortunately, this led rather quickly to conflicts with Indians who still claimed that same land as their own. Having a nomadic way of life centering on the use of the buffalo (bison), the Indians came into conflict with the Americans who wanted to live in one fixed place.

The Plains Indians depended on the buffalo herds for their very existence. Every part of the buffalo was used either for food, clothing, shelter, weapons, and utensils. The buffalo were worshipped by the Indians, who were polytheistic. On the other hand, the Americans shot the buffalo for sport often from trains, like target practice. Once the buffalo was decaying, it was useless to the Indians. These herds were slaughtered by the thousands and today are a protected species.

The Indians feared the gun, the "thunder rod," and the locomotive, the "iron horse," and were often swindled out of land when they made deals under the influence of "firewater." Whether drunk or not, it is important to remember that every land contract signed between Congress and the Indians was eventually vacated as the completion of manifest destiny overrode those edicts. Eventually, all the Indians were herded onto reservations and forced to adapt to the white man's culture, often the antithesis of their own. For example, "Braves" were forced to cut their hair, which was a sign of weakness in their world and it was only a matter of time until wars erupted.

The Battle of the Little BigHorn (1876) was the high water mark for the Indians' fight against the Americans. Often referred to as "Custer's Last Stand," it was one battle of the Great Sioux War involving the large Lakota Tribe against the U.S. Army under the command of George Custer, a Civil War hero for the North. Fought in the southeastern corner of the Montana Territory, Custer and his men were surrounded by Crazy Horse and Sitting Bull, leaders of the tribe. About 300 Americans were slaughtered that day.

Crazy Horse would surrender much later on. Under U.S. custody, he was bayoneted to death in 1877. Sitting Bull escaped and would be killed by the Army on a reservation as he threatened to join the wide-ranging Ghost Dance Movement of the Great Plains. This movement utilized Shaman, who were religious leaders, to unite all the tribes by using ceremonial Ghost Dances that predicted the removal and death of the white men. The Dance included war drums and smoke signals to scare away the white men. Once the U.S. government determined that the Ghost Dance Movement threatened the western lands, it was outlawed all the way to California.

In the same year (1890) there was an infamous event known as the Massacre at Wounded Knee in South Dakota. An Indian on a reservation refused to give up his rifle and then discharged it. Immediately the U.S. Army detachment opened fire on over 300 mostly unarmed women, men, and children. Twenty-five soldiers from the Army were also killed. The Congress admitted the Army overreacted. Today Wounded Knee is a National Historic Site. There are many documentaries you can watch recalling that fateful event.

In the southwest, another famous Indian, a shaman and fighter, was arrested for condoning the Ghost Dance—Geronimo of the very warlike Apache Tribe. He was not killed, but perhaps worse, became a prisoner of war until his death in 1909. He was paraded in front of political leaders and mocked for his beliefs.

The last great Indian chieftain to meet an ignominious end was Chief Joseph of the Nez Perce Tribe from the Pacific Northwest. His tribe had been pushed out of Idaho and forced Northwest into Washington State. They fought back valiantly over the years, killing U.S. Army soldiers, but were never able to make it back to Idaho, or at least Canada for sanctuary.

Chief Joseph was escorted to Washington, D.C. where before Congress he uttered his famous "I will Fight no more Forever" speech before a respectful yet unsympathetic Congress. They did not let the Nez Perce return to Idaho, settling them on a reservation in Washington State. Like the massacre at Wounded Knee, there are television movies and documentaries you can view one of which is entitled, "I will fight no more Forever," which is a television movie from around 1975.

Profile: American Cowboy

The cowboys in a western movie may seem to be romanticized and picturesque. Actually, all the things that make up the picturesque equipment of the cowboy were designed to help him in his work of looking after the cattle. The saddle was the cowboy's "home" and workbench. In it, he spent most of his working hours. His six-shooter (gun) was used to turn a stampeding herd, to shoot a crippled horse or steer, or to kill a rattlesnake.

The cowboy's clothing was adapted to his trade—leather chaps protected his legs from thorns, from the horns of cattle, and from falling horses. The high heels of his boots gave cowboys a lurching gait, but these high heels kept his feet from slipping through the stirrups. They were also useful when he was throwing the lasso on foot because he could dig the sharp heels into the ground. A handkerchief around his neck could be pulled up over his face to protect him from stifling dust stirred up by the moving herd. The cowboy's ten-gallon hat gave him shade from the blistering sun. It could also be used to scoop up water for drinking and washing or to signal other cowboys when the herd was on the move.

A cattle drive of twelve to sixteen miles a day was considered successful, since the cattle had to graze along the way. At night a noise might cause the herd to stampede. Believe it or not, the cowboys would sing to the herd at night to prevent stampedes!

Totem poles

Totem poles are one of the most iconic examples of Native American art. They're found in the Yukon and British Columbia regions of Canada, as well as Alaska and Washington state in the U.S.

While the Northwest Coast Indians mostly passed down knowledge by word of mouth, more important information would be carved into totem poles, some over 100 feet tall. The details would be told to a carver who would visualize the right symbols and encode the story into a sculpture. This symbolism could range from who owned the rights to what territories to genealogical records

Memorial poles honored chiefs and other ranking officials. Accomplishments were memorialized, and the Haida Tribe topped the pole with ashes of the deceased.

Less common were shame or ridicule poles, which criticized neighbors for being offensive or not paying their debts. Chiefs also used these poles to taunt and belittle their rivals. Family poles featured animals that made up a clan's crest of honor.

CHAPTER 34

Industrialization and Urbanization

THE TRANSFORMATION OF AMERICA from a rural agrarian society to an urban industrial one was the biggest visceral changes in the American landscape in the latter part of the nineteenth century and into the early twentieth century. Modern America as we know it today was largely shaped during this time period.

Immigrant labor was invaluable to the completion of the first transcontinental railroad. In 1869 many otherwise able-bodied men were tired from the recent Civil War so Irish rail builders were hired along with Chinese workers. The Irish started to lay down tracks in St. Louis and worked west while the Chinese did the same job working east from Sacramento, California.

The Chinese "Coolies" though smaller in size were able to work much faster than their Irish compatriots. Why? The Irish were bare-chested as they worked in the hot sun while the Chinese wore light-fitting clothing repelling the heat. They were ridiculed at first but lauded later on. They needed less rest with fewer water breaks and were more work-efficient than the Europeans. The effects of dehydration on work efficiency were unknown in those days. They kept their cool hence the nickname Coolies.

Shortly thereafter, three more cross-country train lines were completed that led to the growth of the urban (city) areas in San Francisco, Los Angeles, Denver, Phoenix, Chicago, St. Louis, Houston, and elsewhere. Before the ongoing Industrial Revolution, eighty-five percent of America was rural and agricultural with the other fifteen percent urban and industrial. Today about ninety percent of America is urban and industrial and about ten percent agricultural. [Most of today's farmers do not own their land. They lease their acreage. Guess who owns the most farmland in America today? None other than Microsoft mogul Bill Gates. Why should you care? Gates is planning on giving, selling, or leasing a majority of his nearly 300,000 acres of farmland to his corporation cohorts, who in turn want to replace natural produce with an artificially engineered variety of crops. Allegedly, Gates wants to force the American people to eat the fake crops thereby profiting his cronies while the natural crops are, of course, exported to other nations!]

The great wealth that was created during this time period was not shared equally, and the gulf between the very wealthy and the rest of us has gotten wider over the past 125 years. Today about ninety percent of the wealth generated by America is owned by a relative handful of billionaires. That is the price to be paid for living in a competitive capitalistic society with private ownership of businesses. Soon the government and the labor unions would attempt to equalize the distribution of wealth in America and to enact laws that restricted corrupt business practices.

There were many inventions and innovations of this era that caused the meteoric rise of the American nation, leading it to become the most powerful nation in the world, envied by one and all. Some of the innovations/inventions were:

1. 1856 - Bessemer Steel process
2. 1859 - Discovery of Oil
3. 1860s - Food Processing
4. 1866 - Transatlantic Cable
5. 1876 - Telephone
6. 1877 - Phonograph
7. 1879 - Electric Light Bulb
8. 1887 - Elevator
9. 1895 - Wireless Telegraph
10. 1898 - Rubber Tires
11. 1902 - Hydroelectric Power
12. 1903 - First Airplane Flight
13. 1913 - Assembly line production (cars)
14. 1923 - Farm tractor

The first train tracks were made of iron ore. The problem was that the trains and their cargo became too heavy for the tracks that began to break down. Henry Bessemer developed a process of combining iron ore and coal with the furnace—creating heat to produce steel, a much stronger version of iron that did not oxidize (rust). America had large deposits of coal and iron ore in Pennsylvania, Michigan, West Virginia, and Alabama. Pittsburgh became the Steel City, hence the name of their pro football team, the Steelers.

Pennsylvania also had the first oil strike near Titusville in 1859. Later on, much bigger oil strikes occurred in Texas, Louisiana, California, and Alaska. Oil is a lubricant and also processed into gasoline and used in the vast majority of motorized vehicles in America. The internal combustion engine was not invented until the late 1800s in Germany, but the technology quickly arrived in America, via cultural diffusion.

The transformation of farm crops and livestock into food in the 1860s became known as food processing. The canning of fruits and vegetables became a new food source and improved nutrition around America. Before the canneries came to be, here is one woman's journal of what she baked in a single year—1,038 loaves of bread, 2,140 donuts, 421 pies, and 152 cakes. A different journal from 1895 noted, "The men are more robust and erect now" and the women "have greatly improved both in feature and carriage."

Unfortunately, canned goods and other fast foods today are loaded with chemical preservatives that lead to obesity. Today, the average male is five foot nine and nearly two hundred pounds! Women are proportionately worse at five foot two and 164 pounds. This tells you a great deal about our present culture. You can arrive at your own conclusions.

Cyrus Field's transatlantic cable took twelve years to construct and was completed in 1866. This cable runs under the ocean from Europe to America. At first, it was used to transmit morse code messages across "the Pond" as the British refer to the Atlantic Ocean. It was invaluable during WWI to coordinate the war effort against Germany.

Alexander Graham Bell's telephone was first used to complete a two-mile call between Boston and Cambridge in 1876. By WWI, calls to Europe were possible. Another famous inventor, credited with over 1,000 patents, Thomas Edison perfected the phonograph (record player) and a year later the light bulb in 1879. Edison resisted prolonged sleep that he referred to as "little pieces of death" as he had too much to accomplish knowing the one thing he was not gifted with was immortality. He often took cat naps and is portrayed sound asleep in a chair while sitting next to then President Franklin Roosevelt for a now famous photoshoot.

When you combine Bell's telephone with Marconi's wireless telegraph you have the genesis of the entire wireless mobile cell phone industry we all seem to rely on today.

Skyscrapers would be a lot less practical without the installation of elevators. Though James Otis owns the original patent dating back to the 1850s, it wasn't until 1887 that the elevator unit was completed by the installation of closing doors patented by African-American inventor Alex Miles.

Charles Goodyear saw an opportunity for the creation of a new product. Cars needed something to ride on, so Goodyear's company perfected the vulcanization of rubber, a process that hardened and elasticized rubber into the shape of tires that were weather resistant.

The Algonquin Indians referred to Niagara Falls as the "Thundering Waters." With the creation of the dynamo, water power could be converted to electricity and carried across thin strands of wire to cities, factories, and local villages miles away. Niagara Falls was the first distributor of electric power in the U.S.

Though it lasted just fifty-nine seconds and covered about one twenty feet, the Wright brothers successfully tested the first airplane at Kitty Hawk, North Carolina near the coastline. The timing of this invention was perfect, as the U.S. would require an Air Force to help win WWI.

Although the first automobile originated in Europe, Henry Ford's assembly line production enabled the average citizen to buy his Model T, the most mass-produced car of its day. Each car would progress down a large conveyor belt where different people would install different components of the car. This is called the *division of labor*. Cars were well-made, as a specialist would take care of only one aspect of the construction. Replacement or interchangeable parts were also in the factory for repair jobs. It only took a little over two hours to produce a car using the assembly lines.

One problem that was a byproduct of this specialization was job boredom, doing the same task day in and day out. Workers would leave empty cans inside the car panels then weld them closed. Imagine the panic one experienced buying a new car and hearing a loud rattle driving out of the showroom the first time because someone was bored and playing a joke on a potential customer.

For the record, and again you can draw your own conclusion, the first two cars ever produced managed to crash into each other in the early 1900s. No doubt the entire car insurance industry came about rather quickly after this incident.

Though the first tractor was patented earlier, John Deere and Company patented the first farm tractor in 1923. The science of agriculture was expanding and getting more diversified with bigger farms that needed more land to be plowed more quickly.

George Washington Carver was a famous African American agronomist from this time period. He created many uses, some surprising, for two common farm products—peanuts and sweet potatoes. He derived 300 products from the peanut, not including peanut butter, but the following: chili sauce, shampoo, glue, shaving cream, soap, and grease. From sweet potatoes came flour, vinegar, stains, dyes, and paints as well as inks. Who knew?

Famous Industrialists

In addition to Henry Ford, who began the automobile industry, there were many other entrepreneurs who saw opportunities in other industries. The history books define them as either negatively, the Robber Barons or positively, the Captains of Industry. The Robber Barons, in one view, were a group of powerful nineteenth-century industrialists, pilloried by the press, who used questionable business practices to amass their wealth. They were viewed as ruthless and cutthroat and their alleged corruption was often caricatured by political cartoonists in the newspapers. On the other hand, the Captains of Industry, who were the same group, contributed positively to the overall growth of America by creating thousands of new jobs and raising the standard of living for the general populace. They often gave away huge sums of money in the area of philanthropy. Because there were no laws to restrict their business practices, they used a type of economic Darwinism in the business world meaning that only the strongest company will survive in a given industry. This led to the rapid growth of trusts (monopolies) that concentrated a great amount of power and wealth in the hands of a few.

There were many famous (infamous?) industrialists. I selected three to illustrate their great influence over the control of the newly industrialized American Economy:

1. John D. Rockefeller
2. Cornelius Vanderbilt
3. J.P. Morgan

John D. Rockefeller was the wealthiest man to ever walk the face of the earth. He once owned two percent of the entire U.S. economy and if he were alive today he would be worth many billions more than Bill Gates and Jeff Bezos combined! He took control of at least ninety percent of the oil industry in America by underselling all his competitors who he then bought out. Eventually, new laws of Congress would break up his monopoly.

Hated by the defeated competition, he was loved by his employees, to whom he routinely gave generous bonus checks. It is estimated that he gave away almost a billion dollars to education, medicine, and the arts. As a result of his funding, the scourge of yellow fever was eliminated by eradication and vaccine. His name is attached to a university and perhaps most famously to Rockefeller Center, New York City.

Cornelius Vanderbilt began life in the steamship business, eventually, monopolizing sea trade to and from America. His nickname was Commodore. Sensing a new opportunity in swifter transportation, he entered the railroad industry and eventually took over thirteen independent railroad lines. He had a gruff personality and was not liked by many, especially the female gender whom he treated poorly. He was not a generous philanthropist only giving away about one million dollars but also endowing the formation of Vanderbilt University in Tennessee, one of America's more prestigious universities.

John Pierpont Morgan was the epitome of the Wall Street Robber Barons to many. He avoided conscription into the Civil War in 1863 by being able to buy his way out of duty. Learning and manipulating the financial world, he eventually got himself in control of railroads and two gigantic companies—U.S. Steel and General Electric. His dealings strangled his competitors as well as the U.S. economy.

During the Panic of 1893, he had to pony up sixty-five million dollars to help the U.S. avoid a potential stock market crash. Today his name is associated with Chase Bank, the largest private bank in America. Morgan did have a charitable side, giving money to churches, hospitals, schools, and museums. He also funded the U.S. Army when they needed help buying additional rifles for the military.

The bottom line is, however you choose to view them and their ilk, they had an inordinate amount of power that was a threat to our democratic way of life. [The Big Tech companies of Silicon Valley may prove to be a bigger threat to democracy in 2021 and beyond if not controlled]. Big money influences our lawmakers. People knew controls were needed. The American worker was demanding a bigger share of the pie. Change was on the horizon.

CHAPTER 35

The Progressive Era

IN 1776 SCOTTISH ECONOMIST ADAM SMITH penned his famous opus "The Wealth of Nations" that put forth a philosophy of laissez-faire capitalism to ensure the economic growth of nations. Laissez-faire "hands-off" philosophy states that the government shall not interfere in the business world. If nations are to prosper they must be free to accrue as much wealth as possible without government interference.

This de facto philosophy went unchallenged in America until the Progressive Era of the late nineteenth and early twentieth century. This era revolved around social activism and political reform having to do with problems arising from industrialization and urbanization. This also included the rise of labor unions whose purpose was to check the corrupt/harmful/unfair practices of the capitalist factory and business owners. Unions wanted a larger share of the profits along with job security and safer conditions in the factories.

The factory system was a simple three-tiered arrangement. The top tier were the owners(s) of the factory or business who controlled the means of production—the physical plant, its assets, and the money (capital) needed to run the operation. They paid managers a salary to run the enterprise and supervise the workers. Management had the power to hire and fire workers, at random if they chose. The workers were the lowest tier. They received wages, not a salary. A wage is an hourly rate of pay while salaries are yearly payments. Before the advent of the Progressive Era, workers were completely at the mercy of their boss or owner of the plant. The owners looked to keep wages low so they could maximize their profits. If factories or businesses were successful, owners looked to expand their operations and make additional profits, at the expense of the workers.

Labor unions came about in the late nineteenth century to call attention to the plight of the worker. People were emigrating to America or leaving their farms to flock to urban areas in search of a more exciting life and the prospect of a good job. By joining together workers hoped for improved working conditions, avoiding random firings, and improving their standard of living.

Some of the earliest American labor unions were the following:

1. Knights of Labor (1869)
2. American Federation of Labor (AF of L) (1886)
3. International Workers of the World (1905)

The Knights of Labor attempted to unite all American labor—skilled and unskilled—into one union. They were the first organization to propose an eight-hour workday. Before this precedent, a boss could have you work up to sixteen hours a day if he so decreed. This union had many internal conflicts concerning the use or non-use of strikes. The Haymarket Square Riot of Chicago (1886) led to protesting for an eight-hour workday when someone threw a bomb near the police. After this incident, the union began to splinter apart.

The AFL was founded by Samuel Gompers in 1886. Its membership would be limited to craft or skilled workers. [Today it is the AFL-CIO, the largest combined union of skilled and unskilled workers.] Gompers was pro-capitalist and opposed strikes and violence to achieve gains for his members. He realized that the unions were already being seen in a negative light by both the capitalists and the general population. He urged co-operation between unions and management that would generate the positive publicity the unions needed to become accepted. A giant of the labor movement, Gompers was re-elected every year to lead the union until his death in 1924.

Diametrically opposed to the AF of L were the IWW aka "the Wobblies." They were of pure Communist persuasion. According to IWW doctrine, there should be only one class of people, the workers who shall control the means of production that would in the end make everyone happy. Karl Marx's *Communist Manifesto* describes the takeover process. Like Fascism, power resides with a single leader but in a Communist State, this leader is anointed by the proletariat (workers) after they have replaced the current government. This leader is supposed to distribute all goods and services equally to the people resulting in a Utopia (perfect society). These attempts at Communism ultimately fail as humans are innately competitive achievers. Competition by its nature leads to inequality, the way of the world.

These people were anarchists, like today's Antifa, who were not afraid to use violence to take over business and other institutions. These people made a lot of others nervous. This is why the early labor unions were feared in America leading to the Red Scare and the Palmer Raids in the 1920s. Fortunately, America was about to be run by Teddy Roosevelt who was more than happy to confront them, or anybody else for that matter.

Although Massachusetts passed the first child labor law in 1866, it would take a historic tragedy to tilt the new Progressive laws in favor of the labor force. In 1911, in lower Manhattan, 146 garment workers, mostly young girls between ages fourteen and twenty-three, were burned to death in the historic Triangle Shirtwaist Factory Fire. Management had decided to lock the doors and the exit stairwells to prevent employees from taking unauthorized breaks and to prevent theft of clothing. The owners were operating a now-illegal sweatshop, an overcrowded factory with no protocol for safety or breaks from work. After this tragedy, there were age and hour limits set for employees and safety procedures and inspections mandated for categories and businesses.

Meanwhile, the government was taking some steps to rein in corruption in its own bureaucracy as in the business world. To wit:

1. Pendleton Act (1883)

2. Interstate Commerce Commission (1887)

3. Sherman Antitrust Act (1890)

4. Clayton Antitrust Act (1914)

The Pendleton Act was designed to end the spoils system and replace it with merit-based civil services positions in the federal bureaucracy. The U.S. government is the largest employer in the U.S., granting job security to those who are able to pass the testing. Before this reform, it was "who you know, not what you know."

The ICC was originally set up to regulate the rates that railroads could charge. Later on, their jurisdiction was expanded to cover all modes of transport.

The Sherman Act was the big hammer the government used against monopolies. Under tremendous pressure from both sides, Congress finally passed this act that outlawed the existence of businesses "in restraint of trade," another way of saying that monopolies were no longer legal and had to be dissolved. The most recent victim of this act was AT&T "Bell" Telephone (1984) that was forced to divide into eight smaller companies at the time known as Baby Bells. [Many people today are hoping that Congress applies the Sherman Act to the oligarchs that run Silicon Valley. This is not likely as the current Biden Administration has hired many former Silicon Valley executives to help run the White House.]

The Clayton Act reinforced the Sherman Act and protected labor interests. This act prevents mergers of companies that could lead to monopoly. It also outlawed price gouging and legalized strikes and boycotts for labor. This does not pertain to the police or fire departments of America, which are not allowed to strike.

Muckrakers

Coined by President Theodore Roosevelt, this term was used to describe the investigative journalists of the late nineteenth century who exposed the abuses of capitalism, industrialization, government corruption, and immigration. They illustrated the plight of the more needy "victims" of the Progressive Era. Among the more prominent writers were:

1. Ida Tarbell

2. Jacob Riis

3. Upton Sinclair

Ida Tarbell probably was the original investigative journalist. Her book *The History of the Standard Oil Company* led Teddy Roosevelt to invoke the Sherman Act to break up the monopoly of Rockefeller's oil production. Her writings also directly led to the passage of the Clayton Act that further regulated monopolies.

Jacob Riis was one of America's earliest photo-journalists. He photographed the slums (run down areas) of New York City and exposed the extreme overcrowding of tenements (run-down buildings) that housed thousands of new immigrant families. Laws that limited the number of people cohabiting in one apartment were soon to follow, as were fire codes that also limited occupancy.

Upton Sinclair's fictional account of the meatpacking industry was entitled *The Jungle*. Without any safeguards or inspections, contaminated meats had been sold over the counter and were assumed to be safe. Congress quickly enacted the Pure Food and Drug Act (1906) and today food sold in bulk, especially meats, must be tested and approved by the FDA.

All of these writers were greatly influenced by political cartoonist Thomas Nast. His claim to fame was his takedown of Boss Tweed and Tammany Hall, a mob enterprise that ran a good part of New York City in the late nineteenth century. Tweed would offer immigrants jobs and a place to live only to shake them down later for bribes and the promise of their vote in precinct elections. Nast began to lampoon the Tweed Gang using political cartoons in the New York City daily newspapers. Tweed feared Nast's caricatures so much he offered him $500,000.00 to go study art somewhere else.

Nash declined. The Tammany Hall gang was eventually voted out of office.

Nast was also the creator of the Santa Claus image, of the elephant represented the Republican Party, and the donkey to represent the Democrats. Lincoln referred to Nast as his best recruiter getting soldiers to enlist in the Civil War. Nast also criticized the government for the Chinese Exclusion Act (1882) prohibiting the immigration of more Chinese laborers. His cartoon asked, "What group will be next?"

Overcrowded conditions in cities led to a myriad of social problems including illness, crime, bad housing, and a feeling of anomie (being lost). One person decided to do something about these conditions.

In 1899 Jane Addams established the Hull House settlement in the heart of Chicago. It was a gathering point, where people could meet and take classes in citizenship, cooking, education, dancing, etc. Children were encouraged to meet others and get educated and eventually, anomie was replaced by a feeling of belonging to a community. Social work became a large and very important occupation in American life. Credit Jane Addams as the founder. It seems that Addams may have been a role model for Barack Obama, who began his career as a Chicago "community organizer."

Wyatt Earp…. Boxing referee?

Western lawman Wyatt Earp, who along with his brothers and Doc Holliday became renowned for their role in eliminating the outlaw Clanton Gang at the iconic gunfight at the Ok Corral, reinvented himself after his shoot-em-up days came to an end.

On December 2nd, 1896, Tom Sharkey defeated betting favorite Bob Fitzsimmons in a controversial heavyweight boxing championship in San Francisco. Prior to the match, the combatants could not agree on a referee but finally settled on Wyatt Earp, who had a stellar reputation in California and Arizona but was unknown nationally.

Earp officiated the bout with a revolver strapped to his hip. Fitzsimmons dropped Sharkey in the eighth round, but Earp ruled that Sharkey was hit below the belt. The press lampooned the lawman's decision to award the fight to Sharkey, and the controversy followed Earp to his death at age eighty in 1929.

CHAPTER 36
Spanish American War
(1898)

AMERICAN BUSINESS WAS BEGINNING to look overseas for new markets in which to buy and sell goods. Ninety miles to the south of the Florida Keys lay Cuba, a Spanish possession. Spain had given permission to America to cultivate the sugar cane industry in Cuba. Sugar was processed into rum, one of the world's most potent potables. As the impoverished native Cubans began to rebel against the Spanish oppressors, Americans were also being injured and business interests threatened. President McKinley sent a battleship, The Maine, to Havana Harbor in 1898 to protect American interests.

On February 15th, a great explosion occurred upon the Maine. To this day, no one is sure who detonated the bomb but the ship sank so quickly almost all on board were killed. "Remember the Alamo!" was updated to "Remember the Maine!" as the U.S. quickly declared war on the old and doddering Spanish Empire. Admiral Dewey quickly destroyed the once-proud Spanish fleet in the Philippine Islands. Not a single American was killed. At the same time, the American Army overwhelmed the Spanish Army at the Battle of San Juan Hill with the help of Theodore Roosevelt's Rough Riders, a cavalry unit.

This was a very one-sided war and critics blamed the U.S. for its instigation. They believed that the U.S. had cast its eyes on the Spanish Empire as a market for its goods. For the first time, the U.S. was derided as an imperialistic nation—one looking to add colonies for resources and expansion. As a result of this war, the U.S. took possession of Cuba, Puerto Rico, Guam, and the Philippine Islands. These lands became U.S. territories. Theodore Roosevelt was seen as a war hero and "rode" his popularity into the White House as a two-term president.

CHAPTER 37

The Oriental World

THE ORIENTAL WORLD (CHINA, INDIA, JAPAN) had isolated itself from western civilization and as a result did not experience the Industrial Revolution. That changed in 1853 when Commodore Matthew Perry sailed a U.S. fleet into Japan's main harbor to initiate trade and discuss the treatment of ship-wrecked U.S. sailors.

The Japanese were scared to death by the size of Perry's "Black Ships" and quickly realized they needed to modernize their country. Unfortunately, Perry's introduction of guns into the Japanese culture created a monster as the once pacifist nation would become very warlike and aggressive.

China was the next country to feel the effects of dealing with the West. Around 1900, China was a weak nation but had large deposits of iron ore that became the basis of steel production. China was already a very populated nation that would become a large market for western goods. Great Britain, Russia, France, Germany, and Japan wanted to divide China into sections with each country having a sphere of influence (area of control).

The U.S. was opposed to this "invasion" and instead opted for an Open Door Policy of trade with China in 1899. The Open Door Policy would allow all nations to freely trade with China but allowed China to maintain its territorial integrity. The U.S. received Chinese respect for this attempt but Chinese nationalists attempted to rid China of all foreigners.

The Boxer Rebellion (1900) was composed of thousands of Chinese nationalists using martial arts fighting techniques and weaponry to oust foreigners from China. This was a failure. Ultimately the rebellion was put down by an international force of mostly European nations. This was a rare moment when China and the U.S. were actually friendly.

CHAPTER 38

Theodore Roosevelt

(1901-1909)

THOUGH ELECTED AS A LINCOLN-ESQUE REPUBLICAN, later on, he swung more towards the Democratic side as he offered the nation a Square Deal—honesty in government above the narrow interests of the rival political parties. On the one hand, he favored militarism, imperialism, "a proud place in the world for America," law and order and self-reliance while, on the other hand, he embraced the embryonic stages of the welfare state—government pensions, workmen's compensation, low-income housing, and unemployment insurance.

Born a sickly asthmatic, through sheer determination and hard physical exercise including boxing, that caused left-eye blindness, he gained the confidence to excel in a number of careers including New York City police commissioner, legislator, New York State governor, vice president, and two-term president. It did not hurt that, along with Thomas Jefferson, he was the most widely read president. His favorite expression of approval was "Bully!"

Roosevelt was willing and able to take on any obstacle that befell his presidency. His biggest headache while being in office was dealing with the shenanigans of his daughter Alice, who was a born rebel, one of the first women to create a scandal by smoking in public as well as carrying a live snake in her purse. Roosevelt once famously remarked, "I can either run the country or I can attend to Alice, but I cannot possibly do both."

Ranked as one of America's five greatest presidents—and my personal favorite—he is enshrined on Mt Rushmore. He was a doer who overcame extreme physical limitations to lift himself and his nation to an exalted status in U.S. history. Some of his accomplishments:

1. Mediated the Great Coal Strike (1902)
2. Received funding for Panama Canal (1903)
3. Roosevelt Corollary "Big Stick Policy" (1904)
4. Established National Park System (1905)
5. Trust-Buster (1902-1911)

The coal miners were threatening to strike in 1902. They wanted to work fewer hours and get more pay. Roosevelt was the first president to personally mediate a labor-management dispute. He persuaded the owners of the mine to agree to fewer hours and more pay. He had threatened to call out the federal troops to stop this strike. Sending a message to the radical "Wobblies," he warned coal workers *not* to unionize. Roosevelt would not tolerate violent strikes against management.

Roosevelt's pet project was the digging of the Panama Canal to shorten the trade route from the east coast of America to the west coast. He had to twist a lot of arms both in Panama and in Congress to get the project started, but his efforts were successful. No longer did ships have to travel around the southern tip of South America to get from the east coast of America to the west coast.

Roosevelt sensed that the new German Republic wanted to build a world empire. Kaiser (king) Wilhelm's functionaries were in the area of the new Panama Canal—and Roosevelt did not like it! He induced Congress to reaffirm the Monroe Doctrine by enacting the new Roosevelt Corollary that said the U.S. will not tolerate European interference in Latin America. His method of enforcement was summarized thusly as, "Walk softly...but carry a big stick," a passive-aggressive statement of U.S. police powers in the Western Hemisphere.

The Big Stick Policy has been utilized by many presidents, especially Ronald Reagan. Critics point out that too often the U.S. had interfered in the affairs of the Latin American countries of Central and South America.

During the younger and older phases of his life, Roosevelt spent time on a North Dakota ranch where he became a hunter and also involved in the conservation of natural resources. Some people viewed him as they did Andrew Jackson—as a cowboy President. Roosevelt used his love of the outdoors to create the U.S. Forest Service and from this agency was created five national parks covering about 150,000,000 acres of land. Roosevelt wanted to conserve even more land but Congress realized the expanding western population needed land to live on.

Monopolists and some historians refer to Roosevelt as a trust-buster, one who wanted to put an end to all trusts. Roosevelt demurred saying that there were good trusts and bad trusts. When trusts created unfair trade practices, that is when he brought the hammer down in terms of the Sherman Antitrust Act.

For example, in 1902, the Supreme Court broke up the Northern Securities Company, a railroad monopoly partially owned by J.P. Morgan, not the most popular guy in America, as you now know. It was made up of only three railroads, but they controlled most of the transport of goods throughout America. After reading Ida Tarbell's book about Standard Oil, Roosevelt persuaded the Supreme Court to haul Rockefeller and his attorneys into the Court's chambers. This break-up was so massive that Standard Oil was forced to divide into thirty-four companies. Up to this point, Rockefeller had been the wealthiest man in the world, as previously noted.

As America entered the twentieth century, they had the right man as president at the right time and in the right place. Roosevelt was a tremendous ambassador for American interests and unafraid to talk about them. He gave America a certain equilibrium between the forces of labor and the industrialists, much like a competent referee hired to officiate the big game. He raised the consciousness of the American public in regards to conservation and appreciation of the natural world. Old injuries and physical limitations caught up to him and he died at the relatively young age of sixty. A word of gratitude to one of our greatest presidents—Bully!

Upon leaving office in 1909, Roosevelt was invited by Kaiser Wilhelm of Germany to review the organization of the new German Army. Roosevelt was impressed by their organization but the size of the army worried him. When he returned to America, he warned president Taft that the German leadership viewed America as weak and were preparing for war. His prediction, unfortunately, proved to be correct.

Statue of Liberty

The Statue of Liberty was a centennial gift to America that did not arrive until 1884. Designed by Frederic Bartholdi, it was shipped to America from France in 214 cases. Set up on Bedloe's Island, it required $280,000 to erect a pedestal to hold it in place. As part of her contribution to the fund-raising campaign, Emma Lazarus wrote a poem now attached to the base of the pedestal. "Give me your tired, your poor, your huddled masses yearning to breathe free, the wretched refuse of your teeming shore. Send these, the homeless, tempest-tost to me, I lift my lamp beside the golden door!"

CHAPTER 39
World War I

WORLD WAR I, aka THE GREAT WAR, began as a European war amongst a number of countries who did not much like each other. Tensions had been building up in Europe for many decades and it only took the assassination of a minor political figure to set off the "powder keg" of Europe that would escalate into a World War as the U.S. and other nations got sucked into the mania (madness) of war.

When I taught European history in high school, I used the acronym M.A.N.I.A. to help my students remember the five underlying causes of the Great War:

1. Militarism

2. Alliances

3. Nationalism

4. Imperialism

5. Anarchy

Otto von Bismarck of Prussia organized the German States into one country in the late 1860s. He was guided by a German-based philosophy which stated, "History is written by the winners or more succinctly might make right." As early as 1871, Germany flexed its new military muscle by seizing the iron-ore rich territories of Alsace-Lorraine from bordering France. After they lost these territories France immediately began to build their military, well aware of the totalitarian philosophy of the Germans dating back to the days of Attila the Hun. Though slower to mobilize, Russia was another neighboring country that had issues with Germany. England, of course, was already fully militarized as it had a global empire to administer.

Alliances are agreements signed between nations for mutual support in times of war. If one nation is attacked the others are pledged to help. In today's vernacular, "I got your back!" Two rival alliances were formed to prevent the onset of war—The Triple Alliance and the Triple Entente. The former consisted of Germany, Austria, Hungary, and Italy; the latter Russia, France, and England. There was a balance of power between each side but could quickly become a balance of terror if war broke out. Both alliances also had smaller countries within their respective alliances. In retrospect, all of these countries had agendas and they certainly were militarizing for a reason so this war was inevitable.

Nationalism is a two-edged sword. It can be a positive force, especially in sports competitions like the Olympic Games where there is a lot of cheering and flag-waving. These games show pride in one's nation, which is the definition of nationalism. However, aggressive nationalism is another issue. In this scenario, jeering replaces cheering and guns replace flag-waving. The German philosophy of might makes right, in my opinion, instigated this war.

Imperialism became the new word for colonization. The young country of Germany wanted to test the British Navy at sea, while on land the Germans wanted to build a railroad from Berlin to

Baghdad in Iraq and take control of the new oil fields. They also had their eyes on control of the Suez Canal where trade was done between Europe, Asia, and the Middle East. Roosevelt warned America of this "saber-rattling" and now the rest of the world was aware of German world expansion. France of course wanted the return of Alsace and was willing to go to war to get those regions back under their control. Austria-Hungary was a willing partner of Germany with similar ethnic roots, especially in Austria. Italy had its eyes on Africa and getting back a portion of its once-mighty Roman Empire.

Anarchy means lack of government, "chaos." In this time period, there was no international union of countries to police the aggressions manifested by the competing alliances. Unfortunately, the U.S. would have to fulfill that role as its own interests and well-being were threatened by Germany.

One of the reasons WWI was referred to as the Great War was because of numbers never seen before in conflict. There were twenty-eight countries involved in the war with 60-70,000,000 personnel in combat. There were 9,000,000 combat fatalities, 7,000,000 civilian casualties, and the Spanish Flu that began in 1918, the last year of the war, claimed another nearly 50,000,000 deaths.

Although only in the war for eighteen months, the U.S. lost 60,000 personnel and had another 200,000 injured. The U.S. initiated a draft that netted an army of between one and two million including 300,000 African-Americans, many receiving the distinguished service cross, one of the highest honors bestowed by the military brass (leaders).

After the Statue of Liberty was erected, millions of European immigrants flocked to America. It is estimated that by the turn of the twentieth-century immigration increased the U.S. population by 35,000,000 for a total of over 100,000,000 now living on American soil. Unlike the draft riots of 1863 during the Civil War, this new influx of people was willing to fight without objection.

The German plan to win the war was to quickly knock out France on the Western Front then defeat a slow-to-organize Russia on the Eastern Front. When Germany attacked and overran the neutral country of Belgium to get at France, England declared war on Germany the next day, but more importantly it soon put an end to the U.S. foreign policy of isolationism as Americans began to fear and distrust an anti-democratic Germany. America had been selling goods to both the Allies (Triple Entente) and the Central Powers(Triple Alliance), but since the British navy controlled the seas most of those goods wound up in the hands of the Allies.

One of the new weapons of war proved to be the deciding factor for the U.S. entry into the war. The Germans had designed the first functional submarine that they called a U-Boat. Armed with torpedoes, these U-boats were silent assassins and forced the Allies to quickly invent primitive sonar to detect them underwater. In 1915, the Germans sank the British luxury cruise ship the Lusitania, killing over 1,000 British and over 100 Americans. According to international law if an enemy sinks the ship of an opponent they must rescue the survivors. The U-boats were too small to save passengers, so many innocents were lost at sea. The Germans also did not guarantee the safety of future victims if they attacked again. To combat the U-Boats, the U.S. Navy instituted the convoy system where warships would guide cargo ships across the sea lanes. Gradually the threat was diminished, but this was the main reason for the U.S. to declare war on Germany in 1917.

The icing on the cake was the U.S. interception of the Zimmerman Note. This secret German telegram was an offer to

Mexico to help fight against the U.S. The Germans promised to overturn the Mexican Cession of lands won by the U.S. after the Mexican-American War. This made the U.S. even more motivated to end the German threat to our democracy.

Until the U.S. entry into the war, the land battles had resulted in mostly a stalemate. The reason being that both sides had engaged in Trench Warfare, which involved digging deep into the earth for protection then erecting barbed wire to blunt frontal assaults. Another new weapon also led to stalemate—poison gas. First employed by the Germans, it was a lethal mass killer before the first gas masks arrived in the trenches. But if the wind quickly shifted, the gas became a fickle killer. It is estimated that along the Western Front in France there were 600 miles of trench, sometimes only fifteen yards away from an enemy trench. Many hand grenades were lobbed over the barbed wire fences producing a lot of injuries and fatalities. Germany also used zeppelins (blimps) to drop bombs on the British/French lines. The British countered with the RAF (Royal Air Force) and the U.S. Congress utilized the Elastic Clause of the Constitution to create the USAF (US Air Force), which became an official branch of the military in 1947. The dogfighters of WWI were under command of the U.S. Army.

Dogfighting was a new form of warfare. This involves rival air forces attempting to shoot each other down, usually in one-on-one plane combat. The American "Ace" pilot was Captain Eddie Rickenbacker, who was credited with twenty two kills. The first planes were not constructed like the fighter jets in the movie Top Gun. These planes were more flimsy like the Wright Brothers first airplane. Today machine guns and rockets are used in dogfighting. In the early years of WWI the key to a dogfight victory was to fly above the opponent and have the bombardier drop bricks on the thin wings of the plane that would cause the plane to spiral downwards then crash. There are archival films of the early dogfighting, which was part warfare and part gymnastics. The bombardier actually stood atop the plane, in the wide open sky, and dropped bricks on the enemy planes below.

The Allies finally got the upper hand in Trench Warfare when the British invented the tank. They were able to smash through the barbed wire and trenches and eventually the Germans were in full retreat. Because the British and French were receiving most of the supplies, the Germans were also losing the war of attrition. Attrition means to deplete the enemy of any and all war supplies. Even though the Russians signed a peace treaty to get out of the war, the AEF (American Expeditionary Force) under General John "Black Jack" Pershing proved to be the undoing of the Central Powers. This million-man army overwhelmed the Germans and led to their surrender in 1918.

The bravery of the American soldier was best exemplified by the exploits of Sgt. Alvin York. By himself, he attacked a German machine gun set up and killed twenty five Germans and took 132 as P.O.W.'s. He received the nation's highest honor, the Congressional Medal of Honor and his story became the subject of the 1941 Oscar-winning movie Sgt York. This movie was used as a motivational tool for those soldiers who were going into combat in WWII.

I also have to credit the women behind the scenes. For every one man in uniform, it takes ten to provide for his needs. Rifle ammunition was in short supply and was needed quickly. Women were entrusted with the supervision of the production of rifle bullets. Without their help, we lose. We also give credit for all the nurses who saved lives and got our soldiers back on their feet.

The U.S. used many types of propaganda against the Germans. Cartoons portrayed the Germans as barbarians wearing pointed Prussian helmets and having bloodshot eyes and crooked teeth. German books were removed from the shelves in schools and libraries and the teaching of German was verboten ("forbidden" in German). Sauerkraut was renamed "liberty cabbage." In short the German culture was being expunged or censored out of existence.

Congress was able to pass the unconstitutional Espionage Act of 1918 that took away any right to protest the war.

Treaty of Versailles (1919)

Because Germany was viewed as the instigator of the Great War, they were forced to pay a heavy price. The terms of the treaty are as follows:

1. Germany had to give up all its colonies - mostly to France and England.

2. German citizens were now forced to live in the new countries of Poland and Czechoslovakia.

3. The German Army was reduced to 100,000 and the Navy, U - boats, and Air Force were destroyed.

4. Germany was forced to pay billions of dollars in reparations (damages of war) to many countries.

5. Germany was forced to sign a war guilt statement, taking full responsibility for instigating an entire world war.

The collective anger aroused in the German people forced to live under the terms of this treaty was a motivator for the rise of Adolf

Hitler and a direct cause of World War II that would ensue a mere twenty years later. As history does often repeat itself, you may recall a similar scenario put forth earlier in this book of how one war, in this case the French and Indian War, led directly to and was a cause of the Revolutionary War in America.

The League of Nations (1920)

This was the first international attempt to form a co-operative "police" force that would prevent the occurrence of future multinational wars. This might have become a success, but the refusal of the U.S. to join the League left it with little enforcement power. The U.S. had been hesitant to join World War I and after it was over a sizable number of Congress wanted to retreat back into Isolationism, the foreign policy defined by George Washington. The U.S. was split almost in half, some for, some against—and in the end would not join. The League proved to be a failure, but its progeny, the United Nations, was put into effect after World War II.

CHAPTER 40

The Roaring 20s

THE 1920S WERE THE ULTIMATE ROLLER COASTER ride for America—great prosperity in the middle of the 1920s bookended by economic depression that both began and ended the decade, especially the Great Depression of 1929. The first Depression was caused by the shutdown of the wartime economy. Many factory workers were suddenly unemployed and farmers were really hard hit as the rebuilding European nations were growing their own food again.

Unions lost power as there was a surplus of labor and factory owners used lockouts and yellow dog contracts to suppress the power of unions. Lockouts barred workers from the job site if they joined a union while new workers signed yellow dog contracts agreeing not to join a union as a condition of employment. After a while, industrialists begin to earn large profits again as conservative presidents would not use the Sherman and Clayton Antitrust Acts to curb the growth of big business. A rebuilding Europe needed goods made in America to reconstruct their countries.

In America, mass production ramped up in three relatively new industries—automobiles, radios, and refrigerators. One in five people now owned their own car, and because cheap electricity replaced coal, to a large extent, every household now could afford a refrigerator that replaced the old ice box and each home had at least one radio.

Most people associate The Roaring Twenties with the rise of the entertainment and sports industries. Movie houses sprung up everywhere as people gathered there to watch the newsreels that showed people current events and depicted the battles of World War I. The first "talkie" or motion picture was the *Jazz Singer* in 1927. Hollywood became an identity and a destination like a second gold rush to California.

The passage of the Nineteenth Amendment in 1920 encouraged the liberation of women. They had finally achieved the right to vote. Flappers were the young women of the 1920s who disdained tradition by wearing short skirts, bobbing their hair and smoking in public. Dance halls soon became pervasive throughout America as people began to break away from the more staid and traditional church socials.

Professional sports became big business as the Industrialists looked for new and more profitable ventures. Even though the Eighteenth Amendment was now in effect—banning the production and sale of alcohol—the law was not strictly enforced and speakeasies and Bootlegging (illegal alcohol) became a big if not illicit business. Off the coast of Long Island operated a famous rum runner by the name of Bill McCoy. A rum runner was a seaman who attempted to break through a line of police boats who were attempting to stop the transport of illegal alcohol to the mainland. McCoy had a reputation for running in high quality booze, giving birth to the term "The Real McCoy."

This was the era of real gangsters—Al Capone, John Dillinger, Pretty Boy Floyd, Baby Face Nelson, Bonnie and Clyde, etc—not the pseudo gangsters created by the hip hop culture of today. The cities of Detroit, Chicago, and New York had a lack of gangster control until the FBI under the direction of Eliot Ness and The Untouchables busted the Capone Syndicate in Chicago.

The coming-out party of America involved many fads or crazes. Some of these fads went to great extremes. Over 200 people took part in a foot race between Los Angeles and New York City. The winner crossed the finish line eighty four days later. Other fads included flagpole-sitting, goldfish swallowing, and dance marathons. Dance marathons turned deadly during the Great Depression. Prizes were awarded to those who could dance the longest and the promoters charged entry fees for both participants and the audience. If you are so inclined watch the 1969 movie *They Shoot Horses, Don't They?* a bitter commentary about people literally dying on the dance floor attempting to win badly needed Depression money. But for most of the decade this was America's post-war celebration, however not everyone was invited.

Because of the events of the recent Great War and the looming threat of Communism creeping into America from abroad, there was an entire culture of intolerance that came to be in the twenties. The government feared that Communism was infiltrating the union movement. This was known as the Red Scare, and was countered by Nicholas Palmer, Attorney General of the U.S., who carried out the Palmer Raids, arresting 6000 potential Communists and ultimately deporting 600. Because of the Red Scare and the end of wartime production, there were severe quotas put on European immigration for the first time. Extreme intolerance toward immigration was exemplified by the 1927 trial of Sacco and Vanzetti, Italian immigrants who had supported the growth of unions. On flimsy evidence they were convicted of murder during the course of a robbery, found guilty and sentenced to death. Paranoia and xenophobia (fear of foreigners) had surfaced again and were taken to the extreme.

This intolerance extended into the black community. The Ku Klux Klan rose again, this time north of the Mason-Dixon Line. As many as seventeen blacks were lynched as those unemployed and angry looked for scapegoats. Race riots broke out in twenty-six cities. Black soldiers still in uniform were killed as well as members of their family. The worst riot was in Chicago, lasting two full weeks and taking the lives of thirty-eight people and injuring 500 more. Unfortunately Jim Crow was still alive and well. The Tulsa race massacre took place in Oklahoma in 1921, when White mobs attacked Black residents and burned down thirty-five square blocks of the Greenwood District known as "Black Wall Street," at the time one of the wealthiest Black communities in the U.S.

The entire reform movement seemed to have been abandoned in this decade. Prohibition was the only half-hearted attempt at reform, but Richard Hofstadter characterized it as "a pinched parochial pseudo reform carried out in America via rural-evangelical virus." In short, alcohol was frowned upon by the Bible Belt of America.

The thought police were involved in what was called at the time, the trial of the century. The Scopes Monkey Trial had to do with the teaching of evolution in the classroom. John's Scopes was a Tennessee teacher who went against Christian tradition and said that man had evolved from the ape, where the accepted truth was that man had been created in God's image in the Bible. The issue became freedom of thought versus tradition. In the end, Scopes was found guilty and had to pay a fine. The law banning the teaching of evolution remained in force.

The two major presidents of the 1920s were Warren Harding from Ohio, and his successor, Calvin Coolidge from Massachusetts, both conservative Republicans and pro-business. Criticized for his lack of oversight, the Harding Administration was one of the most scandal-plagued of all the presidential administrations. For example, his Secretary of the Interior, Albert Fall, initiated the Teapot Dome Scandal, where Fall sold government oil lands to his friends in return for kickbacks. He was indicted and sent to prison. Harding died in office in 1923.

Calvin Coolidge was a man of few words, but he did believe that "the business of America is business" and easily won reelection after replacing Harding in office. Reporters tried to trick Coolidge into opening up on issues. One reporter said, "I bet I can make you say more than three words.." to which Coolidge coolly replied "you lose!" Though business was his main concern, Coolidge had one eye on world events. Under his watch, the U.S was involved in the Washington Conference, the Kellogg-Briand Pact, and the Stimson Doctrine that collectively had the purpose of preventing another World War. However, like the League of Nations, there was no enforcement of these ideas.

The 1920s saw a seismic shift in American culture. The old Puritanical ways were being replaced by Leisure Time and entertainment. The culture was changing. For the first time, more than half of the population lived in urban areas and the growth of suburbs was not far behind. There were cars, roads, movies, sports, and new forms of entertainment. Unfortunately, it all came to a crashing halt in the last year of the 1920s.

A singular event encapsulated the mania and energy generated by The Roaring Twenties. A New York Hotel owner promised a prize of $25,000 to the first person who could fly non-stop from New

York to Paris. Several contestants failed, but finally in 1927 Charles Lindbergh decided on a solo flight in his single-engine plane named The Spirit of St Louis. Leaving from Roosevelt Field, Long Island, he took off on May 27th bringing along only two sandwiches and a bottle of water. Known as "the Lone Eagle," Lindberg was forced to fly low because of the lousy weather and barely missed hitting the masts of French ships. For thirty three and a half hours, he flew through terrible conditions. Fighting to remain awake, he spotted the coast of France and landed near Paris. Lindbergh became an international hero and the symbol of what could be.

In a revolutionary but much quieter way, Dr. Alexander Fleming developed the compound penicillin in 1928. Though it did not become commercially available right away, its impact has been immeasurable, preventing and curing bacterial infections that otherwise would have killed millions. It is still largely used today to treat strep throat, which if left untreated can become heart disease.

One of my three favorite books, *The Great Gatsby* by F Scott Fitzgerald, was published in 1925. Fitzgerald saw in the 1920s a brittle, empty way of life. People had their sports heroes such as Babe Ruth of the New York Yankees, their movies, their new jazz music, the Charleston dance, and their alcohol sold at illegal Speakeasy bars. But Fitzgerald saw them searching for some deeper meaning in life. Many people, in retrospect, would agree that he was right. The words ring true even today. I have read the book several times and highly recommend it.

To counter the intolerance of the KKK, the Harlem Renaissance sprang to life. Leaders writers such as William E. B. Dubois, Claude Mckay, and Langston Hughes wrote about the black experience in America, taking pride in their race but also showing the problems of the world were universal and did not have to be seen through a racial lens. The Harlem Renaissance had a profound effect on the upcoming Civil Rights Movement of the 1960s.

Gertrude Ederle (1905-2003)

The Roaring Twenties was a decade fraught with tremendous energy and achievement. Emblematic of this decade was swimmer Gertrude Ederle, from Manhattan, nicknamed "The Queen of the Waves." Though the Nineteenth Amendment had certified suffrage for women, there was still a pervasive bias of male superiority especially in the world of athletic competition. Ederle set out to put that myth to rest.

Being nearly completely deaf from childhood measles, Ederle overcame her disability to become an Olympic swim champion. But her claim to fame came on August 6th, 1926 when she became the first woman to successfully swim across the 20-mile English Channel, beating the best male swimmer's attempts by 2 hours! This record stood until 1950. "people said women couldn't swim the channel, but I proved them wrong."

She received a ticker-tape parade in New York City's Canyon of Heroes. Sadly, she never married and taught deaf children to swim the rest of her life. Even sadder she died alone in an old age home in the Bronx and is interred there in the Woodlawn Cemetery.

CHAPTER 41

The Great Depression

(1929-1939)

THE DEFINITION OF A DEPRESSION is a sustained long-term downturn in business activity in the economies of one or more nations. Characteristics of a depression are an unemployment rate of 25%, bank and business failures and deflation. The Great Depression affected economies to the four corners of the earth but especially war-torn Europe and the United States. The Great Depression in the U.S. was triggered by the October 1929 stock market crash, as the American economy went from boom to bust overnight. One thing I learned in economics is that stock markets and commodity markets where goods are exchanged do not like uncertainty. Once one major market has a meltdown, it spreads quickly to the others. The U.S. was in relatively good shape after World War I but not so for the other nations. These are some reasons for the Great Depression:

1. Poverty in Europe

2. High U.S. protective tariffs

3. Overproduction of U.S. goods

4. Overvalued U.S. stock market

5. Dust Bowl

Similar to America, the shutdown of the wartime production of goods badly hurt the British economy. Workers were laid off and England was losing control of its empire in places like Ireland, Egypt, Afghanistan, Australia, and New Zealand. Most of the war had been fought on French soil. France thought that German reparations would rebuild their country, but Germany only paid a fraction of their war debt, which left both countries in poverty. Russia was in the middle of a messy and protracted Communist takeover of the former czarist regimes.

The U.S. had to use tariffs to protect its industries during the post war rebuild. The government made a serious error raising the tariffs during the 20s with the result of losing a great number of European contracts.

Additionally, the expansion of U.S. business led to a surplus of goods. With an insufficient number of buyers, deflation set in eventually resulting in rising unemployment as workers were let go by employers.

Too many Americans got greedy and invested in a stock market that was overvalued. Some companies let larger investors buy "on margin," only putting down a small percentage of the worth of the stock. When people began to panic and sell their stocks, they took tremendous losses as did the banks who were also short of funds. There became a widespread bank "run" in America, where everyone got as much money out of a bank as they could before the bank shut down. Many people had previously withdrawn large sums of money to invest. Now everyone was a loser.

To add insult to injury, the Great Plains of the U.S., especially Kansas and Oklahoma, had to endure a decade-long Dust Bowl with very little rainfall for many years. Wheat and corn production were way down as was livestock breeding and ranching. The "Black Blizzard" of blown away soil was so widespread that it darkened the skies over the Atlantic Ocean.

The nation blamed President Herbert Hoover for this dilemma and mocked him by erecting "Hoovervilles" for the unemployed and homeless. These were makeshift shacks constructed out of packing boxes, scrap iron, and anything that could be picked up free from the city dumps. Entire families that had been evicted slept on automobile seats carried from vehicular graveyards and warmed themselves before the fires of rubbish in grease drums on America's streets.

As more and more people sank into abject penury, basic food was hard to come by. Eventually the government rationed out bread and the urban lines were incredibly long waiting just to obtain a sandwich or plain bread. Many other people decided to take the easy way out rather than living in poverty; they simply jumped out of buildings and committed suicide by the hundreds if not thousands in the cities.

CHAPTER 42

The New Deal

THE HOOVER ADMINISTRATION ATTEMPTED to take steps to mitigate the effects of the Great Depression. These attempts were inconsequential and as a result Hoover was trounced in the 1932 Presidential election by Franklin Delano Roosevelt (FDR), who promised a New Deal to solve the ongoing misery of the Depression. On the night of his inauguration, FDR gave a down-and-out America hope by proclaiming the now iconic rallying cry "...the only thing we have to fear is fear itself..."

FDR was a distant cousin of Teddy Roosevelt and was born in Hyde Park, New York on the Hudson River. He was a two-time governor of New York State and like his distant cousin also had to overcome severe physical limitations. In his case he developed polio at age thirty nine and had to use leg braces the rest of his life. On the night of his inauguration before going to bed, he asked his son James, who would become his biographer, to say a prayer for me because "I may not have the strength to do this job." James noted, "I stood there for a moment unable to say anything. Then I left my father alone in his room about to embark on the great loneliness of the presidency...."

FDR was aided greatly by his wife Eleanor who was almost as high-profile as her husband. She held regular press conferences, wrote a daily newspaper column, a monthly magazine column and hosted a weekly radio show. She sometimes publicly disagreed with her husband's policies and was a powerful voice for civil rights. When the U.S. joined the United Nations, she became the first U.S. delegate.

FDR's New Deal was going to attempt to steer the United States through uncharted waters with a new and controversial philosophical change—the introduction of socialism into the governance of the United States. They say that desperate times require desperate measures. Capitalism has failed America (and the world). The New Deal was a radical change in government and the pro's and con's are still debated today. FDR was the most influential Democratic president of the twentieth century and many rate him top five status in the rank of presidents.

Until the Great Depression, the government had adopted a mostly laissez-faire "hands off" policy in regard to the growth of business. As previously stated, both the Sherman and Clayton Act began to somewhat control the corrupt growth of business and industry. FDR saw the need for more government control to get America back to its preeminent position in the world.

If you look more closely at the New Deal, it is an Alphabet Soup of agencies and acts, some long gone and some still in existence, that were initiated to get America back on its feet. These acts and agencies were created for the most part in the first 100 days of the New Deal to resolve the three aims of this unprecedented initiative: Relief for the poor and unemployed. Recovery for getting the economy back to normal. Reform to set up a financial system to prevent another depression.

Rather than going through the entire "alphabet," I want to concentrate on the results of the New Deal—or the lack thereof.

In one of FDR's first government-funded programs he hired 300,000 young men, boys, and former war veterans to do conservation jobs such as plant trees, rake leaves, fill in holes, and other menial outdoor jobs. Critics referred to this as "make work" projects, but FDR argued that it gave those who were down and out a sense of purpose.

The next round of government job hirings had to do with infrastructure projects such as the construction of airports, dams, public buildings, and bridges. This employed about 8,000,000 people and cost the taxpayer eleven billion dollars. Relief was brought to many but still many more idled.

Probably the most important reform was the institutionalization of Social Security and unemployment insurance in 1935. Social Security is a pension plan where the recipient and the government join together to provide a monthly stipend. Today a person is eligible to collect this at age sixty two, but you receive more each month the longer you wait (Just don't wait too long!). Should you be terminated at a job but not fired, you may collect unemployment insurance for a set period of time, usually less than a year. The amount you receive is based on your salary, but there is a maximum benefit.

Another important reform had to do with banking. Before the Depression you could have become bankrupt if there was a bank "run." Today you are insured by the government up to $100,000.00. This creates peace of mind and lends stability to the banking industry. Yet another reform had to do with stocks. The SEC (Security and Exchange Commission) is a government agency that regulates the entire stock industry and tries to spot fraud in the market and has the power to arrest brokers for selling bogus stocks or are involved in insider trading (cheating).

FDR did not overlook the Indians. He persuaded Congress to pass new legislation that allowed Native Americans to once again be landowners. Rights to tribal lands are still being litigated in the courts today. Reforms were also made in the energy and labor sectors of society. Overcoming opposition from private power companies, the government set up a power generating facility centered in Tennessee that converted the river flow into electricity. This had been a depressed economic area, but now Tennessee and parts of Virginia, North Carolina, Kentucky, and Alabama are involved in the government owned and operated Tennessee Valley Authority that has produced millions of dollars in wealth in this area over the years and employment for many who work for the TVA.

FDR was firmly pro-labor and his Congress passed what came to be known as the Wagner Act in 1935, giving workers the right of collective bargaining. This put labor and management on equal footing when negotiating work rules and contracts. Between 1933 and 1940 labor unions grew by 6,000,000. In this time the AFL-CIO merged into one powerful union of skilled and unskilled workers. Workers would do a lot better financially, but many feared the unions might become too powerful or Communistic in their ideology.

One of FDR's strategies of recovery was to begin the New Deal with a ninety-six hour bank holiday. All the banks were shut down and inspected. FDR then went on the radio for one of his very effective fireside chats, where he appraised the people about the status of the banks. He proclaimed that seventy-five percent of the banks were on solid footing and persuaded people to redeposit their money in the banks.

Once the banks were functional, he was able to give subsidies (government money) to farmers to not grow crops that were in surplus. The farmers decreased production and began to make money again and eventually were profitable once the Dust Bowl subsided. With federal bank funds, government loan agencies were able to offer low interest loans to lower income families looking to buy modestly-priced homes. Despite an early 2000s scandal, this program has been very successful for lower-income home shoppers and there are a number of different grants potential owners may qualify for to buy modestly-priced homes.

It is important to note that some of the New Deal was ruled to be unconstitutional by the Supreme Court. The partial takeover of the economy by the government crossed some legal lines, and FDR's Congressional foes were successful in derailing some of his programs. FDR did not take this setback lightly. He attempted to "pack" the Court with a half dozen more judges sympathetic to the New Deal. This became another loss for FDR in the courts, and public opinion was beginning to turn on him, comparing him to "King" Andrew Jackson, trampling on the Constitution. The mounting opposition to both FDR and his New Deal can be evidenced by the record 635 vetoes issued by FDR against Congressional bills seeking to undermine, limit, and prevent the expansion of New Deal programs. With the looming specter of another world war, voters did not want a new president in office to conduct the war effort, if there was going to be one. Roosevelt was elected yet again.

The New Deal brought about many changes in America. The coalition cobbled together under FDR united many different groups such as labor and the various minority groups into a more powerful Democratic Party that would dominate his presidency. The era of white Anglo-Saxon Protestant (WASP) rule in America, though not over, would slowly leak power to the multiethnic "Big Tent" philosophy of the Democratic Party. The New Deal era became the crucible of the secular war being fought in America today.

One thing that did not change was wealth distribution. Despite FDR's best efforts, 95% or more of the wealth in America still resides with one or two percent of the population. My opinion is that FDR did what he had to for the good of the country. Some pros and cons of the New Deal:

Pros

1. Protected the banking system
2. Increased power of labor
3. Employed millions
4. Helped farmers
5. Social Security instituted
6. Unemployment Insurance available

Cons

1. Increased National Debt (higher taxes)
2. Unemployment remained high
3. Creation of Welfare State (Nanny State)
4. FDR had too much power over the economy
5. FDR in office too long
6. Attempted Supreme Court packing
7. Government in competition with private industry - Tennessee Valley Authority, the prime example

There was more to the decade of the 1930s than just the Great Depression. People graduating from high school with a simple diploma or from college with a liberal arts degree were having a difficult time finding jobs. (Sound familiar?) As a result, people remained in school longer and changed over to vocational education or to the hard sciences. Those reading the tea leaves saw that there would be more opportunities by getting into these programs. This is even more true today as college tuition is beyond ridiculous and the amount of debt to be repaid is absurd. Partially in response to the Covid Pandemic, look for education to be almost completely online in the future, which will put greedy, overrated colleges out of business who offer too many non-specific degrees.

In 1933, Congress enacted the twenty-first amendment that repealed Prohibition. Once legalized, alcohol became more affordable and people had something to lean on to help soothe the pain of the decade-long misery. The legal sale of alcohol put much needed funds in the coffers of the U.S. Treasury and put an end to the era of gangster bootlegging of alcohol.

There were some famous sporting events that gave America pause and proved to be omens to the outcome of future world events. In 1935, American heavyweight boxer Joe Louis defeated the reigning Italian world heavyweight champion Primo Carnera. A recent Italian immigrant, Carnera was controlled by the Mafioso and was linked to Benito Mussolini, the Fascist dictator of Italy who would shortly be at war with the American democracy. By knocking out the much bigger Carnera, this became a propaganda victory for freedom over Totalitarianism. A year later at the Berlin Olympics, Jesse Owens, a Black American, won four Olympic Gold Medals in track and field with Hitler observing just a few rows away. Hitler was sure that his Master Race of White athletes would defeat Owens, but the results were not even close. Hitler said that the "black athletes have bigger bodies and should be banned from future Olympic Games." This was another symbolic win for the U.S. against the rising tide of Fascism, with which they would soon engage in a world war.

However, FDR did not congratulate Owens or invite him to the White House. Was this slight due to Owens's support of the Republican Party or something more sinister?

In 1938, FDR got a chance to redeem himself before the "Fight of the Century" between Joe Louis and the German champ Max Schmeling, who had upset Louis two years prior. Before the fight, Louis was summoned to the White House where FDR implored him to victory saying "Joe, we need your muscles to defeat Germany." Recall now that WWII had not started yet, so this was going to be a big propaganda win for one side or the other. Louis was already seeking revenge and after his meeting with FDR remarked, "I knew I had to get Schmeling good... The whole damn country is depending on me." The fight was over before it started. Louis knocked down Schmeling three times in the first two minutes of the first round before the referee ended the fight. Revenge for Louis and another symbolic victory for America. Again Hitler was humbled in defeat. It would not be the last time.

Sensing another conflict with Germany, FDR initiated the Good Neighbor Policy with the nations of Latin America. The Roosevelt Corollary had caused some friction as the U.S. had interfered in the politics of Latin American independence. FDR rewrote the Roosevelt Corollary as an agreement to use the Monroe Doctrine to unite the Americas if Germany and other nations looked to attack. It was a good strategic move though the Nazis were able to infiltrate some areas of South America during WWII.

The book that perhaps best portrays the desolation and rootlessness of the Great Depression Era is the classic John Steinbeck book *The Grapes of Wrath*. It is a fictional novel about the relocation of an Okie (Oklahoma) family leaving the Dust Bowl and hoping for a better life in California. It does not go as planned. This is a must read if you enjoy history.

On the other hand, the exploits of Amelia Earhart provided inspiration for the future of America. Emulating Charles Lindbergh, she also made a solo flight across the Atlantic Ocean, the first female to pioneer such an undertaking. In 1937, she attempted to eclipse his transatlantic flight and fly solo around the world, much as Magellan of Portugal had done by ship sailing for Portugal in 1522. Unfortunately she crashed in the South Pacific and her body and plane wreckage were never recovered. Before her demise, she was instrumental in the formation of the Ninety-Nines, an organization for female pilots. There were 117 women pilots at the time and the group name of Ninety-Nines was named for the ninety-nine who attended the meeting or were interested in the group.

FDR has the distinction of being the only president elected to more than two terms in office. Because of the extraordinary juxtaposition of the Great Depression and WWII, he was elected four times as president but died in office during WWII, being replaced by "Give'em Hell! Harry Truman." With the innate fear of a monarch imprinted in the DNA of the American psyche, Congress quickly passed the Twenty Second Amendment to the Constitution in 1947 only two years after the death of FDR, limiting future presidents to two terms of office.

CHAPTER 43

World War II

THE ONSET OF WWII IN 1939 certainly put an end to the Great Depression that had been a plague to the U.S. and the world since 1929. Since nobody else ever claimed this phrase as their own, I always taught my students that a World War is "good for the economy yet terrible for humanity." Nearly every country in the world participated in WWII with most being neutral in the beginning but only a few nations were neutral at the end. An estimated 300,000,000 soldiers saw combat and the death total was about 72,000,000 combatants and civilians. It turns out that many countries were building up their military forces, under the radar so to speak, in the 1930s despite having only Depression funding. The U.S. was not one of these countries and had to quickly conscript a good portion of the 16,000,000 person military almost at the last minute. In this war the two opposing alliances were the Axis Powers (Germany, Japan, and Italy) vs. the Allied Powers (UK, US, and Soviet Union, China, and France) There were many additional countries that joined the fray and Italy joined the Allies in 1943. They had also switched sides and joined the Allies in the middle of WWI.

From the ashes of WWI arose the "Phoenix" of WWII, which would be Nazi Germany led by Adolf Hitler. A powerful speaker,

Hitler rekindled German nationalism by blasting the Treaty of Versailles that had pointed the finger at the Germans being the sole instigators of the first World War. He scapegoated the Jewish bankers whom he blamed for giving away reparations money to the hated Allies. One of his most effective propaganda methods was to "tell a lie a thousand times and it becomes the truth."

Hitler proclaimed that it was the destiny of the German Third Reich to rule the earth for a thousand years. He believed the Aryan Race—blonde-haired, blue eyes and white—would become the Master Race and enslave all others. The irony was that Hitler was Austrian, not German, and may have had Jewish bloodlines. His nationalist catchphrase for Germany was Deutschland über Allies (Germany over all others).

Amassing a large group of police known as the "brown shirts" or stormtroopers, he was able to overthrow the weak German Republic and proclaim himself Führer (leader). He was saluted with the phrase Heil Hitler! Though for the wrong reasons, he fits the profile of the Great Man in history because he controlled events and nearly conquered the world similar to Napoleon of France and Josef Stalin, who will be discussed soon.

Mussolini (Il Duce "the leader") became dictator of Italy before Hitler rose to power. Hitler's formation of his stormtroopers was a nod to Il Duce, who had recruited an army of "black shirts" to take control of Italy and turn it into a dictatorship. Both Hitler and Mussolini and later Tojo (military dictator of Japan) were known as Fascists. In a Fascist State, the dictator is all powerful and the people have no rights or consent in the governing of a nation. Mussolini's goal was to gain back a large portion of the old Roman Empire centering around the Mediterranean Sea and extending into Africa.

Japan began to modernize its military after being intimidated by U.S. Commodore Perry's "black ships" in the mid 1800's. They flexed their new-found military muscles a bit with a victory over Russia in a war in 1905. In WWI, they sided with the Allies and won some islands in the Pacific Ocean. By joining the Axis, Japan hoped to establish an Empire of the Pacific extending to the west coast of America.

On the Atlantic side, France was fearful of German revenge so they were getting ready to fight a defensive war. They were correct in the assumption of German revenge but were not ready for the German Blitzkrieg (lightning war) tactics. They quickly found themselves knocked out of the war, surrendering early on.

China was still grateful to the U.S. for helping them to maintain control of their country via the U.S. Open Door Policy. Japan was a traditional and more powerful enemy at their doorstep and, like the Russians, China was caught up in a Communist coup to take over the country even as they fought the Japanese in WWII. Although overlooked by the history books, China may have had the most casualties of any nation in WWII.

Another Great Man of history, and again for all the wrong reasons, was Joseph Stalin (man of steel) the dictator of the Soviet Union during WWII. Stalin became history's greatest mass murderer. Practicing genocide (extermination of an ethnic group of people) it was estimated that he executed between nine and twelve million people, many native Russians like himself. Hitler's genocide of the Jews (Holocaust) was estimated to have killed six million people, yet Stalin gets less blame. Why? Because he was an ally of the U.S. during the war, so the media did not expose him as they did Hitler. It became clear that Stalin was exploiting his alliance with the Allies in order to crush Hitler. Once this rival was eliminated, Stalin had his sights set on world domination.

Stalin who dispatched thousands of Communist sympathizers into China during WWII helped Chairman Mao take over China and turn it away from democracy. By defining and building the Communist World (China and Russia), Stalin has membership in the Great Man of history club.

British foreign policy before WWII was a major cause of the war. England was losing its empire and did not want to engage in another major war. Its Prime Minister, Neville Chamberlain, adopted a policy of appeasement with the Germans. Chamberlain agreed to give back large swaths of land to Germany that the Treaty of Versailles had assigned to other nations. In return, the Germans would agree to seek no more land. This was like giving the antagonist in a fight the first punch and hope he doesn't proceed to knock you out. Germany saw this as a sign of weakness, and before you knew it their Panzers (tanks) were blitzing Poland and the Sudetenland in Czechoslovakia, both having unhappy German citizens living inside their respective borders. Chamberlain was quickly voted out as Prime Minister by a worried British electorate and replaced by Winston Churchill, one of the world's best and most famous states-men—the FDR of England. This did not dissuade Germany from declaring war on England, whom they still viewed as their biggest threat to European and global conquest.

After making the world safe for democracy, the US reverted to its decades-long policy of isolationism as evidenced by its refusal to join the League of Nations. The U.S. was almost totally focused on attempting to solve the horrors wrought by the Great Depression that plagued America from sea to shining sea.

Newsreels downplayed the rise of both Mussolini and Hitler, portraying them as comedic figures. Mussolini was seen as a minor Italian politician running around with a bunch of medals pinned to his chest, wildly waving his arms while making incomprehensible speeches. Hitler was compared to Charlie Chaplin, the mustachioed icon of the silent movies in America. Also small in stature, the Chaplin persona was a tragi-comedic figure created by the Depression with the appearance and demeanor of a hobo. In short, America marginalized the threat of Fascism as a threat to world security. It would take the bombing of Pearl Harbor, the armageddon day of the Greatest Generation to catapult the U.S. into World War II. As soon as the US entered the war, employment increased by 5,000,000 people in a very short time, reinforcing the theory of war being good for a country's economy.

World War II was triggered in 1939 by the non-aggression agreement signed between enemies Germany and Russia, which led to the dual invasion of Poland by those two countries in September 1939. Germany used a blitzkrieg against Poland, a neutral country, attacking from its western side and two weeks later Russia attacked it from the East. Again the Russian transgression received little criticism at the time. Two days after Germany invaded Poland, England and France declared war on Germany and the war began in earnest.

For the most part the war was fought in what were called Theaters of Operation. There was the European (ETO) and the Pacific (PTO). I will start with the ETO that began first then lead into the PTO. Due to limitations, I chose the most significant events that have described and defined World War II as the war to end all wars. Because the war was fought on more than one front, there were a number of Turning Point battles. Again, another top ten list:

1. Battle of Dunkirk (1940)
2. Battle of Britain (1940)
3. Holocaust (1941 - 1945)
4. Pearl Harbor (1941)
5. Midway (1942)
6. Battle of El Alamein (1942)
7. Battle of Stalingrad (1942-3)
8. D-day (1944)
9. Island hopping (1942 - 1945)
10. Bombing of Hiroshima (1945)

France updated its World War I trenches into what was called the Maginot Line. It was a longer set of trenches with more barbed wire and machine gun placements to repel the Wehrmacht (German Army). France also constructed "pillboxes" with longer range gunnery to repel the German Panzer (tank) divisions. Through their spy system, the Germans learned that the turrets in the pillboxes could not rotate but only fire straight ahead. The Wehrmacht simply marched around the line and through the undefended forest, and eventually trapped a large Allied Army of British and French near Dunkirk on the beach near the English Channel.

The Germans' failure to move in for the kill at Dunkirk gave time to the Allies to erect a defense and arrange a sea rescue similar to Washington escaping Brooklyn during the Revolutionary War. Thousands of private boats crossed the channel along with some British naval ships and rescued 330,000 soldiers before the Germans could mobilize for the kill. Nearly 70,000 British military lost their lives, but the British people had saved the day, if not the war.

Winston Churchill's speech was a masterpiece of motivation for the rescue. He thundered "...We will fight in the streets. We will fight in the hills. We will fight on the beaches. We will never surrender!!" After the heroic rescue was over, Churchill wisely warned his nation, "Wars are not won by evacuations."

With France out of the war and the Russians not yet a threat, Germany went for the knockout punch against England and the UK (United Kingdom) in the Battle of Britain. Unable to penetrate the naval blockade of the British Isles, Germany decided to use their Luftwaffe (Air Force) to bomb England into submission and force a surrender. The British surmised the strategy. British and American scientists worked feverishly with the British military to perfect aerial radar to track the German bombers as they approached Great Britain. This battle lasted from July to October with the German bombers relentlessly destroying city after city, including swaths of London.

Then two things happened. Radar was perfected that in turn allowed anti-aircraft guns to down bomber after bomber. The next thing to occur was the appearance of the new RAF (Royal Air Force). The British RAF employed small, Spitfire fighting planes armed with machine guns. The smaller size of the Spitfires allowed them to turn in tighter circles than the German fighter planes and bombers with the result of eventually being the hunters not the hunted. Once the Spitfires turned inside of the slow-rotating Luftwaffe, they got behind the Germans and shot them out of the sky en masse until the Germans finally gave up in October 1940.

Britain had been saved again! The toll on the British was tremendous. Churchill knew he could not defeat Germany alone and with Russia still mobilizing looked to the United States for aid. Sentiment was building in America to send aid to the Allies, but it would require a singular event to draw the U.S. into WWII.

Now taking the Nazi war machine seriously, the newsreels of America looked for some good news in the prevention of the spread of Nazi oppression inside Germany. They reported that the Jews were organizing protests against the Third Reich government under Hitler. The Nazi propaganda agency announced that Germany was working on a "final solution" to the Jewish protesters of Nazi policies. The propaganda put out the myth that the Jews were being allowed to slowly leave Germany (actually some did including Albert Einstein) but in reality the Nazis were initiating a holocaust (genocide of Jewish people) that would be carried out in concentration camps in a number of countries. I was surprised to learn that of the six million Jews exterminated nearly 5 million came from three countries outside of Germany – Poland, Russia, and Hungary. The other million or more are from Germany and other countries in Europe. The genocide killed nearly one-third of all the Jews in the world.

A large majority of the executions involved poison gas. Herded together in shower rooms and promised a good cleansing, gas came out of the shower heads rather than water. Death was painful but quick. The more unfortunate became guinea pigs for twisted doctors like Josef Mengele who tortured people to death using gruesome experiments. Gas Chambers were preferable to mass shootings.

At the Nuremberg War Trials (1946), fifteen Nazi leaders were put on trial for crimes against humanity, genocide being the major charge. All the defendants pleaded not guilty. They said they were following chain-of-command orders from Hitler, and if they had not followed orders they themselves would be executed. All were found guilty. Twelve were hanged and three received life sentences in prison. The Nazis that escaped went to the four corners of the earth. The most high-profile captive was Adolf Eichmann, nabbed in South America and hanged in public in Israel in 1960.

The singular event that caused the U.S. to enter World War II on the side of the Allies was the sneak attack by Japan upon the U.S. Naval Base at Pearl Harbor, Hawaii December 7th, 1941. "A day that will live in infamy," proclaimed then president FDR. People in Honolulu were out for early morning walks or getting set to attend Sunday church services at 8 a.m. when the carnage began. Most people initially thought It was a little strange for the USAF to be on training runs Sunday morning, then the awful truth became a deadly reality. After the attack was over, all U.S. battleships were damaged and four sunk. All but the USS Arizona were later raised and six returned to service. The Japanese also sank three cruisers, three destroyers, and 188 aircraft were blown to pieces. 2403 Americans were killed and another 1178 were wounded. [For the record, in 2015 Japan finally issued a statement of remorse for this heinous act but has never apologized for this historic misdeed.]

Literally overnight the American wartime economy kicked into high gear. The war-production industry immediately hired 5,000,000 people to produce whatever was needed. The government raised additional money by putting a payroll tax (salary tax) on people's weekly paychecks. To save steel for the war machines, new car production was disallowed and car factories were retooled into wartime factories. As noted, the U.S. conscripted an army and naval force of 16,000,000 including nisei (Japanese-Americans) to fight against the Axis.

The government created the WAC (Women's Army Corps), an auxiliary branch consisting of 150,000 women helping the army with nursing, mechanics, uniform design, communications, and office personnel. The Navy received 100,000 women to work in their auxiliary who were known as WAVES. Farmers were happy as well. Their Dust Bowl disaster came to an abrupt end as they had to feed a nation at war and send surplus food to the Allied countries opposing the Axis. Meat had to be rationed for a time as was wheat. "Save the wheat…Help the Fleet…Eat less Bread," became a famous slogan of conservation during the war. One of the most iconic recruitment tools used by the US government to encourage females to join the war effort was the issuance of the Rosie the Riveter poster. Portraying women as physically strong, almost immediately 8,000,000 women became employed as hard-goods producers for the war effort.

Japan had awakened the giant and would pay a heavy price for their treachery. Unfortunately there was a xenophobic backlash in America against Japanese citizens who were American. Through U.S. intelligence the military learned that the west coast of America could be the next objective of the Japanese invasion. Similar to earlier Presidents, FDR went outside of the law, in this case denying due process, and interned hundreds of Japanese who resided on the west coast in relocation centers for the duration of the war. Hysteria had once again trumped the rule of law.

The PTO was not going well for the U.S. early on. With a wounded fleet facing a superior Japanese Navy, the upper hand went to the Japanese who were collecting strategic islands in the Pacific, including the Philippines. The U.S. signed the Anzus Pact (Australia, New Zealand, U.S.) to help stop the advance of the Japanese toward Australia. Anzus fleets turned back the Japanese in the Coral Sea and gave the U.S. more time to build and fix ships. Through intelligence, the U.S. learned that Midway Island near

Hawaii was the next target of the Japanese. Though a small island, it had refueling stations midway across the Pacific. Though vastly outnumbered, the U.S. naval command knew the Japanese game plan and with the help of the USAF were finally able to control Midway and stop the advance of the Japanese. This was the turning point in the PTO.

How did the U.S. know the Japanese PTO game plan? Our communications officers were able to decode the messages being sent to the Japanese fleet directing them where to go. The Japanese could never decode U.S. messages because of the Windtalkers. These were native Americans who spoke in the Navajo language, indecipherable to the Japanese. The result was that the U.S. was always one step ahead of the superior Japanese fleet and it drove the Japanese crazy. All historians agree that without the Navajos we lose the Pacific War.

Returning to the ETO, Germany set its eyes on the conquest of Russia now that France and Great Britain had been humbled. They wanted to take over the Russian oilfields and defeat Russia as quickly as possible before the United States arrived in Europe.

The Battle of Stalingrad (today named Volgograd) was probably the biggest single battle in all human history and along with D-Day was one of the two turning points in the ETO in WWII. It was a battle of egos (Stalin vs. Hitler) as well as a battle of the ISM's (Communism vs. Fascism). The winner would be able to control history; the loser consigned to the ages. This battle lasted five months and ended in the winter of 1943. Each side lost nearly 1,000,000 men along with hundreds of tanks, airplanes, and rifles destroyed.

In the end, the Germans violated a historical imperative—do not attack Russia in the winter on their home land! Napoleon's quest for world power in the nineteenth century was crushed by a similar failed attack. The Germans had the option to withdraw and resupply their forces, but Hitler's ego demanded that the Germans keep on the attack. In the winter of 1943 thousands of Germans did surrender. The remaining armies retreated. The air of Nazi invincibility had been broken. Germany was forced now to defend its own boundaries. George Santayana the Spanish philosopher summed it up best. "Those who do not remember the past are doomed to repeat it."

Also in 1942 the Germans received more bad news from North Africa. One of the goals of Hitler was to take control of the Suez Canal and the oil fields of the Middle East. The second battle of El Alamein was a battle of the tank brigades fought in the desert near Egypt. Erwin Rommel aka the Desert Fox was the German Panzer commander, and his opponent the flamboyant British General Bernard Montgomery, who had the ego of George Custer but was a brilliant field commander as was Rommel, who had won the first battle near the same site. This time Montgomery's tanks broke through the combined German and Italian ranks and captured 30,000 prisoners and while Rommel was not captured wound up in the hospital, replaced by an inferior commander. Great Britain had won an important and much-needed victory. The Axis would not threaten the Suez Canal or the oil fields again.

The Tuskegee Airmen, an all Black squadron of the USAF played a pivotal role in WWII. The pilots shot down numerous Italian and German planes during the battle of Anzio, which was the Allied invasion of Italy. Because of their effort, it forced Italy to surrender, execute IL Duce, and join the Allies. The Tuskegee Airmen continue to have an active squadron of fighter pilots today utilized in recent warfare.

D-Day: The Invasion of Normandy Operation Overlord. On June 6, 1944 the Allied forces of Britain, America, Canada, and France attacked the German forces on the coast of Normandy, France. You may recall that in the year 1066 the Normans of France attacked and conquered the British across the English Channel. At the same location with a huge force of over 150,000 soldiers, the Allies attacked and gained a victory that became the other turning point in the ETO. General Dwight D. Eisenhower of the U.S. was appointed Supreme Commander of the entire ETO and put Bernard Montgomery in charge of a land invasion that would lead to the liberation of German-occupied Western Europe. The horror of war can be best seen in the opening frames of the movie "Saving Private Ryan," as thousands of men were gunned down attempting to exit their LST (landing ship tank). The small aqua-colored waves lapping against the beach quickly turned crimson red and stayed that way. Soldiers were pinned down on Normandy Beach and four other beaches, and it took five full days of airforce shelling and incremental ground assaults to finally get the Nazis to retreat from the beachfront.

Reinforcements came in the following weeks for both sides. The Allied Army approached 2,000,000 opposing almost 650,000 German troops. By the end of the summer, Allied casualties numbered about 230,000, while the Nazis lost more than half of their army and had to retreat. The Allies pushed eastwards toward Paris and arrived there on August 24. After a short battle the overwhelmed Nazis surrendered to the Allies the next day. Paris was liberated.

Eisenhower needed a bulldog to complete the mission of pushing the Germans inside the boundaries of their own nation, so he chose General George Patton and his Third Army to finish the job. Patton had to survive the Battle of the Bulge, which was the last Nazi offensive attack against the Allies. Patton noticed all empty gas and oil drums and concluded the Nazis were in retreat and he was correct. His decisive actions in western Europe and the Mediterranean led to the Germans seeking a ceasefire, followed by a formal treaty of surrender.

During the Allied occupation of Germany, Patton was relieved of his command for making aggressive statements against the Soviet Union. In the movie Patton (1970), George C. Scott playing Patton raises his glass to toast the Russian commanders who helped to bring down Germany. Through a clenched-teeth fake smile he raises his glass and says, "Those s.o.b's are the real enemy."

Back in the Pacific, after the battle of Midway, the U.S. launched a counter-offensive strategy known as "island-hopping", the goal being to capture certain key islands, one after another, until Japan came within range of American bombers. Led by Admiral Chester Nimitz and General Douglas MacArthur, the U.S. embarked on a two-plus year campaign to bypass the Japanese strongholds and attack the weak points, suffering through endless bloody battles from an enemy that would choose suicide over surrender and butchered American POWs much as the Indians scalped the pioneers in the Old West. In both cases they were referred to as savages by the U.S. military.

The U.S. forces were forced to traverse the Pacific from the Philippine Islands to the Aleutian Islands near Alaska then on to Iwo Jima and Okinawa, in range of the Japanese mainland. Mac Arthur promised the citizens of the Philippines that, "I shall return to set you free," which he and his army succeeded in doing. [A great book to read is called American Caesar, the biography of Douglas MacArthur.] Another force of 100,000 American soldiers and sailors were dispatched to the Aleutian Islands to get rid of 2,000 Japanese soldiers who refused to surrender. It took two weeks of frostbitten fighting to end the Japanese threat to Alaska.

Iwo Jima and Okinawa were the two bloodiest battles fought between the Japanese and the Americans. Both involved hand-to-hand combat to decide the outcome.

70,000 American soldiers landed on the beach at Iwo Jima, and thirty six days later the 27,000 Japanese force was defeated. Iwo Jima is the site of the famous raising of the American flag at Mt. Suribachi. By procuring Iwo Jima, the US ended the majority of the Japanese Kamikaze (suicide flights) against the Navy.

The U.S. was now in bombing range of Japan and the battle of Okinawa would bring the U.S. even closer. This American victory was the bloodiest battle of the war as Japan put 100,000 men in caves with orders to fight until death. The U.S. suffered nearly 61,000 casualties. [My father was in charge of communications on an LST anchored at Okinawa. He describes the hell created by a typhoon that almost scuttled the entire operation. He did bring back a souvenir - a Japanese Samurai sword - which I could barely lift up from my hip when I was young.] In retaliation for Pearl Harbor, the U.S. Navy launched a series of nighttime, low-altitude raids on the capital city of Tokyo. Flying low avoided radar detection but there was not enough fuel for some of the bombers to return safely. On the other hand, some of the manufacturing ability of Tokyo was compromised but at the cost of civilian deaths. This is known as collateral damage, one of the sins of warfare. President Truman was contemplating a land invasion of Japan that would have been next to impossible because of logistics. Then the Manhattan Project came to fruition.

The Manhattan Project was the program that led to the creation of the first nuclear (atomic) bomb. Based on the theories of Albert Einstein, the design of the bomb was created by Robert Oppenheimer and Enrico Fermi. Ironically, all three had Axis blood in their veins being German and Italian. It was no secret that the Nazis were also racing to create the bomb but the pre-Holocaust exodus of German scientists worked against them and for the U.S. After a couple of successful tests in the New Mexico desert, the components of the bomb were loaded onto the U.S.S. Indianapolis, sent on a classified mission to the new naval and air force base at Tinian, in the South Pacific, where the components were offloaded.

Observing radio silence, the Indianapolis was hit by a random Japanese torpedo that sank the ship. It went down too quickly for an SOS message to be relayed. In the movie Jaws (1975), Robert Shaw tells the rest of the story as 300 men were rescued but 1200 were eaten alive by sharks. The 300 saved were picked up by a freighter ship in the shipping lanes.

Harry Truman now had a historic decision to make, one that was never contemplated up to that point. Do I drop an atomic bomb on Japan? The alternative would be a near-impossible land invasion, and Truman did not want more unnecessary deaths on his conscience. In Late July 1945, Truman and the Allies demanded the surrender of Imperial Japan or face "prompt and utter destruction."

On August 6, the bomber Enola Gay dropped the bomb "Little Boy" on the city of Hiroshima. It was dropped in a parachute and detonated two thousand feet above Hiroshima. The structures of the city instantly disintegrated as did 99% of the population. The Japanese did not respond, so on August 9th the "Fat Man" Plutonium bomb, more powerful than the "Little Boy," was dropped on the city of Nagasaki. Nearly 200,000 people had been vaporized in both cities. Truman implied that the next target would be Tokyo. On August 15, Emperor Hirohito Announced Japan's surrender in a radio broadcast.

<u>That Fateful Day</u> In Chicago, on Wednesday, December 2, 1942, the thermometer dropped to ten degrees and a raw wind blew in from Lake Michigan. People bundled to their ears walked the streets, unaware of an experiment being carried on at the Universiy of Chicago.

The experiment was being conducted in a temporary laboratory under the west stand of Stagg Athletic Field. Enrico Fermi, the scientist in charge, was about to try *to release and control* the awesome power of the atom.

In was midafternoon when Fermi gave the signal. The small group of observers stood tense and silent. If anything went wrong, they would be destroyed in a single blinding flash. Stagg Field would disappear, and much of Chicago along with it.

Cautiously, a man began to draw a control rod from the pile of graphite blocks at one end of the room. The deadly uranium began to work. Slowly, then faster and faster, the needles on the meters began to move upward. Atomic energy was being released. But could it be stopped? Could it be controlled? No one knew. Suddenly, Fermi gave the command, "Throw in the safety rods." For an instant, everyone held his breath. Then the needles began to move back around the dials.

The experiment had succeeded. For the first time in history, man had released and conrolled the terrifying energy locked in the atom. Mankind had entered a new era, and the world would never be the same again.

Chuck Yeager (1923-2020)

He was America's best combined test and fighter pilot and the inspiration for the book and movie "The Right Stuff," which vaulted him to A-list status. His most famous individual feat as a test pilot was being the first to break the sound barrier in 1947, dispelling the myth that a plane would be torn apart by the sound waves. He was able to accomplish this feat despite entering the cockpit with two broken ribs courtesy of a horse race with his wife a few days before.

When asked what motivated him to become a pilot, he quipped, "I was in (airplane) maintenance, saw pilots had pretty girls on their arms, and didn't have dirty hands, so I applied."

As a WWII fighter pilot, he shot down an unheard of five German planes in one day and thirteen overall. As a test pilot, he flew over 360 different types of aircraft. The development and success of the NASA Space Program would have been impossible without the exploits of this daring flyer!

CHAPTER 44
Aftermath of WWII

THE WORLD CHANGED IN SIGNIFICANT ways after WWII. Some of the more important changes:

1. Allied occupation of Nazi Germany and U.S. occupation of Japan

2. Founding of the Republics of Italy and Israel

3. Birth of the United Nations

4. Beginning of the Nuclear Age

5. U.S. and Russia become rivals superpowers

6. Onset of the Cold War

In the spring of 1945, the Western Allies and the forces of the Soviet Union met in the middle of Germany. They rounded up thousands of German soldiers then threw open the gates of the prison camps holding German political prisoners and Jews. On May 7th, 1945 Germany surrendered and the world learned of Hitler's suicide in a German bunker with his long-time mistress Eva Braun, who he married just before their demise. In Italy, the people captured Mussolini and sentenced him to death followed by a public hanging. Germany was divided into four occupation zones. One was British-controlled, another American, a third French, and the last zone was Russian–controlled. Berlin would become the main symbol of the Cold War.

In theory, Japan was to be occupied by the Allies and Douglas MacArthur was put in control of this occupation that lasted from 1945-1952. The Japanese war machine was dismantled and seven military leaders executed by the Americans. The Japanese Emperor had become a ceremonial leader, as MacArthur had Japan draw up a constitution that allowed women the right to vote. A centuries-long tradition of monarchical rule would slowly evolve into a republic with the guidance of the United States.

The State of Israel was created in 1948. The British ceded land to the Jewish people to finally have a place they could call home. It is despised by most of its Arab neighbors but protected by the U.S., which were happy for an ally and a democracy in the Middle East.

On April 25,1945, fifty governments met in San Francisco for a conference and began to draft the U.N. charter. The United Nations began to operate later in 1945 replacing an ineffective League of Nations.

There are six organs to this body that is headquartered in New York City on the East River.

There is a General Assembly of all nations but the Security Council is the most powerful body. China, France, Russia, the U.S. and the U.K. are the permanent members with fifteen other nations that rotate in and out of power. The big problem with the Council is that it *takes only one veto* to stop a resolution put forth by the rest. The U.N. does have a standing international army known as "peacekeepers" who are called out to stop skirmishes from becoming wars. They would not have the muscle to prevent a major war from occurring. The U.N. seemed to be more effective early on, but countries such as Russia, China, and the U.S. have the real power in today's world.

Fortunately the U.S. developed the Atomic Bomb before the Germans were able to finalize it. By 1944, Russia had tested and produced an effective atomic weapon. In succeeding years other countries have joined the Nuclear Club. The worry today is that a rogue nation such as Iran or North Korea randomly decides to use such a weapon. Most sane nations who have nuclear capabilities are wise enough (I hope) to keep the atomic arsenal only as a deterrent.

When the dust settled after WWII, the U.S. and the Soviet Union were viewed as the world's two superpowers. Most observers were stunned by Stalin's defeat of Nazi Germany. Russia was now positioned as a history maker with Nazi Germany in ruins. The U.S. had saved the world again. Stalin was grateful for the U.S. assistance in defeating Germany, but now he would be exposed as a dictator who wanted omnipotent power. All of Stalin's pogroms (genocidal raids) came to light and quickly the ally was becoming the frenemy, just as Patton had predicted.

The result of this new alignment of power was the Cold War, a war of ideologies, propaganda and occasional fatal clashes but the clear avoidance of another world war. Both the U.S. and the Soviets looked to amass the support of other countries. One side was selling freedom and democracy, the other side Communism and oppression. The threat of the Cold War becoming a hot war was very real until the symbolic fall of the Berlin Wall in 1989.

As previously stated, the ideology of Communism was promulgated by the German political philosopher Karl Marx in his writings *The Communist Manifesto* and *Das Kapital*. Published in the 1800's, Marx decried the abuses of Capitalism thrust on the proletariat working class. He encouraged the working world to unite to take over the ownership of business and have the government run the business world. The government would then decide what jobs the people would do.

The Bolsheviks initiated the Communist Revolution in Russia and took Marxism to the next level. They claimed that a dictator would run a country more efficiently and denied basic rights to the people. In the Communist paradigm, there is no God as the dictator assumes that role. In atheistic Communist countries, freedom of religion is disavowed as are all other First Amendment rights of our Constitution. People are encouraged to spy on one another and, like the Nazi Fascists, there was a secret police (KGB) to keep the people in line in Russia. People who resisted the Communist Party were executed or sent to Siberia to the hard-labor work camps. Siberian prisons were thousands of miles away from central Russia and did not have walls. To escape meant a quick death in the ferocious Siberian winter climate.

The Communist apparatchiks under Stalin quickly spread Communism to China and under Mao Tse Tung (Chairman Mao) overwhelmed the U.S. backed democratic forces. From the rubble of WWII was born the clash of today's two dominant ideologies—Communism vs. Democracy.

With freedom in the air after WWII, why did democracy not take root in Russia and China? The answer lies in their similar histories. Czars (tsars) had ruled over Russia since its inception in 1547. The 1917 Bolshevik Revolution replaced the czar (king) with a dictator. In short, Russia was accustomed to and abided by the will of a strong leader. China had family dynasties of leaders dating back to nearly 2200 years before the birth of Christ. The Chinese people have always obeyed a strong ruler. It is in their DNA or so it seems. Whereas democracy has a persuasive approach to gaining allies, communism is much more Machiavellian using force when and where necessary.

Winston Churchill, in a speech given to the American nation, affirmed what George Patton had claimed—that Russia was the new enemy. Churchill reasoned that the huge Russian Army did not overrun all of war torn Europe after WWII because the Russians feared the use of the atomic bomb against them by the Americans. This standoff led to the beginning of the Cold War and the buildup of nuclear arsenals by the Russians and the U.S.

In a feeble attempt to appear democratic on the world stage both Communist Russia and Communist China used misleading formal names for their respective countries. Russia was called the USSR (Union of Social Soviet Republics) and China was called the People's Republic of China. They both advertised "free" elections to the world as a propaganda ploy. The reality was that there was only the Communist Party in each country and in the slang of the day the people got a chance to "elect their favorite Commie." So much for democracy in those nations.

CHAPTER 45

Cold War and Containment

WINSTON CHURCHILL WAS QUICK TO NOTICE that the Soviet Union was building an "Iron Curtain" around the countries of Eastern Europe that it took control of as the war ended. These countries were known as "satellite" countries totally under control of a domineering Russia. Because Russia feared the bomb, which gave the U.S. and its allies time to counteract the spread of Russian Communism. The Allied policy employed was called Containment, preventing the spread of Communism with monetary programs, alliances, and a continued military presence.

Both the Marshall Plan and the Truman Doctrine were U.S. monetary policies of aid to Western and Southern Europe. The Marshall Plan gave sixteen billion dollars to the countries of Western Europe such as France, Austria, Italy, UK, Ireland, Sweden, Switzerland etc. to help them rebuild their countries that were largely in ruin. Later on the Truman Doctrine gave money to the military of Greece, Turkey, and Yugoslavia to resist attacks from the Iron Curtain countries.

The formation of NATO (North Atlantic Treaty Organization) was a second way to obtain the spread of Communism. Thirty countries in North America and Europe signed an alliance to back any member that was attacked by Communist aggression. It was a powerful tool of deterrence and still is today. Russia formed a similar alliance with its ten satellite nations of Eastern Europe known as the Warsaw Pact. By 1949, only four years after the end of WWII, Europe was again divided in half by opposing alliances. It did not take long for that peace to be challenged.

The Berlin Airlift (1948) was the first confrontation between Russia and the NATO Allies. Germany was half Communist and half Democratic as was its capital city of Berlin. East Berlin was Russian-controlled and West Berlin democratic with a gigantic wall that divided the city in half. Russia devised a plan to get the Allies out of Berlin. Berlin was in East Germany so the Russians closed off all the roads and bridges into Berlin hoping to force the Allies out. The United States and Great Britain used airplanes to fly over the closed roads and bridges, land in West Berlin, and unload their supplies. This lasted for 321 days until the Russians gave up. To shoot down unarmed planes would have been a propaganda nightmare for the Communistic cause.

On the other side of the globe, the Korean Peninsula had also been split into two nations, Communist North Korea and Democratic South Korea. Stalin and Mao were fomenting aggression in the area by sending "operatives" into North Korea with the intent of overthrowing the regime of South Korea. It did not take long for the Korean War (1950-1853) to break out. The U.S. had signed another alliance called SEATO (Southeast Asia Treaty Organization) with Korea, Japan and others having the same obligations as the NATO treaty.

Truman had another war on his hands and decided to put Douglas MacArthur in charge. The "American Caesar" had the upper hand pushing back the North Koreans into their own country until China sent a much larger army to prosecute the war. MacArthur knew China was the instigator of the war and insisted that the air force could end the war quickly by utilizing the Bomb. Truman worried that Russia would join the Chinese and WWIII would break out.

When MacArthur complained to the media, he was fired though much of America supported him. In the end, the war concluded with a ceasefire in 1953 but never a treaty signed. The U.S. had 140,000 injured casualties—40,000 killed and 100,000 injured. In the end it was seen as an Allied victory as Containment had been maintained.

Because of the paranoia surrounding the spread of Communism, President Truman signed an executive order stating that all federal employees were to be screened. If they were found to have any Communist ties or sympathies for Communism they could be prosecuted. This new Red Scare was referred to as McCarthyism named for U.S Senator Joseph McCarthy who went on an extended witch hunt. Looking for Communists beyond the realm of government into education, sports, and Hollywood. For a period of time, certain movies were blacklisted (not shown) if the producers were deemed to be "left-leaning." McCarthy compiled an "enemies list," much as Nixon did during the 1960's.

McCarthyism became an updated version of the Salem Witch Trials in colonial America and claimed two victims in 1953, Julius and Ethel Rosenberg were arrested for espionage after having allegedly handed over atomic bomb information to the Soviet Union. The trial was quick as was the decision—guilty as charged. They were both executed. Critics said that the government prosecutors were scapegoating the Rosenbergs for being of Jewish faith and left-leaning Communist sympathizers who were convicted based on flimsy evidence. Others say the evidence was damning. Soon thereafter, McCarthy was derided as being out of control and was voted out of office.

In 1956 the U.S. had to get involved in the Suez Canal crisis. Egypt was angry at England and France for establishing the Jewish State of Israel right in its backyard, so it nationalized (took over) the Suez Canal that had been built by England with help from France. The U.S. was worried that Russia would seize the opportunity to move in. By using all its persuasive powers, the U.S. eventually got the canal reopened and kept out Communist operatives though it did take a number of years. At this point it would be safe to conclude that the old U.S. policy of Isolationism was gone forever.

Russia achieved a propaganda victory in the Cold War in 1957. There was a budding space race to see who would be the first to put a satellite into orbit. The Russians were able to orbit a very small satellite named Sputnik (Russian for spouse or traveling companion). It orbited for three weeks before its batteries died. Its radio signal was easily detectable around the world. After the death of the batteries, it was relaunched for another two months. The success of Sputnik led to fear in America that we were losing the technological race to the Russians. It was a significant Cold War triumph for Russia and hastened America to fund NASA and hopefully win the Space Race. A major propaganda victory for Communism was the takeover of Cuba by Fidel Castro, who quickly aligned with the Soviet Union. You could hear them clapping in Russia as only ninety miles from the United States the Iron Curtain had a base of operations. This was the classic case of one dictator replacing another, but the previous dictator was pro-American to a degree whereas Castro was all in with the Communist program. The U.S. cast a wary eye towards its closest Latin American neighbor.

Though there was international turmoil, domestic America was a very safe place to reside in during the 1950's, characterized by conservative leaders and a conservative culture. People were tired of war, so they elected Republican Dwight Eisenhower president for two terms, trusting that he would use his military and foreign policy experience to keep the U.S. out of another major world war, which he did. America became a prosperous country in the 1950's and "Ike" Eisenhower used a lot of U.S. Treasury money to complete the finest interstate highway system in the world. Superhighways and interstates now connect America like never before. It was now possible to travel from New York to California in three days if you pushed it. [My friend and I once drove from Long Island to San Diego, California in four days in 1973.] Because people had money to spend and travel was easier, this decade witnessed extensive growth in suburbia. "Suburban Sprawl" today can now be seen outside of all the major cities because cars were affordable and the roads were modernized. The expansion of commuter trains and buses also allowed people to live outside city limits and enjoy a different way of life.

There were two scientific breakthroughs that increased the quality of life in the 1950's. The first organ transplants were in a Boston hospital in 1954 and by the 1960's heart transplants were initiated. In 1955 Dr. Jonas Salk perfected the vaccine against Polio, the crippling disease prevalent in children.

CHAPTER 46

The 1950's:
The Influence
of Television

THE WORLD WOULD BE FOREVER CHANGED when television burst onto the scene in the 1950's. The most popular model was the RCA Victor 19" black and white console. Although the dial had numbers ranging from two through thirteen only three channels headquartered in New York City offered programming—ABC, NBC, and CBS. Color TV would not become popular until the 1960's. I was a young child of the 1950's and because my father was a well-known Park Ave television marketing and advertising executive producer, my memories are still very vivid in regards to how television depicted American culture and helped to shape the mindset of the Baby Boom Generation. My father and his company employed a number of very famous and near famous people in the production of the radio and television show known as the Lucky Strike Hit Parade that birthed the Billboard Top 40 and later the music video craze of the 1980's.

The show ranked the top selling records of the day—mostly jazz—and employed the likes of Frank Sinatra, John Forsythe, "Dynasty," "Charlie's Angels," Priscilla Presley—wife of Elvis and western TV star Dale Robertson. Bob Fosse directed the television version and Johnny Carson's bandleader Skitch Henderson conducted the television orchestra. So how did these people help to impact the culture of the 1950's?

The White Bread Culture dominated the decade. Blandly conventional in a way that is regarded as characteristic of the white middle class in the 50's, it was nevertheless the guiding ethos of that time period. Frank Sinatra, the iconic singer of his generation, helped to keep jazz music in the mainstream through most of the decade before Elvis Presley and Rock 'n Roll began to steal its thunder toward the end of the decade. Some of my love for music emanated from Hit Parade singers who came to our house and sang to my sister and myself at a very young age.

Dale Robertson's show "Tales of Wells Fargo" probably had the biggest impact on my young life. His show revolved around the deeds of the Pony Express and the culture of the Wild West. It was not long before my cousin and I would be playing "Cowboys and Indians" in the driveway with plastic guns and ammunition. I also began to watch television shows that depicted the West including "The Lone Ranger" and "Broken Arrow."

John Forsythe's "Bachelor Father" was one of the shows that we watched that encouraged strong American values and the importance of family. Other shows in the same vein were "The Adventures of Ozzie and Harriet," "Father Knows Best," and "Leave it to Beaver."

The ultimate family-bonding show was Sunday night's "Ed Sullivan Show." By the way, there were no morning news shows like Good Morning America or Fox and Friends. On the weekdays you were off to school but on the weekends you watched "Captain Kangaroo," "Howdy Doody," and "Andy's Gang," along with "The Little Rascals," and "The Mickey Mouse Club."

Television did offer commentary on current events and did speculate about the future. The movie "Godzilla" predicted that one day atomic bombs might create a "monster" we could not control and Godzilla was the perfect metaphor. Television also raised concerns about the Space Race. Movies such as "Invasion of the Body Snatchers" and the original "War of the Worlds" sent the message that the exploration of space might have unintended and dire consequences.

As a counterbalance to serious television there was the rise of slapstick comedy. While my parents laughed along with Bob Hope, Milton Berle, and Jack Benny I was more taken by "Abbott and Costello," "Laurel and Hardy," and "The Three Stooges."

Though television helped to shape culture in the 50's decade, it did not create a "couch potato" generation. That would occur many years later. Television was a nocturnal activity. During the daytime, when not in school, we were outdoors learning how to hula hoop, throw a frisbee, hopscotch, and play marbles. I learned how to ride my Schwinn bicycle with a little help from dad, and in the winter we found the nearest snow-covered hill to test our Flexible Flyer sleds.

Without helicopter parents, we learned the rules of life by playing games. It was okay to fail as tomorrow would be an opportunity to win. There was little league baseball but no trophies for finishing in seventh place. The advent of TV raised the profile of the big three professional sports—baseball, basketball, and football—and gave kids goals to shoot for. The bottom line is that because we were given freedom to play and interact and solve our own problems many of us became strong, independent thinkers utilizing our own resources to deal with life situations. My father, for example, would have me look at a situation and ask me, "What do you think?" rather than rushing to supply the answer. If I remarked that a TV commercial was flashy, he would always test my critical thinking by asking "But what are they selling?" Thank God for that type of parenting by Mom and Dad.

One of my favorite activities was reading comic books. I liked sci-fi but Mad Magazine was my favorite. They cleverly satirized the Cold War standoff between the U.S. and the Soviet Union with the cartoon Spy vs. Spy. My favorite Mad parody concerned the classroom and the threat of an atomic bomb detonation. In grade school we practiced drilling in case of armageddon. The teachers would line you up, march you to your classroom, and you would have to crouch underneath your desk while the teacher locked the door and drew the curtains. Mad Magazine satirized the entire scenario by providing the artwork showing all the steps and in the last cel were these words that I still laugh about decades later, "KISS YOUR ASS GOODBYE!"

This decade taught me self-reliance, resilience, co-operation, and problem-solving while reaffirming the American work ethic. You were not subject to the public vulgarity and coarseness of the succeeding generation. In a way, this decade was like the "Era of Good Feelings" in the early 1800's, a time of peace and prosperity that would not last long. Western TV stars Gene Autry and Dale Evans sang a famous duet that may have best summed up the decade, "Happy Trails to You!"

White America had to deal with the thorny issue of school desegregation in the 1950's. In the 1896 Supreme Court Case of Plessy vs. Ferguson, the Court seemed to invalidate the Civil War Amendments by allowing separate white schools and separate black schools so long as they were "equal." The Great Depression and two world wars had commanded the nation's attention so this issue had been put on the back burner.

In 1954 there was a petition put forth to allow a black student to enroll in all white Arkansas Central HS in Little Rock. Thurgood Marshall, who would go on to become the first black nominated to the Supreme Court, argued for the plaintiff stating that "separate is inherently unequal" and in a unanimous decision the Supreme Court overturned "Plessy-Ferguson." The 1954 Brown vs. Board of Education Case became the law of the land allowing for the integration of all public schools in America.

The last chapter to this story has been omitted from the history books. Democratic Governor Faubus called out the Arkansas National Guard and refused to let Blacks into the high school, defying the Supreme Court. Republican President Eisenhower was abiding by none of this. Eisenhower nationalized (took over) the Arkansas National Guard and sent a division of the U.S. Army to enforce this ruling. Television was there to capture the unfolding standoff. Faubus blinked first and relented. Integration would begin. However the stage had been set for a Southern backlash against this ruling and the tumultuous 60's provided the perfect vehicle for the radical violence that would ensue.

This entire episode illustrated that yet again, as in the Civil War and before, it was the Republicans who stood up for the rights of the blacks, not the Democrats who are always portrayed as the ones looking out for minority interests.

Less than a year later Rosa Parks would bring national attention to more inequality in America. She refused to obey an Alabama state law that relegated Blacks to the backseats of public buses. Her arrest led to a racial brouhaha and again the spotlight of television turned this into a national issue. The Black Community staged a year long boycott of the Montgomery Bus Company eventually resulting in its going out of business. Parks became an icon of equality and earned the moniker as the "First Lady of Civil Rights." She collaborated with the local chapter of the NAACP and the Reverend Dr. Martin Luther King Jr. who, like her, believed in using passive resistance (civil disobedience) to bring about meaningful change. This incident would provide the impetus for the burgeoning Civil Rights movement that went to another level in the 1960's. After her death in 2005, the U.S. Senate passed a resolution setting the stage for her to become the first woman in U.S. history to lie at the Capitol Rotunda.

CHAPTER 47

1960's: Decade of Upheaval

OF ALL THE DECADES IN MY LIFE, I would have to say the 60's were the most consequential. Not only did my generation come of age, but it is my opinion that this decade had the most profound effect on shaping the events of every succeeding decade. No matter if you see America as irredeemable or to be passionately defended, the events of the 60's have clearly defined the American experience going forward. Without a doubt the deep political divide originated in the 1960's and clearly created social revolution as well. The Baby Boom generation has given a great deal to Americana on one hand but on the other hand has assisted in a good deal of the resistance to what has been referred to as the American Way i.e. traditional America.

The decade began with some quiet excitement as my father announced plans to move into a much new and much larger house on the waterfront. After only a couple months our joy was tempered by reality—a major hurricane had its sights set directly on our new abode. "Donna" would turn out to be one of the three most powerful storms of the century. As the storm drew near, we tied down the boat the best we could then went upstairs in the house. We watched in horror as a windswept storm surge easily came over the dock and completely flooded the basement. When the surge receded, my father tried to distract from the trauma by joking, "There goes our yard right down the street." In retrospect it was an omen of things to come in the 60's.

John Fitzgerald Kennedy (JFK) became president in 1960 and the media proclaimed that "Camelot" had come to the White House. Television played a pivotal role in the 1960 Presidential election. During the first debate Kennedy appeared to be tanned and at ease in front of the camera. He had a younger appearance than Nixon, who had recently been ill and seemed nervous in front of the lens. There were three ensuing debates but first impressions helped to carry Kennedy across the finish line. The Kennedy Administration signaled a new direction and energy to a populace weary of the staleness and conformity of the 50's. Like our flooded home, the Kennedy "Camelot" would have a short period of grace before troubled waters rushed in from many sides.

With far too much material to cover I will summarize the major themes of the 60's by dividing them into three categories—foreign affairs, domestic affairs, and the social revolution—with the understanding that all three are connected in many ways.

Foreign Affairs.

The Communist Party of Russia awaited the results of the 1960 Presidential election. They were a collective smile, no doubt, when the young and untested JFK defeated Richard Nixon for the Presidency.

The Russians made immediate plans to bully the young president and his nation. Nikita Khrushchev, the Premier (leader) of the Communist Party, gave a speech before the U.S. General Assembly in 1960 that shocked the world. He removed his shoe then arose to make a speech and while he was ranting at the U.S. "We will bury you," he was simultaneously pounding his shoe on the lectern! Though some dispute the word "bury" in his speech, the threat was real. Kennedy did not overreact, the world did it for him, condemning Khrushchev as a madman with his finger on the trigger of the bomb. The fear infiltrated the Communist Party, which worried that their leader was becoming unhinged.

Shortly thereafter in 1961 Kennedy quietly authorized the Bay of Pigs Invasion, a secret mission of CIA operatives organized by the U.S. government to sneak into Cuba and assassinate Fidel Castro thereby ridding the Communist threat from our doorstep. Unfortunately this attempted coup backfired completely and now JFK would have to handle a publicity nightmare. With attention deflected, Khrushchev quickly sent military supplies to the Cuban Isle. American reconnaissance planes noticed the activity and on closer inspection realized that Russia was building missile bases in Cuba!

The Cuban Missile Crisis (1962) was the most scared I have ever been. Kennedy sternly warned the Russians to get the bases out of Cuba "or else." For thirteen long days the media airwaves were silent. Everyone alive was holding their breath. Khrushchev blinked first. The bases were dismantled. The U.S. Navy blockaded Cuba. Khrushchev would soon be replaced as Premier. The world exhaled a large sigh of relief as the existential threat of a nuclear holocaust had been narrowly averted!

In the 1950's the U.S State Department articulated the Domino Theory. This theory said that if one country became Communist in an area then other surrounding countries would as well. When the Berlin Wall (1961) was erected it created two Germanys—one free and one Communist. Kennedy knew that the Marshall Plan and Truman Doctrine contained the spread of Communism in Europe but he feared what might happen in Asia. In 1962 Kennedy sent military "advisors" into French Indochina to help stop the spread of Communism. In the middle of Indochina was Vietnam and the rest is history. The French bailed out of Vietnam and Kennedy was assassinated in 1963. Lyndon B. Johnson succeeded JFK and made the decision to escalate the war. Escalation means sending more troops and supplies (blood and treasure) to fight a war at the next level.

The Vietnam War (1962-1975) was the longest war in U.S. history (recently surpassed by the Afghanistan War). Many decades later this is still the only war I can't justify. LBJ knew he was engaging the entire Communist World in Vietnam. There were weapons from the Warsaw Pact nations and soldiers from Russia and Red China. Yet Johnson kept sending more troops. Why? My best guess was to keep the military-industrial complex of the day up and running. As I postulated, war is good for the economy and bad for humanity. Visiting the Vietnam Memorial Wall in Washington, D.C. is always a humbling experience. The Wall is an upright virtual tomb for over 58,000 Americans that gave their lives in service to America, many of them draftees.

Johnson chose not to run for re-election in 1968. Millions of anti-war protesters saying, "Hell no we won't go," and a stalemate of a war were too much for his psyche. Or maybe it was incidents such as the 1968 My Lai Massacre in South Vietnam where hundreds of innocent villagers were killed by U.S. soldiers who could not distinguish them from the Viet Cong. The VietCong were Communist rebels dressed in villager clothing. Or maybe Johnson tired of watching Walter Cronkite, "the most trusted man in America," announce on the CBS evening news the number of Americans killed every day in battle before signing off with his iconic closing, "And that's the way it is," followed by the date.

Nixon won the presidency and de-escalated the war, but it still raged on until 1973. One of the most enduring images was the last U.S. helicopter taking off from the top of the U.S. Embassy Building in Saigon leaving behind U.S. supporters. Those left behind were assuredly executed by the North Vietnamese Army who were only minutes away. It was an ignominious end to a war that should have never been fought.

South Vietnam became a Communist country and Saigon was renamed Ho Chi Minh City in honor of the North Vietnam dictator. This was the only war where the returning veterans were treated like dirt, especially when 90% of them were draftees. Scorned by their own citizenry, many resorted to heroin as an escape from their PTSD lives. Over the years heroin was replaced by cocaine, then crack, then ecstasy etc. It is not a stretch to pin a good deal of blame on this war for the destructive drug culture that permeates America today.

The September 1969 Vietnam draft lottery was the big one that led to a small "nation" of draft-eligible young men between the ages of eighteen to twenty one to be involuntarily forced to fight in Vietnam or dodge the draft in many different ways, leaving the country in extreme cases. 365 plastic cylinders each containing a slip of paper with a date were put into a barrel. The first cylinder picked was number one and the last one was 365. People with numbers under 100 were goners.

I have two anecdotes to share. One guy in my freshman dormitory in college drew number seventy five and was outraged. We tried to injure him in a tackle football game to disqualify him from the draft. We only wound up hurting ourselves and the next morning he was gone. Three months later I received an incoherent letter from him stating that he was living in a cave in Tibet and not coming home soon. Another friend was at a college in upstate New York and was sitting by the radio—as were thousands of others—waiting nervously for his number. The student who was running the radio stations announced September 16 as draft number one. That was the announcer's birthday who then went ballistic destroying the entire radio station's operations center and left everyone else hanging!

Domestic Affairs

The Civil Rights Movement made great strides in the 1960's. Following the lead of Dr. Martin Luther King Jr (MLK), new non-violence tactics were utilized as modes of social change.

In 1960 the use of sit-in protest became widespread. Sit-ins involve people occupying a certain area in order to protest and bring about social change. In Nashville, Tennessee and Greensboro, North Carolina blacks sat at lunch counters that previously were the province of white patrons. News of their success spread to other cities and before long lunch counters were integrated in over 100 cities. In 1961 Freedom Riders rode interstate buses to make sure those buses were now integrated. By 1962 nearly 100 cities in America were on the road to full integration.

In 1964, LBJ and Congress enacted the Civil Rights Act that outlawed discrimination based on race, color, religion, sex, or national origin. President Truman had set the table for LBJ's Civil Rights Act by issuing an executive order in the 1950's banning segregation in the military. This created common ground for race relations and was a foundational block of Civil Rights legislation. It also banned discrimination in employment and reinforced the integrated use of public facilities like bathrooms and water fountains. In 1965, LBJ and Congress passed the Voting Rights Act that outlawed the old Jim Crow literacy test requirement for voting. In the same time period, the 24th Amendment to the Constitution was enacted, banning the poll tax payment prior to voting. In short, legally now the black man had the same rights as the white man. Unfortunately a lot of violent days lay ahead for the Civil Rights Movement.

The assassination of JFK in 1963 abruptly ended the days of Camelot. Though the Warren Commission concluded that Lee Harvey Oswald was the lone assassin, I am with the other 80% of Americans who believe it was a conspiracy followed by an elaborate cover-up.

Without going through all the conspiracy evidence, there was one part of the tragedy that I saw live on television that puts me in the conspiracy camp. The two guards, one on each side of Oswald, the alleged killer of JFK, were escorting him into the courthouse. These guards were looking straight ahead into the camera and not looking sideways where a crowd had gathered. Jack Ruby simply walked up and shot Oswald dead. The guards almost did not react, but Ruby was captured. It seemed they had been told to keep looking straight ahead. Some claimed that Ruby was hired to kill Oswald because he had terminal cancer and would die in prison before his testimony. Many think JFK was killed because he was the first Catholic President. We will never know the truth. All the players in this drama are probably dead now. If you believe that history repeats itself, go on the internet and type in Lincoln-Kennedy Assassinations. There are so many coincidences, some of which have been debunked but many not.

The other major event of 1963 was the march on Washington, spearheaded by Dr. Martin Luther King, Jr. who led about 200,000 African-Americans to the capital where he gave his famous "I Have a Dream" speech. Because the gathering was peaceful, it had a profound effect on America and the U.S. Congress that passed the Civil Rights legislation of 1964 and 1965.

Despite all the gains made via Civil Rights legislation, there was still great anger in the ghetto of major cities. In 1965, rioting began in the impoverished section of Los Angeles known as Watts. Rioting went on for almost a week with thirty four recorded deaths and 3400 arrested. In response to police actions, Bobby Seale led the formation of the Black Panthers in 1966, a militant group not afraid to use violence against the authorities. Taking their cue from Watts, the ghetto area of Detroit rioted in 1967 resulting in sixteen deaths and nearly 500 injured. Domestic terrorism raised its ugly head as well for the first time in 1966.

At the University of Texas, Charles Whitman, a white man climbed up into the clock tower and randomly shot dead fourteen students while wounding thirty two before he was eliminated. Though it is underplayed, Whitman's rampage at the University of Texas has encouraged decades of White Rage. Anti-government and other White supremacist groups besides the KKK have proliferated over the years. The antidote to this violence was the Summer of Love which began in San Francisco in 1967. People were longing for an escape from all the violence in America and Vietnam. They formed a brotherhood with each other. The music spoke of peace and love and the movement did spread eastwards later on. Quite accurately, the Beatles sung "All You Need is Love" and captured the moment and the spirit of 1967, as did Scott Mckenzie's anthem "San Francisco."

Unfortunately 1968 turned out to be one of the worst years ever in U.S. history. The Vietnam War was at maximum escalation then came the assassinations of MLK Jr., and Robert Kennedy, younger brother of JFK and the favorite to become the next president. In April 1968, James Earl Ray assassinated MLK Jr. outside of a hotel in Nashville, Tennessee. Ray escaped to Europe but was captured and extradited to America. He was found guilty and sentenced to ninety-nine years for the murder of MLK. He escaped prison and was caught again and one more year was added to his sentence. He died in prison having been incarcerated for twenty nine years.

A couple of months later in June 1968, "Bobby" Kennedy was killed by an assassin's bullet near Los Angeles, where he was campaigning for president. He was murdered by Sirhan Sirhan, a Palestinian. Sirhan killed Kennedy because he was a supporter of Israel. This killing portended bad relations between America and the Middle East with Israel in the middle.

Martin Luther King Jr. : Eight facts

- He was born Michael King Jr. on January 15, 1929
- King entered college at the age of fifteen, skipped grades nine and twelve before enrolling at Morehouse College, the alma mater of his father and maternal grandfather
- Although he was the son, grandson and great grandson of Baptist ministers, he was considering becoming a doctor or

lawyer instead but decided that the Bible had "many profound truths which one cannot escape" and entered Seminary in Pennsylvania getting a PHD

- He got a C in public speaking his first year but received A's in his last year as the valedictorian

- He won the Nobel Peace Prize at age thirty-five, the youngest recipient ever.

- He was jailed twenty-nine times often on trumped up charges such as driving 30 MPH in a 25- MPH speed zone

- In a speech on April 3, 1968, he told the audience "I've seen the promised land. I may not get there" He was assassinated the very next day.

- He is the only person born in the U.S. whose birthday is a federal holiday. (George Washington was born before the U.S. came into being) In 1983, President Ronald Reagan signed a bill that named the third monday in January as the holiday observance "Martin Luther King Jr.'s Birthday.

The fallout from the two assassinations was immediate. Both men were champions of Civil Rights. This led to the widespread violence in 1968 that nearly ripped this nation apart. There were riots in over 125 cities at the same time and millions were protesting the Vietnam War.

Another militant group, the Black Muslims, came into being. They were founded by Malcolm X, who became the leader of the Black Muslim movement.

Though rightly celebrated as a towering figure of the Black Pride movement, he was also a virulent Anti-Semite. He cast the Jews as a race of white oppressors who utilized "Zionist Dollarism" to block the social, economic, and political advancement of the Black Race. Today, a disciple of Malcolm X, Louis Farrakhan, leads the Nation of Islam, a hate group that wants to rid the world of the Jewish culture.

Sensing his imminent demise, Malcolm X warned about the power of the press, which rings even more true today in 2021. He asserted that the press are image-makers and exerted mass mind control over those who do not closely examine facts: "They have the power to make the innocent look guilty and to make the guilty innocent...newspapers will have you hating the people who are being oppressed and loving the people who are doing the oppressing..." He was gunned down shortly thereafter in 1965. "Burn Baby Burn" became the rallying cry of the black militants.

The rioting culminated at the 1968 Democratic National Convention in Chicago. More than 10,000 Vietnam protesters fought with the Chicago police who were trying to protect people attending the convention. This was one of the first instances of media bias. The media seemed to be against the cops who were just doing their job and were outnumbered by hundreds of unruly protesters. No one was killed but hundreds of rioters were arrested. The fact that there were no casualties tells me that the police were in the right. Of all the radical riots of 1968 the three biggest ones were in Washington, D.C., Baltimore, and Chicago. The latter two still have severe issues with their populace today, and I wonder why the same problems persist there fifty year later!

The fact that America did not disintegrate in 1968 is partially as a result of foreign affairs. Neither the Russians nor the Chinese took advantage of the breakdown of the American society. Why? They were in a bitter feud as to who would lead the Communist world. This dispute lasted a long time and gave America time to heal and rebuild its image.

In 1969 there was finally some light at the end of the tunnel. The fighting in Vietnam eased up a bit as Nixon put forward a plan to slowly exit Vietnam where the U.S. military trained the army of South Vietnam how to better fight. After a decade of one-upping each other, America won the Space Race over the Soviets by putting men on the moon in July of 1969. It was a huge propaganda victory over the Communist world and made Americans feel good about their country once again. (For the record, Yuri Gagarin, a Russian cosmonaut became the first human to travel into outer space. Aboard the Vostok 1, he completed one orbit of earth on April 12, 1961. Alan Shepherd,an American astronaut who would later walk on the moon, became the second person in space aboard the Freedom 7, on May 5, 1961)

Things were not all rosy in the last year of the decade. The SDS (Students for a Democratic Society) a radical group, gave birth to a splinter group known as the Weathermen. These people were dangerous anarchists who espoused the overthrow of America. They bombed public buildings and killed American citizens. These buildings included the U.S. Capitol Building and the New York City Police Department.

Bill Ayers was imprisoned for his role in the bombings but shoddy FBI work allowed him release from prison. I find it unfathomable how a prestigious college like the University of Chicago would hire him as a professor. Worse than this he was a major mentor of Barack Obama.

The Man who Saved the World

During the Cuban Missile Crisis, a decision made by a single Soviet Navy officer potentially saved the entire world. President John F. Kennedy initiated a blockade on shipments to Cuba. Meanwhile, a soviet submarine carrying a nuclear torpedo approached the blockade. The American navy launched several depth charges to ward away the submarine and force it to surface. However, with the threat of nuclear warfare looming, it's believed that the captains aboard the vessel saw this as an indication that the war had already begun.

Soviet protocol demanded that three high-ranking personnel must be in agreement to launch the nuclear weapon. Two of the commanders had their detonation keys at the ready. However, the third, Vasili Alexandrovich Arkhipov, refused. It's reported that he recognized the depth charges for what they were, and not as an instigation of WWIII. Without all three officers in agreement, the launch was aborted and nuclear war averted.

Social Revolution

The upheaval in foreign and domestic affairs was matched if not exceeded by the Social Revolution that swept across America in the 1960's and into the early 70's. What I am about to describe is only the tip of the iceberg, but the ramifications of this movement are still being felt today, for better or worse. The transition began somewhat benignly but became a tidal wave of change by the end of the decade.

In 1961 the Kennedy Administration initiated the Peace Corps. Mostly college students staff the Corps. There is a training period, then you enlist for two years. After the two years are up you can re-enlist. The Corps operates in 141 countries around the world, offering aid in education, technology, agriculture, and environmental science. Over 235,000 younger Americans have joined the Corps since its inception. Kennedy saw this as an opportunity to counteract the image of the "ugly American Imperialist" being promulgated by the Communist propaganda machine. The Peace Corps was a progenitor of modern day multiculturalism. An old adage applies here. It is easier to entice people using honey rather than vinegar.

A second organization was derived from the Peace Corps known by the acronym VISTA (Volunteers in service to America). These organizations raised the consciousness level of Americans. They began to care about others not so fortunate living in remote areas and in poverty within the United States.

A different level of consciousness was addressed by Rachel Carson's iconic best seller *Silent Spring* that was published in 1962. She noticed the "silencing of the birds" in the spring and became curious as to the cause. It turned out that the chemical pesticide DDT would now allow shells to be formed around the embryo so the nascent birds became stillborn. She galvanized the scientific community, which began a crusade to ban the production and sale of DDT in America. The crusade was successful. This was the first step in the Ecology Movement in America.

By the end of the decade the government had created a new bureau known as the EPA (Environmental Protection Agency) tasked with monitoring illegal use of land and looking after endangered species. Countless construction projects have been squashed by the EPA and many species are thriving again since they were placed on the Endangered Species Listing. Americans were being reminded that we all share one planet, so take care of it.

Up until the 1960's the norms and cues of society had originated from and were reinforced by the family, schools, and religious institutions. Now there were two new interlopers creating new norms—radio and color television. Books were still important but visual and auditory learning would challenge the old way of doing things. There were new genres of music that grabbed the attention of younger people, who could now buy their own records and play them on RCA Victrola, which were the most popular record players in the early to mid 60's. Color television quickly became an outlet for Pop Art created by men such as Andy Warhol and Op Art that was geometric and created illusions as you viewed it.

The two Godfathers of Rock 'n Roll were actually 50's icons but had more influence on the music and lifestyle of the 60's. They would be Elvis Presley and Chuck Berry. Trained in Gospel music, Presley added the backbeat of country music to the R+B (Rhythm and Blues) and created the Rockabilly style. Presley's style challenged old standards of appearance. His hair was slicked back and he wore tight pants, but his hip rotation was an affront to many of the White Bread culture living in the Bible Belt who viewed his behavior as risque and rebellious. Presley served in the military from 1958-1960 then began a movie and concert career until 1977, when he died of a drug overdose at age forty-two, still the largest-selling solo artist of all time. Chuck Berry was the original lead guitar soloist superstar of the early Rock 'n Roll Age. His songs have been replicated for years and the best way for me to describe his influence on music is calling him The American Idol. Every guitarist wanted to riff like Chuck Berry! Bob Dylan, the poet laureate of the boomer generation, dragged the acoustic coffee-house folk genre into the world of arena rock and electric guitars. He and

John Lennon are considered to be the most influential songwriters of the Baby Boom generation.

On the West Coast, Brian Wilson was listening very intently to Chuck Berry. He called Chuck Berry and asked permission to rewrite Berry's "Sweet Little Sixteen" into his own lyrics. Berry gave his assent and Wilson along with Mike Love transformed the song into the iconic "Surfin' USA" in 1962 and the Beach Boys became an overnight sensation. The California mystique - not a state but a state of mind - drew many young people (including me) to the West Coast to live life near the beach in the Golden State. They became far and away America's biggest band in the 1960's. [Counter culture guitar superstar Jimi Hendrix was also living on the West Coast in the 1960's and developed his unique sound, "So we don't have to listen to that beach music anymore."]

In Liverpool England, John Lennon was also listening very intently to Chuck Berry. He and his original band the Quarrymen played some Chuck Berry favorites at their gigs in the local pubs. They also listened to the Beach Boys, then they changed their name to the Beatles.

In February 1964, "four guys from England took us all by the hands," as the Beatle British invasion came to New York City. You have all heard the screaming and hysteria, often imitated and never duplicated. Overnight the world changed. Beatle haircuts and garage bands were everywhere. The image of their first Sunday night on the "Ed Sullivan Show" still sends tingles down my spine. In a friendly rivalry with the Beach Boys, they went album vs. album, hit vs. hit over a couple of years. You had the 60's beach culture and Beatlemania coming at you at the same time. Shortly thereafter arrived the Rolling Stones, "The World's Greatest Rock n' Roll Band," who were a bit edgier than the Beatles in music and dress. The Rolling Stones had the longer mullet look and by the end of the 1960's long hair was becoming the norm. Because of the success of the Beatles, Stones, and Beach Boys, single records became passe and albums were in.

Chuck Berry also paved the way for the Motown Sound of the 60's. Motown played an important role in the racial integration of popular music (soul music) into mainstream America. Motown placed seventy nine records in the Billboard Top Ten between 1960-1969. Motown was originally headquartered in Detroit, "The Motor City." Famous Motown performers are The Temptations, The Four Tops, Diana Ross and the Supremes, Marvin Gaye, Stevie Wonder, Smokey Robinson, The Jackson Five, and Gladys Knight and the Pips. Because blacks were gaining equality, the Motown Sound had a good time dance feeling to it and many Blacks were in the middle class by 1970. To summarize, from Chuck Berry and Elvis to the Beatles, Bob Dylan, The Beach Boys, Jimi Hendrix and Motown, the growth of rock'n roll proved to be an enduring and uniting social force in America bonding Americans across racial lines

I want to give you a snapshot of how cheap goods were to purchase in the 1960's. Let's pretend you were driving to the 1969 Woodstock Concert in upstate New York from New York City. You were planning to spend all three days there. This is what you would have paid: Five dollars each for a haircut (optional in those days) and a pair of Levis jeans, four dollars for a case of beer, a dozen candy bars were $1.50 and 15 cents for a McDonald's hamburger. Gas was thirty cents per gallon, roughly ten dollars for the road trip ride to Woodstock and back, and the three album set of Woodstock which you would of course buy upon your return cost ten dollars. For under $100.00 you could have experienced the event of a lifetime!

If you passed up Woodstock (like I did), you could have bought a newspaper for ten cents and read about what you missed. If you had attended Woodstock you could have written a letter to Aunt Mary in Toledo, Ohio and told her about your misadventures, and it would only cost you a four cent stamp. Goods were so inexpensive in the 60's because America was a manufacturing nation in those years. The country did not rely on imported goods. To illustrate the dominance of the U.S. economy, 75% of the global wealth was controlled by one American corporation—General Motors headquartered in Detroit, the "Motor City."

Every revolution involves change. Some are good, and some are bad. Some are necessary and some excessive and evil. The 60's Social revolution had all of these elements. In 1963 the feminist movement raised yet another level of consciousness in America. Betty Friedan's *The Feminine Mystique* spoke of the continuing inequality for women in U.S. society. She co-founded and was the first president of NOW (National Organization for Women), which aimed to bring women into the mainstream of society in equal partnership with men. Today NOW is a formidable voting bloc of women pivotal to winning any election especially on the state or federal level. Friedan was succeeded by Gloria Steinem in the 1970's, who was more radical and therefore received more resistance from the powers-that-be, i.e. the male establishment.

The social revolution had many people looking and acting differently. As people grew longer hair, hats and suits were out and blue jeans were in. You were "cool" if you sported tie-dyed shirts or jeans or wore bell bottoms. Black America began to embrace African clothing and the Afro hair cut for both males and females. You began to notice less censorship of movies and television as the culture relaxed a bit compared to the more monochromatic 1950's.

There was experimentation in other domains besides dress and appearance. People began to experiment with marijuana then some moved on to harder drugs like heroin and LSD (acid) which purportedly took you to alternate states of reality. Author Tom Wolfe wrote the iconic drug tome entitled *The Electric Kool Aid Acid Test* that chronicled the cross-country travels of 60's guru Ken Kesey and his "Merry Pranksters," who drove high on acid trying to make sense of their world meeting everyday people while they themselves were on another planet, so to speak.

Eventually Wolfe united the Pranksters up with Dr. Timothy Leary, a Harvard professor who advocated the use of psychedelic drugs to discover new worlds and leave convention behind. Leary's motto was "Tune in…Turn on…Drop out," which is what he did. He got on his own magic bus and managed to get arrested thirty six times. At the time President Nixon referred to Leary as the "most dangerous man in America." Both Kesey and Leary were responsible for the widespread Hippie movement in America. Thousands of long-haired kids dropped out, dropped acid, and went on the road—the road to nowhere half the time.

The feminist movement and hippie movement emboldened the gay community to begin to come out. In the mid 60's there was not that much violence yet, but you could see the clash of the mainstream and counterculture on the horizon.

The social revolution will always be identified with the Vietnam War. On one side a younger generation with a lot of pent up energy waiting to be put to use; on the other side was the Establishment ready to suppress the agitated resistance. As the war escalated into the horrible year of 1968, thousands of activists were now involved trying to end the draft that was taking friends and family to certain death in Vietnam. Flag burning became more prevalent. Kids burned their draft cards in public and were summarily imprisoned. Muhammed Ali refused to get drafted and was thrown in jail, forfeiting his title of world heavyweight boxing champion. One disclaimer needs to be added. Just before the draft was instituted, Ali had the Christian name of Cassius Clay. By converting to Islam and dropping his Christian name, he claimed he was draft-exempt. Many people saw this conversion as a cop-out, but he did go to prison.

Other people toted signs reading "make love not war" and "old enough to fight, old enough to vote." This issue became a larger driver of the anti-war protests as the draft dragged young people into war yet because they could not vote they had no say in the government that opted to force them into the military. It was not until 1971 that Congress saw the error of its ways and ratified the 26th Amendment allowing eighteen year-olds the right to vote.

In the summer of 1969, THE signature event of the generation occurred- the Woodstock Music and Arts Festival in upstate New York. I had the tickets in my hand but the weather forecast called for rain there the entire weekend. The weather at home was beautiful, so I decided to take my transistor radio and my surfboard to the ocean to catch some waves. From what I could glean from my radio and later from those who attended, the gathering of the 400,000 people at Bethel, N.Y. was not so much "peace, love, and music" as advertised; it was more like drugs, music, and mud. Many were there to protest the war and a couple of songs in particular added an indelible amount of anger to future protests. Jefferson Airplane's "Volunteers" encouraged revolution in America. But the loudest, most strident and vulgar Woodstock song of the counterculture that fanned the fires of protest had to be the X-rated "Fish Cheer" by country Joe McDonald and the Fish.

Less than a month later college would be back in session and protesting would go to the next level. Individual protests now blossomed into group protests as resistance to the war increased. Using the technique of sit-ins, students closed down some colleges across America, the two most prominent being UC Berkeley and Columbia University in NY City. The SDS (Students for a Democratic Society) started to organize a march on Washington that was set for the spring of 1970. The level of anger was high but the release of John of Yoko Lennon's "Give Peace a Chance" brought down the anger a notch or two. Meanwhile Richard Nixon had assumed the presidency and was willing to take whatever measures necessary to maintain order. A few days before the march on Washington, the Ohio National Guard gunned down four students at Kent State University. Crosby Stills Nash and Young quickly wrote and released the song "Ohio" with the iconic opening words "Tin soldiers and Nixon's coming..." Actually Nixon did come to meet with the leaders of the march to discuss issues and though they were not resolved the march went on without a hitch and was non-violent. Because the government had used weapons, the marchers feared that Kent State could happen again. Nixon was bringing the troops home from Vietnam which also dropped the degree of militancy.

As if the Vietnam War, the emerging drug culture, and the burning of American cities were not enough the decade reached its nadir in the personage of Charles Manson. With his cold, hypnotic appearance, Manson and his cult of killers achieved national infamy carrying out the Tate-Labianca murders. Sharon Tate was a rising star in the movie industry which brought even more attention to this cult. This sent a panic through an already unsettled nation that faced the possibility of copycat cults popping up anywhere.

The media fed the frenzy surrounding Manson by associating him with the Beatles maniac song "Helter Skelter," which Manson was using as his motivation to incite a race war in America. Fortunately Manson was incarcerated for murder and died in prison in 2017 and never had the chance to see his "dream" fulfilled. It was a hell of a decade!

Katherine Johnson (1919-2020)

As astronaut John Glenn prepared for his historic launch into space in 1962, he trusted one woman more than any computer.

"Get that girl to check the numbers," Glenn insisted before the lift-off of his rocket. "He knew I had done the calculations for him and trusted my work," Johnson, who worked at NASA for thirty three years, told the Washington Post in 2017. The orbital mechanic guru was also part of the team that supported Alan Shepard, who became the first American to reach space on the fifteen-minute suborbital flight aboard Mercury's Freedom Seven on May 5, 1961. In these days she and her colleague used only pencils, slide rules and rudimentary calculators to crunch numbers for these launches.

Her contributions finally received acclaim in the 2016 Oscar-nominated film "Hidden Figures," which celebrated the Black women who for years toiled anonymously behind the scenes during the space race with the Soviet Union.

During the Academy Awards ceremony in 2017 she was given a standing ovation when she joined the film's cast in presenting an award for these documentaries.

CHAPTER 48

1970's: America in Decline

ALVIN TOFFLER'S BOOK *Future Shock* (1970) describes the psychological toll the 1960's had on the populace of America, especially the younger set. Toffler wrote of the effects of too much change in too short a period of time. The Baby Boom Generation became somewhat displaced, as young people were caught between the nurturing norms of the 50's and the radicalization of the 60's. This normlessness known as anomie results in the maladjustment of the individual who is "feeling lost." On a grander scale, this translates to a criminogenic society along with many people dropping out of the mainstream culture and in the worst case resulting in suicide. For example, in 1960 there were 286,000 violent crimes committed throughout America. By the end of the 70's that statistic exceeded 1,000,000. The 70's was a very unsettled decade as both individuals and society struggled to adapt to a rapidly changing world.

The 1970's were bookended by an international crisis. The war in Vietnam raged on at the onset and the Iran Hostage Crisis was the defining nadir to another turbulent decade. In between there was rapprochement with Red China, more tension with Russia, an energy "crisis" and the Watergate Scandal, up to now the worst political crisis in U.S. history. The decade was also defined by weak presidential leadership and a growing distrust of the government that has only grown more cynical with the passage of time. Similar to the1960's, I want to examine the social, economic, and political trends of the 1970's with the understanding that they are all interconnected.

Social Issues

The Sexual Revolution went into high gear in the early 70's. With the production of the pill and wider use of other male and female contraception devices, pre-marital sex became the norm and not the outlier any longer. In colleges, open dormitories and co-ed dormitories replaced the segregated-by-gender ones of the 1960's. Before the 70's if you wanted to invite a co-ed up to your dorm on the weekend you had to keep the door ajar so the dormitory RA's could monitor any potential hanky-panky. That abruptly changed and not just in the colleges but in society at large. The old paradigm of college graduation followed by employment and marriage in rapid succession became a dinosaur. This was a part of Toffler's future shock thesis and would result in the breakdown of the nuclear family unit. The mid 70's had at the same time, the lowest birth rate in U.S. demographic history.

The major demographic change of the 1970's was the explosive growth of the Latino population whether by birth or immigration. It was either Time or Newsweek magazine that put forth a cover story about the impending explosion of the Latino population in America with the by-line "...they will bring a lot of energy to America..."

There was a national debate as to whether English should be the national language of America. From the start cries of racism rang out and the issue was put to rest by the Voting Rights Act of 1975. This Act said that voting instructions must be printed in at least two languages to accommodate clustered immigrant groups in a particular locale. Over time Spanish became the popular second in America, but I feel that the gang issues of today involving MS-13 and other groups sprang from this law.

In the earlier years America was seen as the melting pot, as many immigrant groups came to America and quickly learned the language and were assimilated into the large culture. English was the glue that bound this country together and reinforced shared customs and traditions. The Voting Rights Acts allowed immigrant groups to live in America but not necessarily embrace American culture with the end result of a pluralistic society segregated by different languages and cultures no longer glued together by one common language. We see the results. The failure to communicate leads to fear, suspicion, and isolation that encourages ethnic gangs to congregate sometimes for survival, sometimes to raise hell. I have nothing against others maintaining their culture and values, but mastering English would help solve the deep divisions in society. As for numbers, in 1970, 4.5% of the population were Latino. That was a little over 9,000,000 people are of Latino descent. Today nearly 20% or 52,000,000 people are of Latino descent. Maybe up to 25,000,000 are here illegally. This is a very simple statement: Either we are a nation of laws or we are not.

Speaking about laws, in 1976 the Supreme Court attempted to deal with one component of housing segregation in America. Black America was frustrated over the fact that they seemed to be limited to where they could live, which resulted in overcrowded ghetto burnings and riots of the 60's. In an attempt to allow black and white integration in reference to housing the Court ruled that low-income housing could be built in the nation's suburbs, the province of white middle-class America.

Though there has been some success in this area, segregation remains a hot topic because of "steering." Steering is the practice of guiding prospective homeowners or renters to certain neighborhoods or away from other neighborhoods or areas based on their identity as part of a protected class such as race. It's illegal because it limits the housing opportunities available to that buyer or renter. Steering is difficult to prove in a court of law and is still a commonplace practice of American life.

The ERA (Equal Rights Amendment) was a proposal to guarantee equal legal rights for all Americans regardless of sex. Proposed in 1972, it required thirty-eight states, which is 75% of the states, to ratify this amendment into the Constitution. Women always maintained that men earned more of a salary for doing a similar job as a woman so economics was the major impetus for this amendment. It was also seen as a door for women to step through and join the managerial and executive class of corporate America. However, conservative women leaders feared that women would be subject to the military draft, more likely to lose alimony cases and perhaps custody of children if divorced. Recently the ERA has been brought back to life but that three-quarters majority vote of the states is still elusive.

The power of rock 'n roll ground to a near halt in the mid 70's after holding sway over the popular culture for a full decade or more. With the deaths of Jimi Hendrix, Janis Joplin, and Jim Morrison all at age twenty seven, the rock culture was also in future shock having lost its direction. That void was filled by the explosive emergence of disco music that took the nation by storm from 1975-1980. People still had longer hair, but it was now more styled and disco dancing was the rage. For my money, "Saturday Night Fever" is still the best timepiece movie ever produced. Most people, whether you liked disco or not, acknowledge the masterpiece album that derived from the movie. As the disco fad began to wane, its symbolic downfall arrived on "Disco Demolition Night" in 1978 at Comiskey Park in Chicago. Promotor Bill Veeck gave out free tickets to all who attended the Chicago White Sox baseball game that night so long as you brought along disco records that were piled into the outfield and torched. This event encouraged the sale of "disco sucks" t-shirts that became the rage and presaged the end of the Disco Era by 1980.

Economic Trends

If I had to choose one word to characterize the 70's in economic terms it would be recession. Just as the Great Depression ruled America for a decade, recession characterized America for the majority of the 70's.

Perhaps the most important cause of this recession was the tremendous transfer of wealth that began in the 60's. In the 60's the government programs of Medicare and Medicaid provided health care aid for the majority of the population. Of course this was at taxpayers' expense. In the 1970's there was an increase in unemployment insurance, but a larger transfer of wealth went to other nations who began to market products that Americans wanted. As stated, GM once commanded 75% of the world's economy. By the end of the decade, a totally different scenario would begin to emerge.

Two events of 1973 helped to weaken the economy. The first event was the termination of the Vietnam War as the military returned home leaving behind a skeleton force to train the South Vietnamese Army. As the wartime economy shut down, war essentials were no longer needed so unemployment grew rapidly. The second event was the Arab Oil Embargo that OPEC (Organization of Petroleum Exporting Countries) used against the U.S. for our continued support of Israel, an avowed enemy of the OPEC cartel.

Seemingly overnight the "oil shock" of the embargo raised wholesale prices 400% per barrel and tripled the price of gas at the pump. This led to an official gas shortage but myself and others suspect that the large oil companies were in cahoots with OPEC seeing a chance to raise gas prices and pump up the bottom line. In any event gas lines became the news story of the day. Gas was rationed in a couple of different ways. Some stations limited you to ten gallons but the most memorable method was known as odd-even days based on your license plate. The idea was to prevent the consumer "topping off" by going to the gas station two days in a row. Many found a way around this restriction by acquiring two sets of license plates. This system lasted several months and only slowly came to an end in 1974.

The shock of high gasoline prices created a new market for smaller cars that were much smaller than the gas-guzzlers being produced by GM, Ford, and Chrysler. The Japanese auto manufacturers were ahead of the curve and before you knew it Toyota, Datsun, Subaru, Mitsubishi et al were dominating the highways and byways of America because their cars were well made and all had high MPG averages.

The Big Three American automakers had been asleep at the wheel, so to speak, and were not at all ready for this foreign car market invasion. They had been warned in 1965 by Ralph Nader's book *Unsafe at any Speed* that described the design flaws of the

Chevrolet Corvair, Nader's prime target. The book also spoke about a lack of quality control in the American auto industry and Nader became an American cult hero and ran for president four times as a third party candidate. It would not be until the 1980's that the Big Three produced smaller cars for a changing market. For the record, Toyota has surpassed GM as the world's largest auto producer. Needless to say the reduced market for big cars in the 70's led to a large spike in unemployment as GM was the biggest employer of people in America outside of the U.S. governmental bureaucracy. Many at Ford Motors and Chrysler also wound up on the unemployment lines.

The advent of the computer also was a double-edged sword. The first computer was created in 1965 but the use of computers in industry took off in the 70's. Automation allowed businesses to produce more and run more efficiently. Those who did not lose their jobs to computers saw a rise in their salaries in the 70's. On the other hand another segment of manual laborers were relegated to the unemployment lines.

Now that GM no longer controlled the world economy, imported goods began to flow into the American economy at a much higher rate. Usually when a country is in a recession with high unemployment prices tend to drop but with the transfer of wealth out of the country for imported goods, prices began to rise and double-digit inflation became the reality. Wage and price controls that limit both the price of goods and salaries of individuals were imposed by all the presidential administrations of all the 70's presidents to no avail. The post WWII boom (upbeat economy) was in a tailspin and no one seemed to have any solutions.

My personal odyssey through the decade exemplified the dysfunction of change I experienced living through those times. I arrived in San Diego in the fall of 1973 and within a month the oil embargo took full effect. I had planned on a permanent relocation but there was no job market to speak of save for menial jobs. Within six months I was on the way home with the full knowledge I would have to live with my parents who had moved to a remote community unknown to me. I was a stranger in a strange land, lost, depressed, and angry. My mother motivated me by charging rent even though I was unemployed. Out of curiosity but mostly desperation I became a substitute teacher in the local school district, which was not much fun. If you strung together enough days during the school calendar year you qualified for unemployment during the summer months. I collected a whopping $35.00 a week for two summers, which had to go a long way in those days.

Then one day came the epiphany. Substituting for gym class a boy asked "Coach whatever-your-name is, can I go to the bathroom?" The word coach hit me like a ton of bricks and resonated. I saw my life in front of me but this being the 70's it took until 1981 to get my first full-time teaching position with coaching as a second job. Persistence became my main message for all my students. Select a goal, work for it, and don't give up! My belief in the Puritan work ethic would now allow me to fail.

Politics

Politically speaking, the 70's were a decade characterized by drawn out political scandals intertwined with international chaos. The first scandal involved the secret and piecemeal release of the Pentagon Papers (1971) by Daniel Ellsberg. As the war continued in Vietnam, the U.S. Government permitted unsanctioned raids of coastal North Vietnam and allowed the bombings of the neutral countries of Laos and Cambodia, none of which had been reported by the media. Ellsberg was charged with treason by the U.S. government but exonerated by the Supreme Court citing freedom of the press in the first amendment. The final release of the Pentagon Papers did not occur until 2011, documenting decades of covert government operations in Southeast Asia, going as far back as the Truman Administration. The military was never sanctioned for incursions into neutral countries! Recall I speculated that the motivation for the Vietnam War was to keep the military-industrial complex in business.

Though Nixon was taking steps to end the now unpopular Vietnam War, he was still viewed in a negative light by the protestors and a large chunk of the general population for the murders at Kent State under his watch. In a shrewd political move to distract attention, he engaged in detente with both the Soviet Union and China in 1972. Detente means the easing of tensions between two adversaries or ideologies. With regard to Russia he got them to sign the 1972 Anti-Ballistic Missile Treaty which was a component of the ongoing SALT (Strategic Arms Limitations Talks) negotiations. With regards to China, Nixon initiated what might be thought of as the New Open Door Policy aided by "ping pong" diplomacy. With the media present both countries entered into a series of friendly ping pong matches between their national teams. It was the first time the U.S. had reached out to Red China since the end of WWII.

Much of Nixon's legacy, as well as the perception of the government in the ensuing decades, may have been shaped by Nixon's inherent paranoia, initiating the Watergate Scandal and earning Nixon the infamous moniker "Tricky Dick."

The 1972 presidential election was between Nixon and Democrat George McGovern, who was seen as a weak challenger with little chance to unseat the incumbent. For some reason, Nixon was worried about the Democratic Party's campaign strategy, so he arranged for a group of his own hand-picked conspirators aka "the Plumbers" to wire the rooms of the Watergate hotel in Washington, D.C. to record all the conversations that the Democratic strategists would employ to unseat Nixon. An alert security guard noticed evidence of a break-in at the Democratic headquarters at the Watergate. The police nabbed the "plumbers" in a hotel across the street, "caught napping," and they were arrested.

Right away the Nixon White House staff tried to distance themselves from the conspirators they had hired by creating an elaborate cover-up conspiracy to hide the first conspiracy. I was unemployed at the time and watched this marathon unfold over two years on TV, and I was struck by the testimony of Nixon's counsel John Dean who had remembered and detailed everything.

To make a long story very short, the key piece of evidence against Nixon was an eighteen minute audio tape that had buzzed out the steps of the conspiracy partially plotted by Nixon himself! Congress drew up articles of impeachment that at first the White House tried to deny. The Supreme Court ruled unanimously that the case for removal could continue. Seeing the handwriting on the wall, Nixon resigned in August 1974 citing phlebitis (blood clot in leg) as his reason for resignation, but he was only fooling himself. Historians agree that of the few presidents ever impeached he would certainly have been the only one removed by Congress had he not resigned.

The cartoon strip Doonesbury by Garry Trudeau illustrated the impending doom for the Nixon Presidency, drawing a brick wall around the White House and adding one new brick every day until the end of the crisis when the entire White House was walled in. Nixon thought he was above the law.

Concurrent with the Watergate Scandal arose another social/political issue that has never been resolved and today may be more intense than ever. In 1973 the Supreme Court affirmed a woman's right to abortion in the case Roe vs. Wade. The court went on to rule that this right is not absolute as a woman's health could be at stake. The rights of the unborn were also a grave concern for the court. Neither the court nor the medical fields nor anyone else has definitely decided at what point this mass of protoplasm becomes a functional human being. Today Planned Parenthood seems to be okay with aborting a baby near its birth (infanticide) while the right to life side describes it as murder. For the most part Democrats line up with the Abortionists while the Republicans with the Right-to Lifers. It is a very emotional debate that seems to intensify each time Roe v. Wade is applied to a new aspect of abortion that arises in other test cases.

When Nixon stepped down as president, he was replaced by his Vice-President Gerald Ford. Ford has the distinction of being the only man in U.S. political history to have served as both president and vice president without going through the Electoral College. Ford was a Michigan Congressman who was selected by Nixon to replace Nixon's first VP, Spiro Agnew, who took bribes while in office. When Nixon resigned, Ford became president. In my opinion, Ford's first official act as President doomed his re-election campaign for 1976. Ford pardoned Nixon "for any crimes he may or may not have committed." Ford did not want to prolong the agony of Watergate and in effect sacrificed his future for a quicker healing of America.

The economic curse of continued inflation also worked against Ford remaining president despite his public relations campaign against inflation featuring WIN buttons (Whip Inflation Now). The death blow for the Ford Administration was when he refused to bail out New York City in 1975 and the New York Daily News issued its now iconic cover headline, "Ford to City: Drop Dead." Personally I thought Ford was a decent man but bumbling and ineffective as the leader of a nation. He was the second inept president of the decade. The third and last president of the decade, Jimmy Carter, may have been the least effective of the trio of 1970's chief executives.

A very close high school friend of mine became a delegate for Jimmy Carter in the 1976 Presidential election where he narrowly defeated Gerald Ford. According to my source, Carter was a nice guy but ineffective as a leader, much like Gerald Ford. Being a peanut farmer and a party outsider, Congress did not support him as Carter tried to govern as an independent thinker and not get caught up in the D.C swamp. Although America dug out the Alaska Oil Pipeline during his presidency, he was not a fan of drilling for oil and wanted Congressional money to develop alternative sources of energy (sound familiar?). Sound economics would tell you that when a country is struggling with high inflation and unemployment, looking to develop new sources of energy is a non-starter. When an economy is thriving with extra money, that is when you might explore alternate sources of energy.

Congress did not support the Carter economic program. As a matter of fact inflation continued to rise during his administration. Carter's signature success came in the realm of foreign affairs with the signing of the Camp David Accords (1978). Carter was able to broker a peace treaty between Israel and Egypt, at that time the most powerful and most anti-Israeli Arab Nation. This treaty worked against any regional Arab wars against the State of Israel and may have set the groundwork for the Islamic Revolution in Iran. Egypt and Israel have remained close since the treaty, with Iran emerging as the major anti-Israeli threat in the Middle East. Carter must be given credit for this unexpected alliance of former foes.

Carter wanted to keep SALT II talks alive with Russia, but when they invaded Afghanistan he ended those talks. He took it one step further by decreeing the U.S. boycott of the 1980 Olympics in Moscow. That was an effective move, calling attention to an illegal and unprovoked invasion. The Russians retaliated by boycotting the 1984 Olympic Games in Los Angeles, but their protest had no merit, with only a few Con munist countries not entering the L.A. Olympics. This was a definie victory for the U.S. in its propaganda Cold War against the Soviet Union, as the free world backed the U.S. against the Soviet incursion into a smaller, neutral country.

However, accolades for the Carter Administration came to a screeching halt with the takeover of the American Embassy in Iran by radical Islamic students in November of 1979, a segment of the Islamic Revolution. The Iran Hostage Crisis would last 444 days and involve fifty two American hostages who were set free on Jan 20, 1981, the day that Ronald Reagan was inaugurated as president. Like he did with the Vietnam War, Walter Cronkite would begin his newscast each night with the day number of the standoff lending more gravity to an already grave situation.

The Shah (king) of Iran, who was friendly with the U.S. but not with the Iranian people, was forced out of office along with his secret police who were allegedly torturing the citizens of Iran. The Shah was in poor health and sought treatment in the U.S. The storming of the Embassy by radicals began when the U.S. would not return the Shah to Iran to face justice. The ouster of the Shah began a revolutionary change in Iran to a theocratic state controlled by Islamic leaders not afraid to use terrorism to achieve their objectives.

Quickly a pattern emerged of Carter's failed attempts of negotiating the freedom of the hostages. Carter would latch on to initiatives offered by the Iranians agreeing to lame but humiliating sanctions. Because he agreed so quickly Carter was seen as weak and this image was reinforced by the press.

Finally in April of 1980 Carter decided to put his foot down and authorized a rescue attempt of the hostages known as Operation Eagle Claw that involved ground forces and a number of helicopters. This turned into a complete debacle as two of the copters crashed during a sandstorm and destroyed a U.S. transport plane. "The Islamic Wind" had worked against the Great Satan, which is what the terrorists call America. The next day Carter had to go on national television and accept the responsibility for this disaster. This faux pas would be a big factor in his losing the presidential election that year to Reagan.

Iran became a major player in the Middle East and a known sponsor of terrorism throughout the world. The crisis finally ended as the U.S. froze eight billion dollars of Iranian money in American banks, money that Iran would need to fight a war against Hussein and Iraq in the months to come.

The seventies ended as it began, with the U.S. embroiled in international affairs after having been led by three mediocre Presidents during the decade. With faith in their democracy at an all time low, the U.S. faced the new decade of the 80's with many challenges ahead.

Rocky (1976)

The American nation was reeling after years of both internal and external strife. The social fabric of America had been shredded by the upheaval of the 60's. There remained a seething anger in the burnt out ghettos of many urban areas. The U.S. withdrew from Vietnam with its figurative tail between its legs. Unemployment was high and inflation was in the double digits. The government had no answers and things got worse not better. The Watergate Scandal destroyed the faith of Americans in the integrity of their government that was already on shaky grounds. No one, not even the president, could be trusted. After the Watergate Scandal, the American press were no longer a neutral watchdog. Going forward they consistently refused to criticize Democratic administrations, focusing all their bile on future Republican administrations. People were looking for a savior. A celluloid hero arose from the streets and provided a downtrodden American with a jolt of energy uplifting the nation who had been victimized by the future shock of the 60's and early 70's.

Rocky (1976) was the biggest Hollywood "sleeper" movie of all time, garnishing three Academy Awards including Best Picture. The movie *All the President's Men* detailing the Watergate Scandal was probably the superior movie, but the Academy did not want to honor the negativity surrounding the Nixon Presidency.

Rocky's message resonated with the American people and provided hope going forward. People related to the underdog persona of Rocky Balboa, and the signature song from the soundtrack "Gonna Fly Now" has motivated millions of people across America for many decades. Stallone's acceptance speech was cryptic but spot on. "This is for all the other Rockys' out there," as he raised the Oscar above his head.

A few years later at Lake Placid, NY, an underdog team of twenty young men would embody the motivation of this movie to energize America and affect the geopolitical world in the 1980's.

CHAPTER 49

The Big 80's!

JUST BEFORE 1980, PRESIDENT CARTER went on national television with his "crisis of confidence" speech to America. He noted the downward trajectory of the United States. The Iran Hostage Crisis had stunned America. The Russians had invaded Afghanistan and flexed their nuclear muscles. People were scared. Perhaps seeking divine intervention, Carter wrung his hands and wondered, "What can America do?"

The answer was a bolt out of the blue that arrived the night of February 22, 1980 forever known as the "Miracle on Ice." In the greatest moment in U.S. sports history, an underdog team of college hockey players upset the heavily-favored Soviet Union professional team that had not lost an Olympic contest since 1968 and had crushed an NHL All-Star team six to nothing a month before.

This victory at Lake Placid had a number of repercussions. It was yet another Cold War victory for democracy over communism, further proof that the American way was the path to be followed. This was not lost on the various republics in Russia under the thumb of the Russian Communist Party. As the decade progressed, the various republics grew more and more restive. The Soviet military and KGB (secret police) were loath to use force to restore order. The

USSR was fraying at the edges. Russia had chosen to overspend on its military and short-change the rest of the Soviet economy with the result that the Russian people suffered, lacking the basics of life. Freedom looked to be an attainable goal for the repressed nationalities forced to adapt to the Soviet Culture.

The 1960's and 1970's had been decades of reform, protest, and change. But after so many tumultuous years, Americans longed for calmer times.

Many leaders of the 1980's called for a return to traditional American values. They praised family life, loyalty, and patriotism. At the same time they spoke out against "big government." In their view, the government was too costly in regards to its social programs. Too many government regulations stifled business growth.

One leading critic of big government was Ronald Reagan. The ex-Democrat was elected as the Republican candidate for president in 1980. He convinced Americans it was time for a conservative "revolution." As a former movie actor, his experience before the cameras helped him win public confidence. Like FDR's fireside chats when Reagan spoke to the people on television, they felt he truly cared. His skill at presenting ideas won him the title "the Great Communicator."

"Reaganomics" was the plan undertaken to clean up the economic mess that was the worst since the Great Depression. Reagan's plan was based on "trickle down economics," involving tax cuts for the wealthiest. Over time the money saved by business would be reinvested to grow industry more and increase the salaries and spending power of the middle class. Critics said it took funding away from the poor and the elderly and referred to his plan as "Voodoo economics," as it also increased the national debt. These objections were muted as Reagan expanded the military to offset the danger posed by Russia. To me, Reaganomics was a godsend. After a couple of years of Reaganomics, I witnessed raises in my teaching salary unimagined and my city, which had been a semi-burnt out wreck in the 70's, experienced a building boom, which we called Condomania in 1985. Besides teachers, thousands of others in civil service saw meteoric rises in salary. This allowed a substantial portion of the population to become homeowners and boost a surging economy.

Reagan won reelection in 1984 over Walter Mondale and the Democrats. During the campaign, he exhibited his humility and his wit. At age seventy three, he was the oldest candidate at the time to run for office and seventeen years older than Mondale. People were worried about Reagan's age but with one famous line he cinched the election before it even occurred. Reagan announced to the world during the presidential debate, "I will not make age an issue in this campaign. I am not going to exploit, for political purposes, my opponent's youth and inexperience." Mondale himself cracked up laughing. Reagan won in a landslide. Today's politicians should take note, honey trumps vinegar.

America felt safe with Reagan at the helm. He pledged to oppose Communism both at home and abroad. There was a new optimism as the angst and the discord of the previous two decades would become a memory. There would be negatives both overseas and domestically, but the positivity of the decade took center stage. There was a very palpable energy that coursed through the veins of Americans in the decade and you could feel it. The media grabbed that energy and the result was the Go Go 80's.

Nicknamed the Decade of Excess, the Go Go 80's found many outlets for this newly-found energy as well as new modes of expression. Big Hair, Air Jordans, Spandex, and Woodstock-esque colors were in. Madonna was the biggest trend setter in terms of costumes and music and was widely emulated by others. Fads came and went as people were always looking to one-up each other and get national attention on the new media outlets of CNN (1980) and especially MTV (1981). Performers such as Michael Jackson, Bruce Springsteen, and Madonna had their profiles raised by their now iconic videos played on MTV. The excitement generated by the 80's was best exemplified by the music genres of Punk and New Wave. The uptempo guitar riffs made these genres sympatico with the upbeat world of the time. Some of the best of the New Wave songs included The Cars "Let's Go!", The Knack "My Sharona," Loverboy "Working for the Weekend," and most appropriately the Go! Go's! "We Got the Beat!"

Hollywood also captured the fervor of the 80's on celluloid. The competition to one-up was captured on film in one of the all-time classic movies "Top Gun." Who could forget Gordon Gekko's famous line, "greed is good," from the movie "Wall Street," profiling the cutthroat competition for wealth at the highest levels of corporate life. On the small screen it seems that everyone was tuned into "Miami Vice," the ultimate glam show that best combined the glitz, glamor, and action of the 80's. CGI (Computer Graphic Images) were seen for the first time in movies such as "Raiders of the Lost Ark" and the first computer-generated TV "personality" starring Matt Frewer as Max Headroom.

The decade of excess infused itself into the world of recreation and sports. Jim Fixx's book *The Complete Book of Running* helped to start the fitness revolution by popularizing the sport of running. He detailed the health benefits associated with regular jogging. Ironically he died at age fifty two while running, having underlying conditions that hastened his demise. But in the decade of excess, casual running begat the marathon craze and triathlons, with the

Iron Man Triathlon in Hawaii being seen as the ultimate endurance test…or was it? Ultramarathons of fifty miles or more were born. Later in the decade the entire subculture of extreme sports was birthed with the prospect of facing down death a major incentive to participate.

In the 60's the Beach Boys romanticized the surf culture, with the ultimate being able to ride the pipeline in Hawaii. By the end of the 80's, surfers were riding waves two to three times as big as the pipeline at Jaws in Hawaii and Mavericks in California. Today extreme surfers ride 100 foot waves off the coast of Portugal and in most cases live to tell about it.

Although they were not yet affordable to all, the PC (Personal Computer) (1981) and the cell phone (1983) allowed a few folks to enjoy the culture a bit more than the rest of us. In the last year of the decade, about 60% of America had cable television.

There were a number of issues that arose in America that showed the down side of the 80's. First of all, everyone got a glimpse of their own mortality on the night of December 8, 1980 when John Lennon was gunned down in front of his New York City apartment by a crazed fan. America has never gotten a handle on the epidemic of mental illness that often leads to suicide and homicidal gun violence.

On a more societal level, the unwanted pestilence of AIDS reared its ugly head as early as 1981 and by the middle of the decade put the brakes on the party train of the 80's. The epidemic has killed over 30,000,000 people worldwide, becoming the sixth largest human killer disease of all time. All of a sudden safe sex became a new standard of behavior in an era that heretofore seemed to operate with no rules.

The 80's took it on the chin again with the Wall Street crash of 1987. Greed was out of control and "trickled down" to affect many people who either lost their jobs or a good portion of their savings. Luckily this crisis was rectified in a short period of time.

Affirmative action programs were set up to promote and hire minorities, women and others who had faced discrimination. By the 1970's more blacks were entering professions such as medicine and law. The black middle class continued to grow.

In the 1980's however, support for affirmative action declined. Discrimination court cases were being filed by males and whites claiming unfair advantages were now being given to minority hires. Meanwhile, rising costs of education and reduced financial aid limited the number of black students in colleges. When pressed for monetary assistance, Reagan said that the state governments had to contribute more. Once again there became a restless "underclass of poorly educated jobless blacks." There would be repercussions.

Maybe it was a token move, but Reagan surprised his critics by pushing for a law that designated MLK's birthday as a national holiday. He signed that bill into law in 1986. Earlier in the decade Reagan again shocked his detractors who viewed him as a male chauvinist by nominating Sandra Day O'Connor as the first female justice of the Supreme Court (1981). Today one-third of the Supreme Court is female.

Though a cure for AIDS was a long time coming, there was one major medical breakthrough of the 1980's—the creation of an artificial heart. Today heart transplants are common.

In terms of foreign affairs, the 80's were a mixed bag of success and failure for the Reagan Administration. On the positive side, the Iran Hostage crisis was ended and the hostages returned to American soil the day Reagan took office in 1981. Always looking to stifle the spread of Communism, Raegan launched an invasion of the Caribbean nation of Grenada in 1983 that was being overrun by Communist revolutionaries from Cuba. Reagan quickly sent in U.S. forces to dispatch the Communist insurgents. Grenada has remained a staunch ally of the U.S. since being rescued from a near Communist coup.

Reagan's greatest historical success in foreign affairs was the termination of the Cold War with the Soviet Union, resulting in the subsequent dissolution of the USSR into many smaller republics. Reagan repeatedly raised the specter of the U.S. development of SDI (Strategic Defense Initiative) popularly referred to as "Star Wars," a system of orbiting satellites with the capability of destroying any enemy attack by utilizing laser cannons orbiting in space. Some began to refer to the President as Ronnie Ray-Gun.

Fearing SDI in 1985, new Soviet leader Gorbachev instituted a new, less restrictive plan of government for the Soviet Union known as the Glasnost Perestroika opening up Soviet society and reducing the power of the Communist Party. The Soviet Union was already reeling from a protracted war in Afghanistan, their unsuccessful boycott of the 1984 Los Angeles Olympics and in 1986 the explosion of their nuclear reactor at Chernobyl that threatened the safety of the world. Perestroika attempted to make socialism work but as usual proved a failure as the economy could not produce enough goods for their nation. The result was a growing unrest in the outer republics. The demise of the USSR as a superpower arrived at the end of the 80's, as the myriad republics became independent nations. The Soviet Union could never solve the economics of the guns vs. butter paradigm. The USSR did not have a large enough economy to finance both the military and food production. By choosing the former they sowed the seeds of their own demise in the late 1980's.

Unlike former Soviet leaders, Gorbachev was willing to work with Reagan to bring about a better world, more peaceful and secure. In an iconic television speech Reagan implored, "Mr. Gorbachev, tear down the (Berlin) Wall," which was the symbol of the Cold War. Officially the wall came down under President Bush in 1989, but Reagan with an assist from Gorbachev is credited for ending the Cold War between Russia and the U.S.

Unfortunately the ending of the Iran Hostage Crisis was only prologue for more terrorism in the 80's, that was most beyond the reach of Reagan to solve. In Beirut, Lebanon (1983) the first truck bombing of a U.S. military compound occurred killing 241 Marines. This event highlighted the need for increased global security with the result that concrete barriers were constructed at U.S. bases around the world. Another tragedy was the bombing of Pan Am Flight 103 in Lockerbie, Scotland killing all 270 on board including many Americans. The instigator of this attack was the Islamic leader of Libya, Gaddafi.

Reagan got a measure of revenge, ordering U.S. fighter jets to target the home of Gaddafi. He eventually confessed and was removed from power in Libya. He was beaten to death by his own countrymen in 2011. It should be noted that Osama Bin Laden formed Al-Qaeda in 1988, the same year as the bombing of Pan Am 103. The downing of flight 103 gave Bin Laden's organization a blueprint for future destruction.

Though he claimed no knowledge of it, the Iran-Contra Scandal (1986) gave Reagan a black eye. After the Beirut truck bombing American hostages were taken. Iran—of all nations—was willing to help the U.S. get back their hostages. Iran needed weapons for the upcoming border war with Iraq and was willing to pay big bucks for the weapons as well as aiding to return the U.S. hostages.

Though Reagan vowed publicly never to deal with a rogue state such as Iran, his CIA operatives hatched a secret plan. In the Central America country of Nicaragua, the Contra Rebels needed weapons to take on and defeat a Communist insurgency. The CIA took the money from the weapons sale to Iran and gave the money to the Contras. The CIA knew their boss would give tacit approval as another Communist threat would be thwarted. Everything went as planned, but when this illegal deal was discovered only a few members of the CIA were imprisoned for a short stint. Reagan was not indicted on any charges. [Had Reagan done this deal in 2020, he would have certainly been impeached by Congress, but in the 1980's he was the Lord Protector of American foreign interests.]

Given the incessant drumbeat of the Go Go 80's, it came as no surprise that cocaine, in whatever form, fueled the rampant drug culture that went viral in the decade. At this time the drug pipeline to America was centered in the Central American country of Panama. Manuel Noriega was the Panamanian dictator and a one-time friend of the U.S. but resorted to distributing contraband drugs, especially cocaine, as the economy of Panama was in shambles. [As a historical note Latin American countries were often referred to as Banana Republics, countries having only a one-crop economy and therefore prone to political upheaval when times were bad.]

Reagan tried economic sanctions to oust Noriega from power to no avail. Noriega declared that Panama and the U.S. were "in a state of war" and several American soldiers were attacked near the Panama Canal. Big mistake.

In December 1989, new President George Bush Sr. sent in reinforcements to protect American troops and to make sure that the Panama Canal, a vital trade route, remained open. The capture of Noriega was achieved in a novel and somewhat humorous way. U.S.

troops surrounded his fortified compound and decided to bombard the compound not with weapons but rather with screeching high-decibel Big Hair heavy metal music playing relentlessly day and night. Noriega could no longer take this torture and surrendered. He was flown to the U.S. to stand trial on charges of drug smuggling.

As in Grenada and Nicaragua, the U.S. had utilized its "Big Stick" to protect American interests in Latin America. Critics in Latin America and Europe worried that the U.S. had again unwisely intervened in the affairs of Latin American countries.

There was a certain innocence to the 1980's. The Reagan Administration had brought order and security back to America that allowed Americans to enjoy those halcyon years. Of course nothing can last forever and not everyone shares in the wealth. There was an undercurrent of unrest that would lead to dramatic changes in the American landscape in the 1990's—changes that are ongoing today. In many ways the air was about to be let out of the balloon. Smiles became frowns.

CHAPTER 50

1990's: Enter the PC Culture

POLITICAL CORRECTNESS IS A TERM used to describe language, politics, and measures that are intended to avoid offense or disadvantage to members of particular groups in society. In public discourse and media the term is usually a pejorative (negative) with the implication that these policies are excessive or unwanted slurs against certain groups. As early as 1990 P.C. was being heard in debates over what should or should not be taught in universities. Soon thereafter the term was increasingly being used in a wider public forum. In the same year, both Forbes and Newsweek Magazine invoked the term "thought police" into the national discussion as a brewing culture war between the Left and the Right would get more strident.

In May 1991 at a commencement ceremony for the graduating class of the University of Michigan, then President George Bush Sr. foresaw the future ideological battle lines taking shape when he said, "The notion of P.C. has ignited controversy across the land. And although the movement arises from the laudable desire to sweep away the debris of racism, sexism, and hatred, it replaces old prejudices with new ones. It declares certain topics off-limits, certain expressions off-limits, even certain gestures off limits."

Left wing protagonists claimed that conservatives created the P.C. construct to declare war on the Left, who were attempting to improve America by addressing structural problems in society. The Right countered that multiculturalism in education would lead to revisionist history and an indoctrination of youth to identity politics. The paradigm shift to the Left would include militant feminism, gay and transgender rights, and the rights of non-European immigrants. The Leftist agenda had a very aggressive tone to its demands and was looking to impose new cultural imperatives in a nation wed to its traditions.

For example, implicit in multiculturalism is ethnic pluralism. Previously America was a melting pot of many cultures that assimilated into an American culture. Ethnic pluralism is a mosaic of ethnic groups interacting with one another *without* having to sacrifice their particular identities. Ethnic pluralism becomes a new form of segregation in America, isolating not assimilating the various components of the American population.

My personal diaries from the 1990's provided ample fodder for this topic. I do not take stock in many paranoid conspiracy theories but one kept circulating throughout the 90's albeit not in the media.

There was discussion of a new World Order that involved totalitarian government, open borders and a sharing of wealth equally throughout the world, a new Communism if you will. As the decade progressed, I saw the roots of it in public education in America. New York State, where I taught, started to insist that the Social Studies curriculum K-12 now be taught with a multicultural approach.

This sounds benign on the surface, but going a little deeper we realized that they wanted us to teach more revisionist history and not emphasize themes that had once been important. How did they do this? By imposing State Testing that covered a New Age curriculum. Many parents quickly figured out the game and refused to allow their kids to be state-tested. We were expected to cover a massive curriculum (this book!) and grade and prepare state tests as well. In October 1999, I noted in my diary, "more State BS to abide by. If they would leave us alone these kids would be educated." The new state curriculum was solidifying the New World Order. Indoctrinate them early and they become compliant.

One more point about the New World Order. In my December 1999 diary I talked about "mailing in my final ten years." Besides the new curriculum, administration came up with a new modus operandi best summarized as "the Tail wags the Dog."

Administrators have no tenure so they tend to run scared at the prospect of job loss. In the 1990's, children and parents were always right and the teacher was always wrong.

This was a distinct paradigm shift from the 60's, 70's, and 80's classroom, when discipline ruled the classroom and teachers did not run scared. Discipline went out the window as soon as a child or parent complained. This upside down philosophy nearly cost me my job, which I detailed in my first book in 2008. School rules now were dictated by the authoritarian P.C. Culture, and the traditional ways were becoming a relic of the past. The thought police of the New World Order had obtained a foothold in the most basic and fundamental aspect of American culture.

George Bush Sr. (1989-1993)

A former WWII Navy fighter pilot and head of the CIA, Bush was Reagan's vice president and easily rode the coattails of his predecessor to the White House in 1989. Historians give him generally high marks for his foreign policy work and on the domestic side continued Reaganomics into the 1990's. Described as a gentleman, he was seen as a good steward of Republican values but not an innovator. He preferred a laissez-faire approach to government until problems arose. Along with second President John Adams and his son John Quincy Adams, Bush and his son George Bush Jr. are the only two family dynasties of presidents in U.S. history.

Foreign Policy

As previously discussed, Bush was able to oust Manuel Noriega from power in Panama, accomplishing two goals: cutting down the cocaine pipeline to America and ensuring that the Panama Canal remained open to all nations who used it as a trade route. Though Reagan did most of the heavy lifting, Bush oversaw the final dissolution of the Soviet Union morphing into Russia and many other now independent republics. Bush then put the nail in the coffin of the decades old Cold War by recognizing the reunification of Germany which quickly became a NATO ally.

Bush's signature success, however, has to be the coordination of the Gulf War in 1991 along with thirty five other nations known as Operation Desert Storm. Saddam Hussein, dictator of Iraq, had fought a long war against Iran and was now short of oil. Hussein decided to invade Kuwait, a neighboring nation which had vast reserves of oil. Hussein was also rumored to be building WMD's (weapons of mass destruction).

With a good chunk of the world's oil supply at risk and to stop the purported production of WMDs, Operation Desert Storm was launched. The actual fighting only lasted six weeks and Hussein's army couldn't wait to surrender.

Domestic Policy

In 1989, early in the Bush Presidency, the U.S. experienced one of its worst ecological disasters—the Exxon-Valdez oil spill in Prince William Sound, Alaska. While the captain slept, the oil tanker Valdez ran aground, resulting in the largest oil spill in U.S. history—11,000,000 gallons of crude oil discharged from the ship into the sound. Because this occurred in a remote area, the clean-up was slow and the oil affected 1300 miles of coastline, killing thousands of birds and fish. It has taken over a quarter century to create a new "normal" in this area that is still being monitored for random pockets of oozing oil. Exxon initially attempted to deflect blame but with the awful visuals and government pressure grudgingly agreed to pay for the clean-up.

Also in 1989, Bush signed the Clean Air Act into law. This act curbed the amount of acid rain by decreasing the amount of sulfur dioxide released into the atmosphere. On the other hand, Global Warming was becoming a political football with the deforestation of the rain forests and ozone layer issues. Bush "dropped the ball" by being mum on the subject and not encouraging the manufacturing of small cars that were more gas efficient and would have helped to mitigate this problem.

In 1990, Bush signed the Americans with Disabilities Act, which mandated wheelchair access to all government buildings as well as to businesses so long as the modifications did not impose "undue hardship" on business owners. In the same year he curried some favor with the immigration lobby by signing the Immigration

Act that doubled the amount of visas granted to immigrants who possessed work skills. He was viewed as being unenthusiastic in regards to the growing AIDS epidemic that was ramping up in the 90's, not offering any new legislation or increased funding to hasten the curing process.

The major downfall of his domestic policy was his inability to deal with a rising budget deficit that he inherited from the Reagan years. Although there was wealth at the top and in the middle classes, the "trickle down" of money did not reach the lower classes, who were resentful that Bush did not want to substantially slash the military budget.

This long term dissatisfaction of the Black Community came to a head in the Rodney King beating of 1991. Four white LAPD officers dragged a drunken King, who was African-American, out of his car and beat him with excessive force. This was filmed on camera. The criminal trial exonerated the officers yet a federal trial overturned some of the exoneration. No matter. L.A. was set ablaze and riots broke out in six other major cities coast to coast. The U.S. military had to be called out to quell the L.A. riots that lasted into 1992.

Though Bush sided with Rodney King and family, perhaps if he had done more for the minority community in terms of economic aid and jobs creation this scenario may have not become so incendiary. These riots tapped into the undercurrent of anger and frustration of those not sharing in the great prosperity characteristics of the 80's and the 90's.

Election of 1992

This was a watershed moment in U.S. political history as the last president from the Greatest Generation was replaced by the first president representing the Baby Boom Generation. Bush still had a numerical advantage over Bill Clinton of likely voters yet Clinton handily beat the incumbent. Why?

Bush did not seem to have a clear agenda for his second term in office. The Cold War and the threat of Communism that united the Republican Party was no longer a factor. Clinton was seen as younger and hipper. He played saxophone on the late night Arsenio Hall Show. Clinton was able to unite all the emerging P.C. power groups as well as the Black voters. Author Toni Morrison went so far as to refer to Clinton as the "First Black President."

Clinton utilized the new Internet to attract voters, as opposed to Bush who was surprised by a barcode reader in a local store. The DNC (Democratic National Committee) used new IMAX-sized picture screens to constantly remind voters that Bush had gone against his 1988 vow not to raise taxes. "Read my lips…no new taxes" was shown over and over again. To my mind this faux pas by Bush cost him re-election.

Nothing was out-of-bounds to the Clintons when it involved methods of voter solicitation.

AIDS became a major campaign issue in the '92 election. On national television an AIDS spokesman described what it was like to live with the AIDS virus. Without missing a beat, Clinton responded, "I feel your pain," a line he would use over and over again accompanied by his crocodile tears. His supporters referred to Clinton as "Bubba," while those on the other side referred to him as "Slick Willie." Love him or hate him, he was one effective politician.

Bill Clinton (1993-2001)

The former Governor of Arkansas was a two-term president who presided over the longest period of peacetime economic expansion in American history. In 1997 with the approval of the Republican Congress, he became the last president to balance the budget for the American nation. Generally this means lower taxes for all except the top one percent whom he penalized with a tax increase. He rewarded low income voters—15,000,000 strong—with reduced personal taxes. To reward Republican lawmakers, he signed the Omnibus Crime Bill in 1994 that expanded incarceration time and the death penalty for many more dozen crimes at the federal level. Joe Biden co-sponsored this bill. [In 2021, he can't get far enough away from this bill that he once proudly bragged about co-sponsoring.]

There is no doubt about Clinton's ability to run the government and get things accomplished, as he was able to work across party lines, especially in his second term. As opposed to Bush, Clinton was more successful in domestic affairs than foreign affairs.

The questions about Clinton concern his integrity. Going back to the late 60's Clinton opposed the Vietnam War which was laudable. However he attempted to use his Rhodes Scholarship to delay entry into the draft, knowing that a year later the draft might not be as dangerous. Luckily for him he drew a high lottery number in the draft and was spared the agony of having to make a tough choice—serve or hide.

Extramarital Affairs

I always viewed the Bill and Hillary Clinton's relationship as one of political expediency as opposed to a loving marriage. As Bill Clinton once remarked, "Vote for me and you get two presidents for the price of one." It was no secret that Hillary wanted to be the first female president from a very young age. Outside of photo-ops, they seemed to spend precious little quality time together and slowly but surely allegations of marital infidelity were made public by a media that fawned over him. Confronted with any number of accusers, Clinton was forced to pay settlements so that the most intimate details of these sexual encounters remained beyond the public view. Just when you thought Clinton had learned his lesson, the piece de resistance occurred with the Monica Lewinsky affair.

Clinton-Lewinsky Scandal

From 1995-1997 there were nine sexual encounters in the Oval Office between the President of the Free World and a government intern. It was the epitome of power and arrogance by a sitting president that damaged this country forever re-setting the moral compass of America. Male sexual predators had a role model in the White House. "If the president can get away with such behavior, why can't I?" Although impeached on two of four charges by Congress, he was found innocent as a ⅔ vote for removal could not be agreed to in the Senate.

"Slick Willie" had skated again. Remarkably, Hillary (sort of) forgave him and they embarked on an apology tour. Soon there was an army of Clinton Apologists blaming the media and Republicans for his predatory behavior. One final thought. I am not sure which came first, but the Clinton apology strategy mirrored a lot of P.C.

school policy now where students could do no wrong as parents and administrators made excuses for bad behavior. A coincidence? I think not. The # MeToo Movement has cast a negative light on Clinton's numerous infidelities while in the White House with the result that by 2018 no Democratic candidate asked for Clinton to campaign for him/her.

Whitewater Scandal

This was a plan to develop a section of Arkansas—Clinton's home state—into numerous vacation homes to be sold to the public. At the time Clinton did not have enough investment capital to get in on this land speculation deal, so he allegedly pressured David Hale into getting him a $300,000 loan to become part of the investment group who were all Arkansas cronies. To make a long story short, fifteen people were convicted of forty crimes associated with the development plan, but the Clintons were not. Susan McDougal refused to testify against the Clintons and was remanded to federal prison with three others. After eighteen months of incarceration, McDougal and the others were pardoned by President Clinton.

The Clintons received yet another reprieve as the media claimed they were bullied again for political reasons. The apology tour continued. An old adage is applicable here: " The dogs bark but the carnival moves on."

Domestic Affairs

When Clinton entered the White House, the profile of the opposite sex was immediately raised. Clinton was the first president to appoint more women and minority judges to the judiciary than white men. The year of the woman continued with Madeline

Albright becoming the first female Secretary of State and Janet Reno the first female Attorney General. Ruth Bader Ginsburg became the second female justice appointed to the Supreme Court and Hillary Clinton raised the profile of the First Lady in the White House. Clinton reinforced Roe vs. Wade arguing that abortion should be "safe…legal….rare," and under his administration the rate of abortion dropped over eighteen percent..

Clinton was the first president to support gay rights. He issued an executive order that outlawed discrimination based on sexual orientation in the federal civilian workforce. Another executive order allowed gays to serve in the military without harassment. This was known as "Don't ask, Don't Tell." On the other hand, Clinton would not support gay marriage until it was legalized and mainstreamed in 2009.

The Clinton Foundation was ostensibly set up to combat AIDS and global warming in the 1990's. There has been much criticism hurled at this foundation over the ensuing decades. Some describe it as a slush fund and favor bank for many shady investors, some of whom do not have American interests as a priority. There are many international players invested in it, so it is next to impossible to investigate.

Clinton's major domestic policy failure was the establishment of national health insurance, a 1993 bill rejected by Congress. Politically this probably hurt Hillary more as she took credit for drafting the bill. This idea continues to be an unresolved issue in America, though in 2021 the Supreme Court upheld the Obama ACA (Affordable Care Act).

Foreign Policy

This certainly was not Clinton's strong suit, as can be witnessed by several case studies.

1993—World Trade Center bombing. The first attempt by Islamic terrorists luckily resulted in mostly failure. Ramzi Yousef, the arrested mastermind of the failed attack, had this to say in Federal Court "...the attack of the WTC would be merely the first of such attacks..." Later he added that "insufficient funding had been a cause for failure." The Clinton Administration had been warned something bigger <u>was</u> going to occur, yet they did not investigate the allegations! Everyone knows what happened on 9/11/01.

1993—Operation Restore Hope. This was a U.S. initiative to carry out a U.S. plan to help abate starvation in Somalia. It quickly led to the Battle of Mogadishu—immortalized by the movie Black Hawk Down—that became a complete fiasco. Two U.S. helicopters were shot down, eighteen Americans killed and television images showed dead American bodies being dragged in the street by Somali terrorists. Clinton had to end this initiative but not until 1994.

1994—Rwandan Genocide. Up to a million tribal Tutsis were slaughtered by the Hutus from a neighboring country. They asked the U.S. for help but the Clinton Administration declined, with the Somalia fiasco still fresh in everyone's mind. Clinton later regretted his decision not to offer aid.

1994—Clinton initiates NAFTA (North American Free Trade Agreement) between the U.S., Canada, and Mexico. It did eliminate tariffs, but many American companies either relocated or outsourced work especially to Mexico to decrease labor and production costs. Overall this badly hurt the U.S. economy and was replaced recently by Trump's USMCA Plan.

2000- U.S. - China Relations Act

This opened the door for normal non-tariffed trade with China. At the time it benefited the U.S. but not so today. U.S. manufacturing has lost 5,000,000 or more jobs since 2000. Since the entry of China into the WTO (World Trade Organization) in 2001 the decline of U.S.manufacturing jobs accelerated.

Exit Polls

Before the end of his second term, another moniker had been added to the Clinton legacy. "Clinton Fatigue" entered the lexicon. The public had had enough of the Clintons and their dramas. Many wished they would just ride off into the sunset but history was not finished with the Clintons, especially Hillary.

Though given high performance ratings, the final CNN/USA Today/Gallup Poll found that 68% of voters thought he (Clinton) would be more remembered for personal scandal rather than accomplishment. ABC News, a huge Clinton toady, declared, "You can't trust him, he's got weak morals and ethics—and he's done a heck of a job." Upon his retirement, I read an article in Sports Illustrated magazine that really did not shock me. He and the author played a round of golf and the author remarked that almost every hole was an ethical adventure— attempted cheating by the former chief executive.

Senator Walking Eagle

Like her husband who joked, "If you elect me, you get two presidents," Hillary was an opportunist who also sought a path to the White House. Knowing they both needed more exposure, the Clintons moved to New York State in the late 1990's. Hillary, my favorite carpetbagger, saw an opportunity to become a U.S. Senator from New York in 2000. [You might recall that a carpetbagger was a derogatory name given to Northern opportunists who fleeced the South during Reconstruction.] I did not know what to make of Hillary as she stepped forward to the microphone for her first press conference, TV cameras rolling. She picked up and put on a Yankee cap and proclaimed "I've always been a Yankee fan!" This pronouncement from a person who grew up a Cubs fan from Chicago. Remember I said the Clintons would do anything for a vote? I saw right through this phony baloney and that's all I needed to know about her, but it wasn't just me. To Wit:

Senator Hillary Clinton was invited to address a major gathering of the American Indian Nation in upstate New York. She spoke for nearly an hour on her future plans of increasing every Native Americans' standard of living, should she one day become the first female president. She referred to her career as a N.Y. senator, how she signed "Yes" for every Indian issue that came to her desk for approval.

Although the senator was vague on the details of her plan, she seemed most enthusiastic about her future ideas for helping her "red sisters and brothers."

At the conclusion of her speech, the Tribes presented the senator with a plaque inscribed with her new Indian name—Walking Eagle. The proud senator then departed in her motorcade, waving to the crowds.

A news reporter later inquired to the group of chiefs of how they selected the new name given to the senator. They explained that Walking Eagle is the name given to a bird so full of shit it can no longer fly!

Global Warming

There has been a great deal of debate concerning global warming over the last thirty years and former Clinton Vice President Al Gore's documentary film <u>An Inconvenient Truth</u> made it a hot button issue. The crux of Gore's message is that humans have messed up the planet and corrective measures must be taken quickly to save the earth.

In 1970, my college geology professor lectured about this subject long before it became an issue. I learned that the earth goes through hundred year and thousand year cycles of variable weather. The earth now is currently in a cold phase. This is one of the few times in the earth's geologic history where there is significant ice at both the North Pole and the South Pole. There were ages where there was ice at only one pole—or none at all! As recently as the late 1980's polar ice glaciers were advancing towards the U.S. at the rate of six inches per year, the next ice age.

About the same time Joe Bastardi, who was the chief climatologist for the Weather Channel, warned his television audience to "buckle up" and get ready for at least twenty-five years of erratic weather patterns. History has proved him correct especially in North America that has always had the most extreme weather of all the continents. That extreme weather has morphed into the bizarre as the last thirty years have clearly illustrated.

Technology and Science

Computer usage became more widespread in the 90's with the advent of the PC (personal computer). Utilizing the World Wide Web (Internet), PC use grew from fifteen percent to thirty-five percent of the population by 1999. In the same year, twenty-five percent of the population had cell phones while fifty percent of the population now had access to the Internet. As noted the Clinton campaign used the Internet to get out its message, while the Republicans were not up to speed yet on the advantages of this new technology. With the invention of CD/DVD technology, the VCR cassette taping system was made obsolete. By 1998 Apple had introduced the iMac PC Computer into the mainstream of America. The 90's saw the birth of all the main online companies utilized today such as IMDB (1993), Amazon (1994), Yahoo (1995), HotMail (1996), and the now monolithic Google (1998).

The Big Three American automakers—GM, Ford, and Chrysler—changed in the 90's and while Ford was stable, Chrysler had to merge first with Mercedes-Benz until 2001 then with Fiat in 2014 to survive. The Toyota Camry became the biggest seller in America from the late 90's into the 2000's.

The scientific world made strides too with its eyes on the future. The 1990 Hubble Space Telescope expanded the sightings of distant galaxies not seen before. Scientists now think the expanding universe may have originated 13.7 billion years ago. In 1992-1993 the GPS System became fully operational. This system involves the coordination of twenty four orbiting satellites and it is the basis for the new American communication using computers. It will need to be updated and protected as Russia and China are building competing systems with the ability to disable the American GPS System.

Back on Earth, in the same year, scientists were perfecting stem cell research and gene therapy. Gene therapy has led to the creation of so-called designer babies. One day maybe all the terminal diseases will be eliminated by stem cell research which would result in a human being with an unlimited lifespan. That is a concern and raises a myriad of ethical questions. The first example of artificial life was a cloned mammal—Dolly the sheep—in the UK in 1997.

Controversial Events

I chose a number of events inside America that have had long-term repercussions beyond the 1990's.

1992—The 500th anniversary of Columbus' discovery of America. Unfortunately there were many protests of this event claiming Columbus was infamous for being a genocidist, killing or enslaving thousands of Caribbean Island natives. In 2020 the statues of Columbus throughout America were one of the primary targets of anarchist's attacks. Spoiler alert—there is very little archival evidence to support the conclusion that he was a mass killer. It simply is not true. There is more of a case to be made for the mass murder of natives in the U.S. during Westward Expansion. Though it is true that Columbus conflicted with the native Caribs on Hispaniola, their overall population was barely reduced with the result that the Caribbean Islands and Central America where Columbus explored have always had large and stable population bases.

1995—O.J. Simpson "Trial of the Century." Simpson allegedly slashed the throat of his wife and a male companion. This event occurred during the 1994 NBA Finals. The cameras left the game and filmed Simpson's slow-motion escape attempt in a friend's Bronco. 95,000,000 people watched the police "chase" a suicidal Simpson. The Bronco ran out of gas and he was arrested.

In the 1995 trial, he was acquitted of all the charges. Shoddy police work and an all-Black L.A. jury, still smarting from the Rodney King incident in L.A., exonerated him. Many jurors were recognized from the community and were threatened by the crowds and surely feared for their lives. I remember being in my classroom when the verdict was announced over the PA system. The Black kids jumped for joy while the others were quiet. It seems like the racial divide in America will never be bridged.

In the same year was the occurrence of the deadliest domestic incident in U.S. history—the truck bombing of a government building in Oklahoma City by Timothy McVeigh and Terry Nichols. These were two white men angry at the government. They loaded up a truck with bombs and destroyed a number of buildings killing 168 people including pregnant women and small children. McVeigh was unrepentant and was executed. Nichols received a life sentence without parole. Government buildings and our foreign embassies now are protected by concrete barriers to prevent future incidents. I have no doubt that these two mass-murderers have been the inspiration for a lot of the domestic terror that is occuring in America right now.

1996—California becomes the first state to legalize marijuana for [wink! wink!] medicinal purposes. Now other states have legalized this drug for sale to the general public. That this happened under the Clinton Administration comes as no surprise to me. As if drunk driving was not a big enough problem, stoned driving is yet another social issue to be dealt with.

1998—Matthew Shepard Murder. A gay man, Shepard was found murdered and left in a field near the University of Wyoming. His murder became a cause that energized the LGBTQ community and brought many more gays out into the open. Today they are a very powerful voting bloc, largely in support of so-called progressive causes and their respective candidates for political office.

Music

As the country became more fragmented, so did the music genres. Compared to the upbeat 80's, the music of the 90's was, in my opinion, downbeat, crude, full of angst, and self-pity, and in some cases suicidal. Unlike the 80's, the web made these genres international. The roots of continuous social unrest and chaos of 2020 in Seattle and Portland have their roots in the 90's. The vibe fostered by the Grunge movement, that emanated from the Pacific Northwest, aided the present mob mentality that seems hellbent on destroying America and its institutions.

Perhaps it was the lousy weather of the Pacific Northwest or maybe it was the cloak of P.C. madness that enveloped it, but Grunge, the leading rock genre of the 90's comes across as depressing. Bands like the Stone Temple Pilots, Collective Soul, Pearl Jam, and Nirvana have a dark edge to their music. Kurt Cobain, the poster boy of Nirvana, joined the rock suicide club also at age twenty seven along with Jimi Hendrix, Janis Joplin, Jim Morrison, and later Amy Winehouse. Big hair metal music and punk rock were replaced by rave music with concert attendees getting their angst out in the mosh pit, gyrating to Moby and others.

Dr. Dre in <u>The Chronic</u> provided the template for Gangsta Rap, the scourge for all teachers trying to maintain discipline in the classroom and attempting to instill values. With pants below their "cheeks" and sneering attitudes toward authority, tradition, and the female gender, gangsta rap was the bane of the educational hierarchy. For better or worse, hip hop became the best-selling music genre of the mid 1990's. MTV moved away from video productions and decided to promote rap in the 1990's, adding to its growth.

On the other hand, pop acts like the Spice Girls presented a different message. Mirroring their success arose other teen acts such as Britney Spears, Christina Aguilera, and boy bands like NSync and the Backstreet Boys. Country music garnered a new audience of rock n rollers who did like Grunge, rave or rap. Garth Brooks broke all the records for record sales and concert attendance during the decade. Other country stars were Billy Ray Cyrus, Shania Twain, and Reba McEntire.

Television

TV was heavily influenced by pop culture. Baywatch became the most watched show in history. Beverly Hills 90210 was not far behind. With 600 episodes, The Simpsons has become iconic TV for its social commentary. Sex and the City's frank portrayal of relationships and sexuality caused controversy and acclaim leading to more progressive subject matter to be covered on TV in the twenty first century.

Related to television was the appearance of Playstation in 1996. It became the top-selling game console but created a nation of couch potatoes who did not see the light of day. This generation has had problems deciphering reality from fantasy that has led to a myriad of social problems besides obesity. Children playing in the streets is music to my ears, as it keeps them away from these mind-numbing and mind-controlling computers programmed with all the attendant trash.

Demographics

Exploring demographics gives context to the 90's. Millennials were still being born during this decade and the oldest members reached their early twenties. Generation X would have been young adults or teens at the onset while older members were nearly forty as the decade concluded. Baby Boomers ranged from their upper thirties at the beginning of the decade and in some cases into their mid fifties at the end of the decade.

The difference in generational values can clearly be seen. The older generations who are more self-actualized have gained their values by real time experience. I am not disputing the fact that the media affects all generations. I do know that as a young person I was outdoors playing and learning to interact and become a problem solver. Education was inside the classroom as well as out of it, so I became an independent thinker reaching conclusions based on many modes of living learned in real time.

As a teacher and sociologist, I have watched the younger generations take their cues from the media while glued to their computers or cell phones. Their values seem to come from media personalities or website information, not the real world but the virtual one. David Riesman's book "The Lonely Crowd" differentiates the inner-directed self from the outer-directed self. In the former people make decisions based on their own life experiences while in the latter judgments and values are made for people by others.

With the changeover to online learning in the classroom it became easier to tap into alternate sources of information. No longer were textbooks written the Bible. "History" could be accessed easily on a Google website. Who is to know if their sources are real or fictitious? Traditions were de-emphasized or challenged by the liberal P.C. educational bureaucracy. The scary reality was that in the late 1990's the indoctrination was just in its infancy.

America was also in its infancy in regards to the widespread coarsening and dumbing down of its culture not witnessed before, at least to this degree. Up to this point in history, America had always sought to better itself, striving for excellence and accomplishment. Now the "slacker dude" and Valley Girl cultures were in vogue with the bar lowered for individual and group behavioral expectations—the new subnormal if you will. Being spaced-out was "in" as illustrated by the popular TV series "Beavis and Butthead" and a Hollywood blockbuster "Dumb and Dumber."

Body piercings and tatting reflected the counterculture of the 90's much as long hair defined the 60's. The Rap Culture encouraged its acolytes to act like gangstas and promoted an air of false bravado and swagger. It also encouraged the disrespect of the female gender and preached messages of anti-authority and gang solidarity embracing the hatred of police and a no snitch policy.

Disrespect became rampant. I almost lost my teaching job attempting to address disrespect in my classroom as the P.C. culture excused all student bad behavior and put me on trial. It took me three years to get my job back.

Today this disrespect has become more virulent and has gone to the next level. The 2020 rioters have expanded the disrespect toward society in general, assaulting authoritarianism, burning down businesses, and tearing down monuments while weak-kneed politicians did nothing in an election year.

Does America again want to become a "House Divided"?

CHAPTER 51

2000's

AS THE CURTAIN CLOSED ON THE OLD MILLENNIUM, the American people looked to the new millennium with optimism, hoping that a plethora of societal problems could finally be worked out beginning with a smooth Presidential election in 2000. Not! Instead the deep divisions in society resulted in a Y2K constitutional crisis triggered by the hotly disputed results of the presidential election.

The election of 2000 should have been a slam dunk win for the Democrats with Clinton's Vice President Al Gore as the new standard bearer. The economy was in great shape with a balanced budget and the Republican nominee George Bush Jr. was seen as a not-too-bright opponent parodied in the persona of Alfred E. Newman by Mad Magazine. What happened?

In my opinion, largely as a result of Clinton Fatigue, the election became the closest in American political history. Although Gore won the popular vote, Bush won the Electoral College vote 271-266. [To reiterate, when I discussed the Constitution, 270 electoral votes is the magic number for clinching victory.] The State of Florida decided the election. Because of voting irregularities, Florida's Supreme Court ordered a recount. In the recount Bush won by a mere 537 popular votes. Even though the Democrats set up the voting rules for Florida they would not accept defeat and took their case to the Supreme Court of America. In a 5-4 vote the Justices would not allow another recount and Bush was declared the winner!

Clinton and his wife showed their disdain for the verdict in a number of ways. Clinton issued an unprecedented, 456 pardons before leaving the White House, 141 in his last official day in office. On their way out of the White House, they fleeced items from the White House that were not their own personal property. This would not be the last public display of arrogance by the Clintons towards the American public.

Besides the disputed election of 2000, the other story that generated the most buzz in Y2K was the hype surrounding the change in the millennium. Fear and rumor abounded. Religious zealots claimed this would be the Judgment Day and life as we knew it would come to and end. In the techno-scientific world there was worry that computer software would not shift smoothly and that among other consequences all of man's satellites would fall out of the sky and the technological world run by computers would grind to a halt.

Fortunately the major companies of the world had initiated installation of new software in 1999 so the world was "saved" from an armageddon of sorts. As I noted in my new diary of 2000 on January 1st, "so much for the hype surrounding Y2K phobia!" As an aside, in January, according to Yuletide tradition, Christmas trees are supposed to be taken down twelve days after Christmas Day hence the Christmas anthem "The Twelve Days of Christmas."

The lame duck year of the Clinton Administration with a few exceptions proved to be remarkably unremarkable. Terrorism was a part of life now, both nationally and internationally. In October two Al Qaeda suicide bombers placed 400 pounds of explosives in a small boat and successfully torpedoed the U.S.S Cole, a naval destroyer at anchor near the shoreline in Yemen, a new hotbed of Islamic terrorism. The explosion killed seventeen U.S. sailors, wounded thirty nine and took the Cole out of commission for a long period of time. In retrospect, this incident became the harbinger of a much larger event that transpired in 2001.

Russia provided some unexpected angst for the world. In August, the submarine Kursk sank in the Barents Sea. Although this sea is near the Russian coast, it was later discovered that the Kursk was carrying an arsenal of nuclear weapons that could have been triggered by its submersion. Fortunately this did not occur. In December, under some pressure, the Russians finally closed the third and last reactor at the Chernobyl power plant, which had been the site of the biggest atomic meltdown in history. The station surrounding the reactor was also permanently shuttered.

The deep divisions in America were seen more clearly than ever in the world of entertainment. Though Faith Hill had the number one single record, "Breathe," rapper and bad boy Eminem sold the most albums by far. Grunge had been quickly replaced by Hip Hop as the culture became more coarsened. By the end of the decade in 2009 Eminem had sold 32,000,000 records. The runner-up were the Beatles, though disbanded for thirty years, with 30,000,000 records sold. The total polarization of American culture could clearly be seen in its musical prerogatives.

There were several precedents that came to be in the first year of the millennium. India joined the one billion population club along with China. Unfortunately, these two neighboring countries do not get along and both have nuclear arsenals. Also on the international front, the ozone layer had its largest single year increase in size. In this case there is good news. The ozone layer has recovered by one to three percent since 2000 and is forecasted to recover completely in the Northern Hemisphere and mid-latitude areas in the 2030's followed by the Southern Hemisphere around mid century and Antarctica in the 2060's. Nationally, Vermont becomes the first state to legalize civil unions for same-sex couples and lastly Hillary Clinton aka "Walking Eagle" is elected to the U.S. Senate from the State of New York.

2000 began with Y2K paranoia and ended with a still hotly disputed presidential election. In between these two goal posts the year was tame compared to the turbulence of preceding years. This relative calm would abruptly change when George Bush Jr. took over the White House and in short order the you-know-what would hit the fan.

George Bush Jr. (2001-2009)

Familiarly known as "Dubya," Bush became the second son of a father to become president, the other son was John Quincy Adams the son of John Adams. A self-described average student, he nevertheless graduated from Yale with a BA in history and, although failing to enter the U of Texas law school, was able to get a MBA from Harvard Business School. He flew warplanes for the Texas and Alabama Air National Guard then worked in the oil industry. He later co-owned the Texas Rangers baseball team before becoming the two-term governor of Texas. He had alcohol issues as a young man but with a strong Christian faith and support from his wife, Laura, gave up that demon early in life.

War on Terror

Every generation faces an existential crisis. For the (mostly) Silent Generation, it was the "Day of Infamy," sneak attack on Pearl Harbor by the Japanese leading to U.S. involvement in WWII. For today's Millennials and Generation Z, it is the unknown and uncertainty caused by the Wuhan Chinese Flu (Covid). For George Bush, the Baby Boomers, and Generation X, it was the 9/11/01 attacks conducted on multiple U.S. targets orchestrated by Islamic terrorists funded by Osama Bin Laden and his organization, Al-Qaeda. George Bush will be forever linked with the events of that day and its aftermath.

Everyone who witnessed the event has a tale to tell. I want to share a few observations. First look at the date the terrorists choose - 9/11—synonymous with the world emergency. The terrorist pilots trained in Vero Beach, Florida at a small airport close to where I used to own a condo. It was reported that the terrorist pilots were only taking lessons in take-offs, not landings. Some of the "pilots" warned some of the locals whom they liked not to go to New York City during the time period of the attack. How did this information not get to the authorities?

I knew a couple of fire department captains who survived the fall of the WTC towers only because they received new site orders at the last minute. Living only twenty miles east of Manhattan, I recall the deathly quiet of the following days and like a nightmare come true, I no longer saw the Twin Towers on the western horizon. It was stunningly surreal and you could barely function, pondering the enormity of what did and *could* happen. Devoid of any air traffic over the metropolitan area of NY, the skies were eerily quiet. On the roadways, the usual obnoxious horn-honking came to a halt as people were respecting the moment in time. George Bush was in a grade school and reading with children when an aid whispered the tragedy in his ear. He sat there stunned yet all the twisted media could do was chastise him for not vaulting out of his seat, as if he could turn back time.

From the Oval Office that evening, he promised the American people a strong response. He also urged the nation to come together and give comfort to the grieving families. Three days later at Ground Zero in lower Manhattan atop the rubble, Bush addressed all present and a worldwide audience when he announced through a megaphone, "I can hear you. The rest of the world hears you. And the people who knocked down these buildings will hear from all of us soon."

Nine days later Bush condemned Bin Laden and Al Qaeda and issued an ultimatum to the Taliban regime in Afghanistan where Bin Laden was operating to "hand over the terrorists or share their fate." These words fell on deaf ears. Operating with almost complete support, Bush set out to even the score by initiating two wars, one in Iraq and the other in Afghanistan. These wars initiated by the Bush Administration became the centerpiece of his foreign policy known as the Bush Doctrine. The idea was for the U.S. to be preemptive and prevent future attacks from happening. There was huge popular support for both wars as the people thought that Islamic terrorism would finally be eradicated from the face of the earth. Bush also pushed Congress to ratify the Patriot Act (2003) that increased the use of wiretaps, coordinated federal and state investigations of terrorism, and expanded the list of crimes and activities that could bring charges of terrorism.

The government also authorized the establishment of the Department of Homeland Security, the largest addition to the federal bureaucracy since FDR's New Deal before WWII. Employing nearly a quarter million workers, this agency is responsible for public security i.e. anti-terror, border security, immigration, and customs. Many of those on the Left who particularly despise I.C.E. agents—the people who round up and prosecute illegal aliens—have reacted by setting up sanctuary cities and refusing to obey federal laws of immigration. According to the Constitution federal law supersedes state and local laws so sanctuary cities are getting away with illegal activity. Again, either we have a nation of laws or we don't.

Besides the Bush Doctrine, there were other notable accomplishments in Bush's first term as president. A big proponent of education, he and Congress enacted the No Child Left Behind Act that required state testing in order to get federal money for school districts. This act had good intentions but the devil was in the details. I was still teaching at the time and the state tests were a nightmare. They required too much classroom time and the language of the questions methodology left some of us scratching our heads. There was no way the kids in middle and high school would pass these tests. The backlash was dramatic as many parents opted out of subjecting their kids to these tests that certainly did not increase the motivation and joy for learning. The result was that the push to maintain this law mostly fizzled out.

Being a member of the Baby Boom generation, Bush also got Congress to pass a bill for Medicare part D that partially offset the high cost of prescription drugs for seniors. Yes, it is a form of socialism, but it makes prescription drugs more affordable for seniors on fixed income. Bush and his Congress increased funding for AIDS research and being a good conservative Christian got the Partial-Birth Abortion Ban Act passed making illegal late-term abortions. How anyone can favor infanticide is beyond me except in very rare cases. Bush was a master politician a la Clinton and was able to work across the aisle. Closely identified with the oil industry he nevertheless, in his first term, made Texas the leading producer of electricity in America from alternative power sources.

Bush's first term of office was a relative success as he kept America safe from further terrorist attacks, but his approval rating sank quickly in his second term of office due to lack of oversight, slow decision-making, and the overwhelming cost to America incurred from the ongoing wars draining the blood and treasure of America.

The military "victory" in the Iraq War was relatively swift. Saddam Hussein was captured hiding in a hole in 2003 and executed in 2004. The U.S. attempted to set up a democracy in Iraq, but it has become a democracy in name only as other pockets of resistance opened up throughout the country. In 2007 Congress authorized a surge of another 21,500 troops to Iraq but did not set up a deadline for their withdrawal. Currently Iraq is embroiled in a civil war with no end in sight. The cost to America is in the billions.

The Bush Administration also came under fire for interrogation techniques used on prisoners, the main target being waterboarding. This technique of enhanced interrogation/torture involves covering the face of the suspect with cloth, inclining the shackled body then pouring water through the cloth to elicit a gag reflex, simulating drowning. This technique became outlawed once Bush left office.

Meanwhile, the Afghanistan War is drawing down under the Trump Administration, but is now the longest war in U.S. history surpassing the Vietnam war. This also has cost billions to conduct and the U.S. has lost thousands of soldiers in the war on terror. [Biden has officially ended the war in Afghanistan and wants to have all the troops on American soil by the end of the summer of 2021. Biden refuses to leave a few thousand soldiers there "just in case." We will see what happens in that war-torn country, which is still the home base for terrorist organizations that want to cripple the United States.]

Because of the wars and other events, the economy took a big nosedive during Bush's second term. There was a housing crisis as two government loan agencies, Fannie Mae and Freddie Mac, granted loans to first-time homeowners who could not repay these mortgages once the interest rate spiked upward. As the housing market imploded, so did the rest of the economy. The U.S. entered its deepest recession since WWII. Banks and insurance agencies toppled like dominoes and the government was forced to bail out these large banks by the TARP Act, government purchase of toxic stocks being sold by these failing lending institutions. An example of this business failure was the gigantic Enron Company, an energy conglomerate. Management made bad decisions leading to every employee being terminated, losing all their assets and pensions.

More fuel was added to the fire with the arrival of Hurricane Katrina (2005). Not only the costliest storm at the time in U.S. history, it created yet another black eye for Bush. Similar to 9/11, he was criticized for a slow reaction to this disaster. FEMA did not send out inspectors until three days after the hurricane had exited. This area around New Orleans is still being rebuilt some fifteen years later.

Mixed messaging and questionable legislation continued to plague the administration. Though strengthening the U.S.-Mexico border with 6,000 new agents, Bush also got the Temporary Guest Workers Program through Congress. This allowed twelve million illegals to stay in America on work visas until the next wave replaced them. Of course they never left and though the country rails about immigration reform, including a path to citizenship for illegals, they are still in limbo in 2021. Many conservatives at the time never forgave Bush for this open-door type of a policy for those entering illegally. Though Bush once said "America is addicted to oil" and pushed for alternative energy, he nevertheless backtracked on a ban to offshore oil drilling when gas prices spiked in 2008. The bottom line is that the national debt soared at the end of his administration along with high unemployment and a glut of houses were vacant in the broken housing market. It seemed like the U.S. was about to enter another depression.

Bush's views on the scientific world also came into question. Being a good Christian, he opposed stem cell research because it used abortive human embryos for research. He did not believe in cloning of any kind. He was also indecisive in regards to the issue of global warming. There was no major legislation proposed as he did not fully buy into the global warming theory.

He initiated an agreement with the country of India that at the time received little notice but today is of enormous importance. India is the world's largest democracy and signed an alliance with the U.S. known as the India-U.S. Civil Nuclear Agreement. Both nations have many nuclear weapons and they allied themselves together. India also sends the U.S. information on terrorist activity in that area. India also has partnered with the U.S. against Communist China, who recently tried to push across their border with India but were rebuffed.

The Bush Administration will be noted as the last president elected by the old Republican Party. That party's base consisted of white middle-class voters, evangelical Christians (moral majority), and old-line Wall Street Fortune 500 companies (not including Silicon Valley). Backing up the base was strong support by the military and police personnel and enough hard-working immigrants that the Bush Presidency welcomed into America.

The Bush Administration began with a full head of steam but ran out of gas nearing the finish line much like a runner who starts the race too quickly only to lose in the end. Bush lost oversight of his government, and his subordinates helped to bring about the greatest recession since WWII. Fortunately there were no more domestic attacks during his eight year run but it was clearly time for a change in direction

Tesla

There has been a lot of discussion but not a lot of success in the area of renewable energy and its practical application. One exception has been the formation of Tesla Inc. formerly Tesla Motors. The Tesla line of electric automobiles has gained a foothold in the automotive industry hitherto dominated by gasoline-powered internal combustion automobiles.

Musk did not want to partner with traditional automakers. He realized that much of car advertising and capital was allocated to repairs and service that his electric cars would require a lot less of. Musk chose to advertise online and direct potential customers to Tesla showrooms in malls and other high-traffic areas. By constantly updating the hardware as well as the software, Musk wanted to show that his cars would be more reliable in the long run avoiding many of the maintenance and repair issues that were expected to occur in the operation of gasoline-powered cars. The Tesla marketing strategy was to target affluent buyers first with flashy, attention-getting high-end cars costing over $100,000 then moving into larger markets with more affordable models.

This strategy has yielded some success. Tesla controls over eighty percent of the electric car market as of 2020. Though their low-end models are still pricey and not sold in great volume, they have made inroads in the market recently surpassing 1,000,000 sales. In 2020 Consumer Reports designated Tesla with the highest "overall customer satisfaction" of any car manufacturer.

CHAPTER 52

Barack Obama

(2009-2017)

THE FAILURES OF THE BUSH ADMINISTRATION led to a watershed moment in American history: the election of the first African-American President in U.S. history, Barack Obama in 2009. Based on a campaign slogan of "Hope and Change," a new coalition of voters rejected the conservative nature of recent administrations and replaced it with an administration that fundamentally wanted to change America in a number of ways. At the time of his ascension to the White House, Obama was the most liberal member of the U.S. Senate and became the most liberal of all the previous forty-four presidents.

Born in Hawaii, Barack "Barry" Obama was the son of a Kenyan father and a white mother originally from Kansas. Growing up in Chicago, Obama graduated from Columbia University (NY) in 1983 and later from Harvard Law School. Returning to Chicago, he became a community organizer and parlayed that into political office as an Illinois State Senator (1997-2004) then subsequently elected U.S. Senator from Illinois (2005-2008). Obama received national attention in July 2004 for his well-received Democratic

National Convention keynote address that further raised his profile and thrust him to the forefront of national politics, even though as a U.S. Senator he sponsored no original legislation.

Before detailing the Obama Administration, it is important to note the influence others had on his formative years. Though not around much in his maturing years, his father nevertheless shaped his values especially in regard to oppression. Obama Sr. had a deep resentment of colonization and especially resented the British Empire. He also disliked the neo-colonialism of the United States, especially when it annexed Hawaii, his adopted home state, under what he and others considered to be questionable circumstances. Barack Obama Jr. would become an advocate for oppressed groups both in the U.S. and abroad and his policies reflected this orientation.

He had a controversial relationship with his pastor, the Reverend Jeremiah Wright of the Trinity United Church of Christ. They first met in the late 1980's when Obama was a community organizer in Chicago and Wright officiated at the wedding of Barack and Michelle Obama, and later at their children's baptisms. ABCNews released excerpts of sermons where White launched into an anti-American tirades refusing to condemn terrorist attacks against America. "God bless America?... no… God damn America!" thundered Wright from his pulpit. Gradually Obama disassociated himself from Wright but only after these news releases were made public. Bill Ayers of the Weather Underground, who bombed government buildings in the 60's and 70's, was an associate of Obama and broached the idea of using violence but because Obama and his wife were devout Christians this method of extreme change was rejected.

An avowed liberal, Obama embraced the teachings of Saul Alinsky, a radical author whose most famous book was entitled

"Rules for Realistic Radicals: A Pragmatic Primer for Realistic Radicals"(1971). In his book Alinsky referred to Lucifer as the original radical opposing the establishment (of God). Alinsky's goal was to create a guide for future community organizers to coordinate low income communities "the have-nots," into a potent political force by using social, political, economic, and legal power. By creating an "enemy" it would unite the masses into a potent political force. To answer criticism for actions taken, Alinsky offered three methods to deal with criticism—deny, deflect and ignore—which became the buzzwords of radical dogma. Rahm Emanuel, Obama's first Chief of Staff, employed this cynical view of change by stating, "Never let a good crisis go to waste." In fairness the Nixon Administration had used similar techniques in the 60's-70's. When responding to a hostile question from the press Nixon would deflect by responding, "That is not the real question…the real question is…" then proceed to answer his own question. No wonder the press nicknamed him "Tricky Dick."

No other presidency in my lifetime had more expectations and hoopla surrounding it than the courtship of Barack Obama. It was as if Moses had descended from Mt. Sinai with the Ten Commandments and was going to lead his people to the Promised Land. The only other president with such high hopes assigned to him was JFK in the 1960's. But even JFK did not have the total protection of the media, as did Obama. Kennedy's scandals were exposed and his Camelot presidency over in an instant courtesy of an assassin's bullet(s) before completing his first term in office. Obama would serve two terms in office with the media firmly in the palm of his hand. Obama's accomplishments were limited; perhaps his biggest accomplishment was breaking the racial barrier to the White House. The general populace would hear little of the scandals during his eight years in office. He was the chosen one, ergo hands off.

The Obama Administration's first significant action was to deal with a country mired in a deep recession as the Bush Years ended. Obama and Congress passed the American Recovery and Reinvestment Act (2009) that bailed out Wall Street and the business world. This was a stimulus package of government funds to prevent the financial world from total collapse. This proved to be a necessary evil as it kept the business world afloat but increased the national debt of America more than the total of all the previous presidencies combined. In 2010 the Dodd-Frank Act attempted to regulate the lending of bank monies to business to offset another recession. It did not however set up guidelines for the usage of the original stimulus money.

It is important to note here a fundamental realignment of business and politics. Before Obama, Wall Street and big business worked hand-in-hand with the Republican side of the aisle. One of the biggest targets of the 60's protests was the military-industrial complex that funded the Vietnam War. With the failure of the Bush Administration and the rescue actions of Obama, was it any wonder that the big campaign donors of Wall Street now patronized the Democratic Party while more-or-less abandoning the Republicans? Obama had helped to create a new money-making machine for the Democratic National Party.

The Affordable Care Act (Obamacare) passed in 2010 will be the enduring legacy accomplishment of the Obama Administration. This was a government program that guaranteed health care to everyone who previously was without this protection. It also granted health insurance to those who had preexisting medical conditions and had been rejected for coverage by other private insurers.

Overall this act has proved to be good for some and bad for others. Some paid less for Obamacare but many had to pay more. Obama stated, "If you like your health plan you will be able to keep your plan," yet by 2013 millions received termination of policy notices. The other sticking point of Obamacare was the individual mandate. This forced everyone without insurance to get a policy or face a fine. This issue went to the Supreme Court, where shockingly a "conservative" court ruled in favor of the mandate. As protests persisted, Congress eventually zeroed out the penalty for not having insurance. The existence of Obamacare continues to be litigated to this day, though in the spring of 2021 the Supreme Court ruled that the ACA was constitutional and will remain the law of the land in terms of health coverage in the U.S.

The Obama Years were also marked by some symbolic accomplishments. In 2009, Obama won the Nobel Peace Prize—not so much for a concrete action taken but more for the general feeling of hope that seemed to emanate from his administration. In 2016 Obama signed the Paris Peace Accord that dealt with the prevention of greenhouse gases that seemed to increase global warming. After signing on, however, Obama did not take a strong leadership standard with the Green New Deal preferring to defer to others or "leading from behind" per his critics. In his second term in office, Obama advanced the rights of LGBTQ Americans. Obama's thinking on this subject had "evolved" and as a result same sex marriage was legalized in America in 2015. [Obama and his wife had never supported same sex marriage and his critics pointed out that his evolution had more to do with political expediency going forward.] However it should be noted that Obama was becoming a firm advocate of the LGBTQ community by signing into law the 2010 Don't Ask Don't Tell Repeal Act that allowed gays, lesbians, and transgender people to serve openly in the military without recrimination.

On the other hand Obama was the first president not to celebrate a traditional Christmas in the White House. This negative symbolism was attached to the birther issue—whether or not Obama was a true American Christian given his middle name (Hussein). This precedent prolonged the birther controversy for a while longer before it was finally put to rest.

Foreign Policy

A common theme that ran through Obama's statements was the idea that the U.S. must atone for its past policy whether it be about its colonialism or war against Islamic terror, etc. [Obama never used the term Islamic terrorism.] The core of his message articulated that America was a flawed nation and must seek redemption by apologizing for its "sins." In Obama's mind there was no such thing as American Exceptionalism. Obama's apology tour was conveyed to nearly three billion people in Europe, the Muslim world, and the Americas. This apology tour with the inherent corollary of "leading from behind" had the net effect of weakening American power and strength by decimating the military budget and leaving the U.S. and its allies more vulnerable to future attacks.

The legacy of the Obama foreign policy especially in regards to the Middle East can best be described as a hot mess. Although Osama bin Laden was killed by U.S. Navy Seals, war was escalated in Afghanistan by a U.S. troop surge. Though Obama claimed he ended the war in Iraq, he left it a decimated and undefended country open to a new enemy—Isis—who formed a large terror-based caliphate in what had been the country of Iraq. Obama mocked Isis by calling it the "JV of Terrorism," which only made the Caliphate larger and more deadly and later required the Trump Administration to destroy the Caliphate, though Isis forces still remain at large.

The Obama Administration also removed another dictator from power, Muammar Gaddafi of Libya. This resulted in the Benghazi disaster. In the process of ousting Gaddafi from power, four American diplomats were left behind in an under-defended American embassy and were killed by Libyan rebels. The diplomats had pleaded for military reinforcements but the Secretary of State, Hillary Clinton never reacted to their plight. This incident would be used against her in her unsuccessful bid for the presidency and removed some of the good vibes surrounding the ouster of Gaddafi who had been a thorn in the side of the U.S. and his own people for many years.

The JCPOA (Iran Nuclear Deal) of 2015 was probably the biggest fiasco of Obama foreign policy. Obama thought he could persuade the mad mullahs (religious rulers) of Iran to give up their ambitions to build nuclear weapons by offering them billions of dollars in bribe money. Iran did not even have to agree to nuclear inspections of their weapons-producing facilities. Iran took some of that money and funded proxy wars against the U.S. Terrorist groups like Hamas and Hezbollah were in effect killing American military personnel with American money! The Trump Administration rescinded that deal but not before countless Americans returned home in body bags. While abetting Iran, Obama was alienating Israel, the only democracy in the Middle East and our greatest ally against Islamic terrorism. Israel supplied information, weaponry, and the use of air force bases. Israel and the Palestinians were bickering over land they both claimed as their own which resulted in a very uneasy peace. A decades long controversy, Obama was the only president not to offer serious negotiations between the two adversaries for his entire eight year term. Things deteriorated to the point that Benjamin Netanyahu—the Prime Minister of Israel—was escorted out of the <u>back</u> door of the White House after a heated meeting with Obama.

Note the irony. Obama won a Nobel Peace Prize his first year of office, yet as he exited the White House, he had funded and emboldened a nuke-seeking terror state in Iran, expanded the war in Afghanistan and provoked the growth of the ISIS Caliphate in the country of Iraq. A hot mess indeed!

Outside of the Middle East, the Obama Administration had some success dealing with Cuba but not much with Russia. Obama normalized relations between Cuba and the U.S. in regard to recognition and trade. Embassies were reopened after decades of isolation. However no solutions were demanded by Obama in the area of human rights. The Cuban people continue to exist under the tight control of a dictator.

Obama wanted to "reset" relations with Russia but when Russia annexed Crimea in 2014, Obama and the U.S. stood on the sidelines and took no action. Obama had also been warned of Russian cyber attacks on the U.S. 2016 presidential election yet stood idly by and did next to nothing. President Putin of Russia exploited the hesitance of Obama to engage and proceeded to expand Russian influence in the Middle East.

Obama drew a "red line in the sand" warning Syrian dictator Bashar al-Assad not to use chemical weapons against the rebel Syrians, who wanted freedom from Assad's repressive regime. When Assad crossed that red line and used chemical weapons against his own people, Obama again stood by and did nothing. Putin, sensing an opening for a Russian presence in the Middle East, sent his troops into Syria to support Assad against his own people. Russia gained a foothold in the Middle East near the rich oil fields that Russia has always coveted.

As far as China is concerned, the Obama Administration more or less followed a laissez faire (hands off) policy towards China that led to the vast economic and military growth of China which now is the chief rival for America on the world stage. With regards to jobs, Obama stood by as high business taxes and regulations allowed American businesses to relocate in China with their employees in tow. Foreign affairs "expert" Vice President Joe Biden was sent to China in 2013 to meet with President Xi of China. He attempted to get China to stop the military buildup in the South China Sea. China was building artificial islands then installing military bases on them. Biden's initiatives yielded no concessions.

With no sanctions in place China expanded its operations in the Pacific. The lack of push back by Obama and Biden not only posed a strategic threat to the United States but also to our allies like Australia, Japan, and Taiwan. By "leading from behind" Obama had given new power to Russia and China, which now was an existential threat to the United States.

Economic Policy

Obama must be given credit for preventing a major economic depression after the Bush Administration exited the White House. The bailout stabilized not only the American economy but the global economy as well. Millions of people were employed once again.

Unfortunately the bailout came with strings attached. The monetary lifeline thrown to the financial world increased the national debt like never before. I explained earlier in the book that the national debt hurts the average American in two ways. First it increases taxes for everyone as we all pay a debt service charge, like a credit card interest payment. Secondly, a large and increasing national debt increases the price of goods for the American consumer. Lastly it forces future generations to pay for bad policy decisions made by their ancestors. The Dodd-Frank Act did not set strict standards for the use of bailout money so many of the large lending institutions grew larger which was not the intent of the act.

With Congressional eyes on them, banks tightened the spigot for loan-making to small businesses who had to look hard to find capital for investment and expansion. Small business makes up fifty percent of the revenue generated by the American economy. Because small businesses did not share in the largesse of the bailout, is it any wonder that the Obama economy limped along for eight years with a one percent growth each year?

Outsourcing of manufacturing jobs has been a major drain on the American economy dating back to the NAFTA agreement of 1994. The Obama team embraced the Clinton NAFTA plan and as a result thousands of manufacturing jobs went overseas especially to China, now emerging as the second largest economy in the world. It is amazing to see the amount of everyday household items for sale with the "made in China" tag affixed.

In 2020 this outsourcing of jobs proved nearly fatal in the medical field. As the Chinese Wuhan Flu (Covid) hammered the U.S. where did we first turn for ventilators? China. Ironic and scary as many of the Chinese made ventilators proved to be faulty, causing more deaths around the world. The U.S. must bring home manufacturing to our shores. It literally is a matter of life and death.

Obama was a proponent of the Green New Deal especially in the production of new renewable energy sources. Many of these are still in the developmental phase. With a chance to import needed energy while these technologies developed, Obama nixed the Keystone Pipeline. Regrettably it was not opened despite getting EPA authorization.

Social Issues

The LGBTQ community probably made the most strides during the Obama Administration. People of this persuasion could now openly serve in the military and became a much more vocal political force in succeeding years. The media shone the spotlight on gay culture with the result that these former "victims" are now a potent bloc of voters, mostly left-leaning.

Women also realized new empowerment under Obama. He nominated two women to the Supreme Court and both were confirmed by the U.S. Senate without the rancor of the Trump nominees. Sonia Sotomayor and Elena Kagan joined the Court respectively in 2009 and 2010.

In the area of race relations lay the greatest possibilities. There was an expectation that Obama was going to become "the healer-in-chief" of the racial divide in America. Perhaps those expectations had been set too high; no major acts of Congress were passed but how much more could have been legislated that was not already done in the Civil Rights Acts of the 60's? This was where the microscope had been focused and sadly a new age of racial healing never came about. In reality things got worse, in my opinion.

Let's examine a few situations that were symbolic failures in race relations that otherwise could have signaled positivity had they been handled differently.

In 2008 the New Black Panther Party intimidated white voters at a polling booth in Philadelphia. Weapons were brandished when white voters approached the polling booth. Obama and Eric Holder, his attorney general, said and did nothing. Eventually the two men with the weapons were sued in court. Only via back channels were the Black Panthers sanctioned. The media basically ignored this story.

In 2009, Professor Henry Louis Gates, a black man, was arrested by a white police officer who saw Gates fumbling to enter his Cambridge, Massachusetts home late at night. Gates quickly played the race card and another national case of racial profiling was born. Obama could have diffused the situation but chose to escalate it by irrationally claiming the Cambridge police "acted stupidly" and continued "… there's a long history in this country of African Americans being stopped by law enforcement disproportionately."

Upon learning the facts, Obama recanted and arranged a beer summit between the three of them. It turns out that Gates and the officer shared a common ancestor. But the damage had been done. With the verbal bomb hurled at police, it only further polarized America. It is easy to see the connection between these two events and the rioting and violence aimed at police throughout America in 2020.

In 2014 there was more fuel added to the racial fire in Ferguson, Missouri. Allegedly, a white police officer shot Michael Brown in the back with Brown's hands up in the air. For some reason, Obama let Eric Holder do the original talking and establish the narrative. *Before* the verdict, Holder indicted the entire Ferguson PD and said there needed to be wholesale changes made or risk a federal take-over of the police department.

The court trial produced a different narrative. Brown was *not* shot in the back, his hands were down and he was threatening the officer who fired in self-defense. Rather than addressing the verdict honestly, Obama saw fit to reprimand the police department not to overreact. "I appeal to the law-enforcement officials in Ferguson and the region to show care and restraint in managing <u>peaceful</u> protests that may occur." Although he did not surmise it at the time Obama was giving license to future groups of rioters and looters!

From 2009-2015 under Holder's DOJ (Department of Justice) there was a five percent drop in federal incarcerations, the largest decline since the Carter Administration. Obama and Holder showed their disdain for the police by emptying the jails, as best they could. Adding to the spike in crime was the expansion of sanctuary cities in America. It is no surprise that these sanctuary cities have safe havens for illegal aliens and other criminals who have set up encampments in the hearts of such cities as San Francisco, Los Angeles, New York, Portland, and Seattle. Chicago, Obama's adopted home city, is the worst in terms of sheer number of homicides, as gangs rule the south side of the Windy City, where the police are vastly outnumbered.

I find it ironic that Obama often quoted Lincoln as his favorite president. Apparently Lincoln's most famous speech about the Civil War "A House Divided" must have escaped Obama's memory.

Obama's immigration policies were rife with contradictions. Although a proponent of open borders, he nevertheless deported over 3,000,000 illegals, the most of any president. As pointed out he condoned sanctuary cities as a haven for illegal and criminal aliens. In 2012, via executive order, Obama announced the DACA "Dreamers" Act giving "temporary" shelter to millions of illegals for two year time periods. Obama wondered out loud how he was able to get away with DACA considering the vocal opposition at the time to the caravans of illegals attempting to cross the Mexican border for asylum in America. Today the status of the Dreamers is still in legal limbo and Congress is afraid to deal with this issue given the strident partisan political divide in America.

Obama himself offered the best analysis of the shortcomings of his administration in his last State of the Union Address when he said, "It's one of the few regrets of my presidency that the rancor and suspicion between the parties has gotten worse instead of better." Bill Clinton had offered a road map for working across the aisle, but because of Obama's thinly veiled disdain of Hillary Clinton, his own Secretary of State, he failed to employ the Clinton deal-making strategy to heal partisan division. The bottom line is that Obama did not focus his clout on enlarging his base—fundamentally reshaping America as he said-rather he sought to protect his legacy. [Much of Obama's disdain of Hillary Clinton resulted from the Benghazi fiasco. Obama's legacy would be historically stained by this incident.] In retrospect there was so much hype around the Obama mantra "Hope and Change" but in the end much more hope than change, more ego than hard work. There was a wooden sign hanging in the faculty room of my former schools that succinctly summed up the Obama years, "In the end, when all is said and done, there is a lot more said than done."

CHAPTER 53

The Sociology of Knowledge

THERE HAS BEEN A PROFOUND DOWNWARD trajectory in the scope of knowledge transmitted by the U.S. educational system in the last 100 years, especially at the secondary level. Visualize an inverted triangle as the best way to think about the shrinking amount of knowledge being handed down and what has become prioritized in the modern classroom.

My deceased parents were members of the Greatest Generation and graduated high school in the late 1930s. I have their report cards from high school that showed an amazing array of required courses to be taken. To receive a New York State high school diploma, they have to pass four years of math, science, English, and history as well as four years of physical education. They also had to take either Greek or Latin, civics, and electives like astronomy or archaeology.

Never heard of civics? No surprise. As Steven P. Dinkin reported in the September 27, 2020 issue of the San Diego Tribune newspaper only nine states and the District of Columbia require U.S. government or civics at the high school level. Nine states out of fifty! Why is the teaching of civics essential? It delineates the rights and duties of citizens. Some teaching points of civics are the support and defense of the Constitution, the obedience of federal, state, and local laws, respecting the rights and beliefs of others, participating in your local community, and exercising the right to vote. Of these teaching points, the rule of law is most abused by 2020 American society while the right to vote may lead to armed conflict in the not too distant future.

Decades later, requirements eased up for Baby Boomers seeking to graduate from a New York State high school. We were required to pass four years of English and social studies and while four years of math and science were suggested in certain cases three years would suffice. We had to take four years of a foreign language of our choice. We alternated physical education with limited electives on opposite days. We also had one full lunch period and one study hall in our eight-period day. [The worst duty for teachers was supervising the eighth-period study hall. They jammed hundreds of recalcitrant teenagers in the cafeteria awaiting the end-of-the-day dismissal. What I witnessed as a student in the eighth-period "study" hall would be fodder for a good short story.] As you can deduce we had two periods of relatively free time, unlike my parents' generation who had none.

Requirements for graduation in New York have again changed, some would say dramatically. Today, students must pass four years of English and social studies. However, next on the list is three and a half years of electives, followed by three years of math and science, two years of physical education, one year of foreign language, and one year in the arts. Lastly, students must pass half a year of health science. The electives is the area where education has been narrowed the most, in a way, as most high schoolers focus on technology-computer classes as their first choice. The computer was an early pacifier for grade school kids. As they moved up to middle and high school, computers began to replace textbooks for knowledge-gathering, never mind the social networking connection. Because of their comfort level with computers, thousands joined the working world as computer techies, software engineers, you name it. The computer world probably employs (and controls?) more people than any other American industry.

What's the big deal, you might argue? First of all from my viewpoint as a former social studies teacher and burgeoning student of history a great deal of American lore and achievement is no longer being taught. Since I have no offspring (that I know of), this is my legacy and payback to my country sharing Americana the way it was presented to me. From the inverted triangle, you can deduce that my parents were taught more subject matter than me and that I was exposed to more knowledge than the kids I was tasked with teaching. You may counter that the younger generations can find out about everything now on the internet. To which I would rebut only if they were aware of such knowledge and are motivated to learn about new subjects. Although painted with a broad brush, it appears that the cybersphere is dominated by social media and entertainment websites pushed by gigantic social media companies as money-making venues.

Further reducing the body of knowledge being transferred to future generations is the philosophy of WOKE education, aka CRT(Critical Race Theory). In their paradigm, class education revolves around identity politics: the binary either you are a racist or you are not. This is all that matters. White guilt is paramount and white guilt-shaming is a method of atoning for the "sins" of the white race perpetrated against people of color. By definition if you have white skin you are a racist. White people should atone for their racism by paying millions of dollars of reparations and becoming second class citizens, ceding their power to non-white groups.

WOKEism is a successor ideology in that it wants to replace liberalism and democracy that are seen as too passive and slow-moving in the area of advancing racial equality in America. Liberalism will let you do your job and keep your politics to yourself. Successor ideology forces you to voice your politics as a requirement for employment. If you disagree or even ask questions of the successor ideology you either lose your job or if entering the job market are summarily dismissed. The major plank of successor ideology is that white supremacy is the only reason for racial inequality which in their viewpoint is the dominant trait of American society. Individual rights and freedom of expression are not allowed in this successor ideology. To demonstrate how far Left this element of our culture has moved, former President Obama is now viewed as an enabler of white supremacy for advising Americans to use the system to bring about change. The new Leftists want to expunge the liberal democracy that is the United States.

The indoctrination of young people from elementary school through college by this new WOKEism is creating a Progressive monolith of Group Think that will not accept dissenting opinions. The bottom line is that the younger generations, the future power brokers of America, are making life-changing decisions based on biased, limited, and censored information. The WOKEsters are setting the table for another Civil War based on manufactured racism. The parents of school age children have to be our front line of defense. Fortunately many states are already fighting back, with half the states in America outlawing the WOKE/CRT education curriculum in their school systems. However because teacher colleges are indoctrinating and encouraging future teachers to teach through the prism of CRT, this will be a long and not easily won battle. This is yet another phase of the Cultural Revolution sweeping across and attempting to overthrow traditional America. {Despite the fact that racial hatred is already being artificially spawned in the classroom between black and white students as well as hate directed at the teachers of this curriculum, the two largest teacher unions in America, the NEA and the AFT, just voted to support the teaching of CRT in the nation's classrooms)

CHAPTER 54

Revisionist History and the Cancel Culture

LET'S EXPLORE THE RELATIONSHIP BETWEEN revisionist history and the Cancel Culture by examining the controversial NY Times <u>1619 Project</u> authored by Nikole Hannah-Jones that recently netted her a Pulitzer Prize. The major thesis of the Project is that America was "born" in 1619, the purported first year of slavery in America, and not 1776 with the ratification of the Declaration of Independence. Jones asserts that slavery was the driving force that forged the nation, not the tyranny of British King George. She asserts that the need to defend the existence of slavery in America, which the British opposed, was the major impetus for the Revolutionary War. Famous historian Gordon Wood disagrees and in the Wall Street Journal argued against this pretext by noting "the momentous blow that the American Revolution inflicted on the system of slavery in the New World" and the fact that "the United States became the first nation in the world to begin to actively suppress the international slave trade." The fact remains that outside of the Southern slave-owning states, slavery was outlawed in every other state and territory north of the Mason-Dixon Line by 1800. Abolitionist societies sprung to life in the early 1800's.

The 1619 Project gave birth to a curriculum that was to be mandated in many New York schools as well as others around the nation. One of the examples of this curriculum is the use of "erasure" poetry, which when applied to primary sources, can supposedly "lay back the real importance of the document or transform it into something wholly new." In the lesson students choose a historic document i.e. the Declaration of Independence and erase, or blot out, whatever content they choose, leaving behind only the words that convey their message. In other words, concoct your version of history.

Fortunately, this has been a serious blowback by hundreds of history teachers and professors questioning the veracity of this project. Somewhat surprisingly the most influential voice criticizing this project belonged to Barack Obama, who in a recent speech extolled the Founding Fathers documents and stated that the only true way to change our country's history is to exercise the right to vote.

Recently the New York Times backtracked a bit. It now asserts that slavery was a component in the birth of America but not the primary reason for the Revolutionary War. Pressure has been put on the Pulitzer board to rescind Jones's award, but to date this has not occurred.

The bottom line is that the Cancel Culture is not only attempting to rewrite the past; it is attempting to rid America of anything or any person that disagrees with its polemic. In a rare moment of agreement, both President Trump and President Obama warned of the dangers imposed by the Cancel Culture.

For the record, the concept of a cancel culture originated in the colonial period of the thirteen colonies. The Puritans forced non-believers to leave the Massachusetts Bay Colony, those included Roger Williams and Anne Hutchinson. They also waged war on the Wampanoag Indians who had helped them survive—forcing them to roam elsewhere for food. The war against Native Americans continued into the 1800s when President Andrew Jackson ignored the Supreme Court's edict and forced the Indians to relocate via the Trail of Tears. In the late 1800s, the Indians of the west were put on reservations and forced to adopt The White Man's Culture. These attempts to obviate Native American culture involved weaponry and armed conflict.

Today's Cancel Culture is much more efficient. The powers-that-be only require a computer and a mouse and poof! Donald Trump and his 87,000,000 supporters no longer exist!

CHAPTER 55

Donald Trump

HILLARY CLINTON WAS GIDDY IN ANTICIPATION of her coronation as next president of the U.S. Riding the coattails of a popular Barack Obama, the first black president, she was going to set her own precedent breaking the "glass ceiling," becoming the first female president. The Democratic Party seemed to have everything in its favor seeking back-to-back precedents in the U.S. Presidency. She was so close she could smell it, taste it, and almost touch it—then something else unprecedented occurred to dash her lifelong ambition. Donald Trump crashed the party and won the election in by far the greatest upset of all the previous forty-four presidential elections.

How did Clinton lose this election? First, she was a victim of her own haughty arrogance that was reflected in two now-infamous quotes that will haunt her the rest of her life. In 2012 as the Secretary of State under Obama she was called in by the House of Representatives investigative committee and asked to explain why the American embassy in Libya did not get the help it requested the night of the Benghazi Incident in Libya resulting in four American deaths. The committee was attempting to find out who was to blame when a flustered Clinton blurted out "...What difference does it make?..." Many Americans including myself felt that she did not give a damn. Her tone and message were so callous.

The Benghazi Incident was part of a much larger problem created by Clinton herself, the deleting of over 30,000 emails that discussed this incident and others relating to national security. Clinton refused to use a government-authorized server to house these emails. Instead, she used a private phone to record this sensitive information. Before being called to testify not only did she scrub all the emails but went so far as to physically destroy the device. She was cleared of any culpability in the Benghazi Incident, however her arrogance was in full public view as she flouted the rules guarding her conduct as then-Secretary of State.

Fast forward to 2016. During the presidential campaign, she inserted her foot in mouth again. In the course of a nationally televised speech, she denigrated the majority of Trump supporters as "mostly a basket of deplorables." She seemed to indicate that she would curtail the rights of gun owners in the "fly over" states and elsewhere. She also took a swipe at those who supported organized religion as she had become much more secular to appease her base.

Secondly, she got lazy. Rather than getting out on the campaign trail especially during the last month, she let her surrogates do the bulk of the campaigning. What her surrogates could not do, she relied on the television media to take care of the rest. CNN (Clinton News Network) MSNBC, ABC, CBS, et al were de facto acolytes, willing to carry water for the Clinton Machine.

Lastly, like James Carville, her husband's former campaign manager, once accurately said, "It's the economy, stupid!" Especially in presidential elections, people vote with their pocketbook interest first. For the previous eight years, the economy had limped along. Home ownership, for example, was at an all-time low as the middle class suffered stagnant wages. They were frustrated and ready for a change in direction.

How did a reality television star and business mogul with no political experience steal the election? His successful strategy was unorthodox, unconventional, and uncouth. During the Republican primary, Trump refused to follow conventional protocol. In the primary, the goal is to get the nomination but not badly disparage the other candidates who are all part of the same "team." Trump dispatched this norm and denigrated his competitors as wimpy, little, or low-energy, while simultaneously loudly tooting his own horn like the impresario he truly was. Many of the establishment were shocked but thousands more liked his honesty that they felt was sorely lacking in the political world. In the manner of Ronald Reagan, he seemed to speak to them directly without the filter of political pandering.

Now under the glaring hot spotlight, he had to craft a platform that would garner him the Republican nomination and carry him to victory in the general election. Trump described his program as America First, as he borrowed and updated ideas from his hero, Ronald Reagan. Trump pledged to uphold the original intent of the Constitution by enforcing all of its laws. The Preamble to the Constitution talks about providing for the general welfare of America and keeping America safe which he planned to do by rebuilding the military and appointing conservative judges to the Supreme Court as well to lower federal courts throughout America. Trump pledged to support the working class, returning manufacturing to America and allocating money for small business expansion and subsidies for farmers. To keep America safe, he pledged to build a wall between the U.S. and Mexico to keep out illegal and dangerous aliens of all persuasions. Like Eisenhower, another hero, he wanted to upgrade the nation's infrastructure.

On the international level, Trump understood that a large, well-funded military was a key to ensuring American security at home. Funding for all the branches of the military including the Coast Guard exceeded the defunding of the Obama Administration. On the other hand, he wanted to end the carnage of war in Iraq and Afghanistan and return our soldiers home. By working with Israel, he looked to isolate Iran and unify the Middle East. He was willing to negotiate face-to-face with North Korea in regards to a treaty eliminating nukes from their arsenal, an avenue Obama refused to explore. Like Eisenhower, he wanted to contain Russia who had annexed Crimea and gotten a foothold in Iraq. With regards to China, he wanted to end the trade imbalance by imposing tariffs on Chinese imports. He wanted to stop both Russia and China from stealing military intelligence and weapons technology via computer hacking. Lastly, he insisted that our NATO allies pay their fair share for the global defense and the funding of the United Nations in New York City.

To win the Republican nomination and institute America First as his vision, Trump would have to campaign as a Populist candidate. A Populist appeals to thousands of people across party lines who feel either ignored or disenfranchised. Many of the potential voters live in the "flyover states," a derogatory term used by the coastal elitists who literally and figuratively looked down on them. Trump despised the elites and vice versa whose members included Hollywood, the Media, Silicon Valley, and the Swamp—the entrenched bureaucracy that performed the everyday functions of the government in Washington D.C. but were awash in corruption. "Drain the Swamp!" became one of Trump's most repeated and effective campaign slogans, along with "Make America Great Again!" Trump was able to defeat about twenty other Republican candidates to become the party standard-bearer in the 2016 election against Hillary. But for Trump to be successful he would have to buck tradition again and remake the Republican Party. Up to the Bush Dynasty, the traditional Republican Party was composed of white middle to upper-middle-class voters, religiously conservative with a large segment of Wall Street, big business, and the military.

Despite fierce establishment resistance, Trump remade the party in his image. Gone was much of Wall Street, who joined the Democrat Party along with their Silicon Valley brethren from the West Coast. Trump marshaled support from blue-collar workers, small business owners from the middle class, women, Evangelical Christians, farmers, and ranches from the "fly over" states and as many young voters, Blacks, Hispanics, and Asians as he could persuade. Fifty years ago this was the electorate of the Democratic Party. In effect two parties had flip-flopped their electorate. Not only have the electorate of each party flip-flopped, so have their philosophies. The Republicans used to be viewed as close-minded, their 1960's campaign buttons advertised, "American...Love it or Leave it." Today censorship is more a tool of the Left.

On the campaign trail, Trump was a relentless dynamo. Widely distributing his red MAGA hats, Trump took no prisoners, repeatedly referring to Clinton as "Crooked Hillary" and exhorting his minions with the refrain "Lock her up!" Besides being a road warrior, he gathered massive audiences to Facebook and Twitter, beating the Democrats at their own game and especially on Twitter, marginalizing the hyper-partisan, hypercritical liberal media. In front of large Black audiences, he would ask, "What do you have to lose (by voting for me)?" Before asking that question he had stated that the Obama Administration had done little to help Blacks. Meanwhile, he made inroads with the Hispanic population by praising their energy. Some were drawn to his brazen energy, to a kindred spirit, who seemed to offer hope.

By the time Hillary awoke from her pre-election nap in October 2016, it was already too late. The train had left the station while she was arriving at the platform. Trump won the election, being the fifth man to lose the popular vote but win the electoral college. Those in the "fly over" states felt vindicated while Hillary and most of the world were in shock. But she was not done with Trump yet, not by a long shot. (Democratic strategists determined that the Internet was the deciding factor in the 2016 election. By controlling the flow of information via censorship of the Republican platform, the Democrats were able to win the 2020 election. In my opinion it seems like the social media outlets are taking their marching orders from the Democratic Party.)

"Collusion!" screamed Hillary and the Democratic Party as well as their toadies who dominated the media. "Trump won the election because he is a Putin Pawn…" And so was born the Trump Derangement Syndrome.

From day one of his presidency, impeachment became the main topic concerning Trump. His myriad accomplishments received little to no mainstream media coverage. Impeachment was everything. To make a long story short, the Democratically-controlled House of Representatives brought formal charges of impeachment against Trump and he was officially impeached by all the Democrats. The Republican-controlled Senate saw through this sham and exonerated Trump of the charges, ending the case. The "Russian Hoax" as Trump labeled the witch hunt was now at an end. Or was it? Unbelievably there would be the second impeachment of Trump in his last week in office!

There is ample evidence in 2020 that the real collusion was involving the Obama Administration and the Deep State, who was attempting a soft coup (removal) of Trump before he assumed office. The Deep State is a shadow government including agencies like the FBI who were concocting false charges intending to oust President Trump in an unprecedented act of regime change. There is damning evidence that Obama, Clinton, and Joe Biden, were all aware of this coup and if not actively involved did nothing to prevent it. [Now that Biden has been elected president, the investigation of the soft coup versus Trump will be swept under the rug. Only if Republicans someday regain the level of power will this conspiracy be investigated.]

By the way, you would not be incorrect to conflate the Deep State with the Swamp. They are pretty much interchangeable entities certainly lacking a moral compass. When Trump pledged to drain the Swamp he understood that it would bite back; survival, not loyalty is its raison d'etre much akin to the Coronavirus that mutates to survive.

Born in Queens, New York, Donald J. Trump was the son of Fred Trump, a Bronx-born real estate developer whose ancestors were German immigrants. At age thirteen, Trump was enrolled in the NY Military Academy, a private boarding school then entered Fordham University for two years. He transferred to the Wharton School of the University of Pennsylvania where he graduated in 1968 with a BA in Economics. Much of Trump's persona was imprinted from his father, also a controversial figure but not as high-profile as his now more famous son. Fred Trump was a firm believer in the Protestant Work Ethic and devoted all of his energy to building his real estate empire just within the boundaries of the law, though others claimed outside the law. Being a teetotaler, Fred Trump was not distracted from the pursuit of his goals.

Because of his strict German upbringing, there were rumors of Nazism in regards to Fred Trump's dealing with some of his tenants who leased apartments in his building. That autocratic streak was also evidenced in the discipline of his children who were raised with very proscribed rules of right and wrong.

Of his three sons, Donald became the chosen one to eventually take control of his empire. After graduating from Wharton, Donald Trump began to assume more responsibility in running his father's empire. His father mentored Trump in a Machiavellian take-no-prisoners way. He exhorted his son to "be a killer" in the cutthroat business world and he continued, "You are king." Backed up by a multi-million dollar inheritance, is it any wonder that his son became so successful yet so narcissistic, egocentric, crude, and enabled? In this case, the apple certainly did not fall far from the tree.

Embracing a strong work ethic, Trump was a doer in the mold of Washington, Lincoln, Jefferson, Jackson, and both Roosevelts who shaped America in so many ways. Let's review some of the accomplishments of the Trump Administration.

Foreign Policy

There have been several triumphs for Trump's foreign policy, some of them historic. Trump's Middle East Abraham accords persuaded the kingdom of the United Arab Emirates (UAE) and the kingdom of Bahrain to recognize and normalize relations with former enemy Israel. They are the third and fourth country to recognize Israel. Sudan and Morocco will be the fifth and sixth Middle Eastern countries to recognize the existence of the Israel state in the Middle East. Egypt was the first in 1979 followed by Jordan in 1994.

The biggest loser in these accords is Iran who is becoming more isolated in the Middle East as other countries fear the aggression that a nuclear Iran could wreak on the rest of the area. Trump ditched the agreement signed with Iran during the Obama Administration.

As previously discussed Obama gave billion-dollar loans to Iran to try to dissuade them from building nuclear weapons. This soft bribery was a failure as Iran continues down the road to the development of a nuke. Trump isolated Iran from trade with most of the rest of the world and the U.S. has helped to suffocate the Iranian economy by freezing their bank assets. For his efforts, Trump has been nominated for the Nobel Peace Prize in 2020. [Just before publication of this book, Biden has decided to ease the sanctions on Iran. This will surely lead to other nations of the Middle East developing their WMDs (Weapons of Mass Destruction) who are scared at the prospect of a nuclear Iran. With Trump deposed, there is no one powerful enough to prevent them from finalizing their WMDs. This could prove to be a fateful decision for the world!]

As mentioned, Trump crushed the ISIS Caliphate in Iraq that grew out of control when Obama mockingly referred to it as the "JV" aka a minor threat to world security. Obama's verbal mockery of ISIS backfired as ISIS metastasized from a regional threat to a global problem. The fact that Iran both feared and loathed ISIS legitimized the Trump initiative to crush the threat posed by the former Caliphate.

Trump is the first president since Eisenhower to not get involved in any new wars and took steps to end the war in Iraq. The war in Afghanistan is now officially over, for better or worse and was the longest-running war in U.S. history. Trump was the first president to actively engage North Korea in hopes of ending their nuclear threat to neighboring Asian countries and the U.S. Although they were not happy, Trump also was able to get billions of dollars from NATO allies, money that they owed to the collective defense of the alliance.

Lastly, Trump's biggest accomplishment was the recognition of China's plans to dominate the globe. Trump's first move was to tariff Chinese goods and his second move was to ally with India, the world's largest democracy, that borders China. In recognition of the Chinese threat, Trump added a sixth branch to the military. The Space Force will be the first branch added since the USAF in 1947 and will protect U.S. military satellites in space from foreign attacks.

Economic Policy

Up until the outbreak of the coronavirus the economy had been a smashing success. The Trump tax cuts seemed to help most American people. By slashing the corporate tax rate from 35% to 21%, Trump was able to create 4,000,000 new jobs in America. When Trump pledged to return 400,000 manufacturing jobs from China and other countries, Obama sharply replied "You would need a magic wand to pull that off..."

Trump wielded that magic wand and presto! 400,000 manufacturing jobs returned to America. As a result, median family income was raised by nearly $6,000.00 with historic lows in unemployment, down to 3.4%. Blacks, Hispanics, Women, Asian-Americans, and college-aged workers were the main beneficiaries. Additionally, 4,000,000 people were now off of food stamps. Unemployment claims hit a forty-nine year low. Because fracking was not banned, the U.S. became an exporter of natural gas for the first time since 1957 and the U.S. also became energy independent for the first time. The average price of gasoline for cars dropped from four dollars a gallon to two dollars a gallon. Many retirees who were existing on marginal IRAs were now living with increased retirement savings. Happy days are here again! (The Biden energy policy has made the U.S. reliant again on the import of foreign oil by shutting down new American energy pipelines and new areas of oil drilling in America. The results have been the doubling of gas prices at the pump, increases in home heating fuels causing runaway inflation not seen since the Carter Administration. Biden has followed the lead of the radical wing of the Democratic Party who want the Green New Deal enacted as soon as possible, totally eliminating the fossil fuel industry.)

The Trump Administration canceled the NAFTA deal and replaced it with the more America First USMCA (U.S., Mexico, Canada) trade agreement. To boost the production of U.S. steel and clothing (textiles) the dumping of cheap steel from Canada and textiles from Mexico into American markets was reduced by tariffs and other means. The U.S. began to show a net gain to the economy rather than losses under NAFTA.

Lastly, the pressure was put on Big Pharma. The war on opioid sales received national TV attention on the show 60 Minutes. The fall-out is still not complete, but America is now aware of the source of this epidemic. The FDA put pressure on Medicare as well. Big Pharma was making a huge profit from the sale of prescription drugs to seniors and others. The Trump administration has seen to it that the prices have come down across the board.

Social Policy

One of the main planks of Trump's campaign platform was his promise to conservative Americans to appoint judges at every level who would pledge to keep America traditional in its trajectory. To accomplish this goal Trump looked to nominate constructionist judges to the courts. Those types of judges read the Constitution as it was written in the guidance of decision making. Liberal activist judges will read *into* the Constitution and loosely interpret it. Trump viewed activist judges as de facto lawmakers contrary to the philosophy of the separation of powers.

During the Trump Administration, nearly 300 federal judges have been appointed as well as three Supreme Court justices. Judges have more influence in shaping America than Presidents as they are, in many cases, in office for decades.

Trump increased the safety of America in another way. By the sheer force of his insistence, he has been able to construct nearly 450 miles of a border wall between the U.S. and Mexico. There had been caravans of thousands of illegals, a silent invasion at the advent of his administration, seeking asylum in America. Despite heavy opposition, he was able to win the public relations battle and pressured Mexico to help prevent the illegal crossings of thousands. What was once a liberal talking point has become a major accomplishment for Trump who also was able to get funding to hire 6,000 more border guards. This avoided a court battle over using the military to guard the border. [Unfortunately Biden reversed all the Trump policies vis-a-vis the border resulting in a totally open Southern border yet the Canadian border remains in lockdown.]

The First Step Act was a triumph of the Trump Administration with the approval of the Democratic House Of Representatives. There were far too many inmates incarcerated in federal prisons for minor offenses. The First Step Act has released thousands from these prisons for petty crimes. Federal judges are nullifying state laws that were too cruel or antiquated for such petty offenses. This is a win-win.

The Trump Administration was a big supporter of the military, both active and retired. Trump promised during his campaign to end foreign wars and reconstruct the VA (Veterans Administration) that had been left in a shambles by the Obama Administration.

There was a lack of clinics with the result that long waiting times lead to many, many unnecessary deaths. Trump summarily fired many of the VA workers and replaced them with others, more compassionate. There was a large increase in the number of walk-in clinics created as well as same-day urgent care. The most important upgrade was in the area of mental health- counseling, and facilities. Trump again had lived up to his promise!

Trump's most enduring legacy may prove to be the total realignment of the Republican Party. The Republicans, somewhat by necessity may become The Big Tent Party of the future. The blue-collar working class is certainly no supporter of the Democratic Party when they advocate open borders that lead to many immigrant workers looking to take jobs from American citizens. Look for the Republicans to be a polyglot part of the future because of Donald Trump.

Headwinds

It is a virtual certainty that some of the Trump legacies will be mitigated by executive orders come Jan 2021. Let's (briefly) discuss the various entities who have resisted Trumpism from the get-go.

Usually, there is a grace period granted when a new president takes office. Not in the case of Donald Trump. When the dust settled and the voters tabulated Trump had shocked the world and the liberal media lost their collective minds. "It's a hoax," they screamed: "The Russians helped Trump to win." Trump, the street fighter, pushed back fiercely on Twitter. "Fake News" Trump repeatedly told his 87,000,000 followers. He claimed this was the biggest political witch hunt in U.S. History. He was proven correct but had to induce a bogus impeachment process. "Fake News" became a widely popular phrase used routinely now in the American lexicon.

Because Twitter had become such an effective weapon for Trump, marginalizing and circumventing the media, the titans of Big Tech i.e Silicon Valley decided to silence the president and censor his tweets. It is obvious that by these actions and the millions of dollars pumped into the Biden campaign by these technocrats that they can no longer claim they are a platform for free speech.

The Socialist Movement is a threat to capitalism and American democracy. Capitalism built much of America and has created much wealth. The Socialist Movement has gained strength lately due to the multitudinous business scandals that rocked America in the '80s and '90s. There are indeed elements of socialism in America—Medicare, Medicaid, unemployment insurance, and welfare.

The problem with socialism is that, unlike democracy which has deep roots, socialism is only a rung on the ladder leading to Communism, deeply rooted in countries such as Russia, Communist China, and North Korea. The radical wing of the Democratic Party wants to mandate the redistribution of wealth throughout all of America. They will not rest until the government controls every aspect of life for the American population. This is totalitarian Communism. Absolute power and control by the government is the goal. Donald Trump and his base are the bulwarks opposing this movement. To achieve absolute power the Socialists realize they can not use force as they simply do not have the numbers. Their method of takeover is much more insidious and largely employs the use of the Cancel Culture in America.

The Cancel Culture also includes the guilt-shaming of "White Privilege" and the push for reparations for the ancestors of slavery, which would surely redistribute most of the wealth in America.

The tearing down of monuments and statues throughout history has always indicated a nation on the brink of a civil or revolutionary war. Hopefully, we are not at that point but this may be wishful thinking. A revolution would be abetted by the defunding and dismantling of the police, a major rallying cry of BLM and Antifa this summer. It is important to note that Congress convened in the summer of 2020 to address the riots, lootings, arson, and killings associated with the unrest. Not one Democrat said a word or voted to condemn the unrest. The record shows that many Biden staffers donated money to get the rioters and looters out on bail, with Vice President Kamala Harris tweeting her support and encouraging further unrest in the streets.

So who are BLM (Black Lives Matter) and Antifa, the firebrands of the Cancel Culture?

Antifa has been around for a long time in history and has existed in other countries. Though they brand themselves as anti-fascist, they employ the same violent methods as did the infamous Fascists of history, like Hitler, Mussolini, and Tojo of Japan, all of who were involved in WWII. Antifa is a mobile paramilitary group made up of mostly disgruntled young white males who have nothing else to do but create mayhem wherever they go. They are organized but the main funder of Antifa seems to be George Soros, a left-wing bomb thrower and the sworn enemy of American democracy. He may be right at the top of the globalist oligarchy who are installing the New World Order. The irony of Antifa is that this organization of mostly white thugs has devastated many urban black communities this summer, the people they are supposed to be helping.

Black Lives Matter is both a diverse social movement and the name of a national organization whose leaders include co-founder Patrisse Cullors, who described herself and fellow co-founder, Alicia Garza, as "trained Marxists." [In fact, Pew Research reports that five out of six members in BLM are white.] BLM took center stage last summer protesting the slow-death slaying of George Floyd by a white police officer, who stepped on his neck until he suffocated several minutes later. A heinous crime to be sure that angered all of America, the initial protests were respectful and very powerful.

Unfortunately, the militant elements of the organization hijacked the movement and the method of peaceful protest was replaced with violence not seen on this scale since the 1960s. In regards to the police, their mantra became. "Pigs in a blanket, fry them like bacon!" This is where they lost me. The resulting carnage included the murder of over 200 police officers throughout the nation. When both federal officers and police have faced assaults from bricks, baseball bats, sledgehammers, Molotov cocktails, mortar-style commercial-grade fireworks, accelerants, IEDS, and other violent weapons by those sporting BLM shirts, those "Peaceful Protesters" are not exactly collecting for the Red Cross!

WOKEism is fast becoming the new state religion. WOKEsters view America as a deplorable, irredeemable nation. Politicians like New York City Mayor DeBlasio and NY State Governor Cuomo have "mainstreamed" WOKEness by allowing rioting and looting while banning Christians and Jews from participating in their religions. Such a situation undermines our founding principles and opens a door to a new reality, a theocracy of the WOKE. Unfortunately, although Trump is aware of WOKEism, the permanent bureaucracy of the Deep State knows it can ignore the directions of any commander-in-chief and continue to remake U.S. institutions in its ideological image.

Perhaps the bigger factor to unseat Trump in 2020 was the unexpected plague of the Chinese Wuhan Flu (Coronavirus) and how Trump dealt with it. Some here as well as some in China think that China concocted this plague in a lab with the expectation that it would reach America. Because it was a new strain of virus, there was no guidance on how to handle it. China may have banked on that premise knowing the American people were about to vote for a President, and Trump would be blamed for its spread. It would be a way for China to rid itself of its main obstacle to world domination, Donald J. Trump.

In January 2020, the CCP used a digital blitz of misinformation to mislead the public and protect the party's image as infections began to soar. By making the disease look less severe, the world lost its best chance to prevent a global pandemic. Fresh evidence published by the New York Times and ProPublica, two left-leaning new organizations, confirms that Beijing has been working to deceive the rest of the world about the virus from the very start of the pandemic.

Of course, the majority of the mainstream media had a field day with this crisis. All the energy that had been put into the debunked Russian conspiracy hoax and the failed first impeachment was now immediately transferred to the crucifixion of Trump's "mishandling" of the virus.

Never letting a good crisis go to waste, the timing of the plague played right into the hands of the radical left-wing of the Democratic Party, who demanded free healthcare for everyone. Oh, you have Covid? No Problem. The government will pick up the tab. I'm sure quite more than a few voters were swayed by this possibility that translated into votes for the Biden Presidency.

Pfizer was one of the Big Pharma drug companies sanctioned by the Trump administration. Did they wait until the election was over to roll out their vaccine and would this have affected the outcome of a razor-thin election? Just before the new year of 2021, Trump's Operation Warp Speed has proven to be a success, administering over fifteen million doses of two separate vaccines to the general population. These vaccines have a ninety-five percent rate of effectiveness and were tested and developed in record time. In retrospect, people will view this as a Christmas miracle.

Legacy

For better or for worse I do not believe we will see another presidency like that of Donald J. Trump. The following are lists of hits and misses that will be forever associated with Trump.

Positives

- Deeply cared for the common man in America
- Made America energy independent
- Eliminated the ISIS Caliphate in Iraq
- Closed the southern border to illegal aliens/terrorists
- American safety increased against foreign nations (Space Force)
- Unity in the Middle East (Abraham Accords)
- Made America a manufacturing nation again
- Identified Communist China as the pre-eminent threat to global security
- Implemented the rollout of Coronavirus vaccines

Trump did not need this job. He viewed it as a labor of love. America had lost its way, and Trump was determined to restore its esteemed position. The size and passion of the Trump rallies were unprecedented and showed that the commoners trusted Trump, and he did his best to reward them. He made America safer at home by building the southern wall and made America safer abroad by beefing the military and confronting our enemies as necessary. Internally America became stronger economically spurred on by the return of manufacturing and the expansion of capital to small businesses for growth. He did the near-impossible and convinced several more Arabic states to embrace Israel as a friend and not as an enemy combatant. He should be awarded the Nobel Peace Prize for his trailblazing efforts. I used to think that Ronald Reagan had the most profound effect on changing the geopolitical world by ending the Cold War. On second thought Trump's initiatives in the Middle East may prove more consequential over time given the fact that the Holy Lord has been contested for 5000 years by various religions and oppositional cultures. The CEOs of Google, Facebook, and Twitter have been deposed by Congress about their rule in censorship. These tech companies have now been exposed as the de facto monopolies. Perhaps in the not too distant future, a new Congress will ascribe monopoly status to Big Tech and therefore be subject to trust-busting by the Sherman Antitrust Act. As it stands now Big Tech is undermining both democracy and the Constitution. While Big Tech may be the biggest internal threat to democratic America, Trump has identified China both by word and deed as the biggest external threat to American society.

Negatives

For all the good Trump has accomplished, much negativity will always taint his presidency.

- Downgraded the office of the president with boorish and unpredictable behavior
- Did not solve the deep divisions within America
- Did not deliver a workable health plan for all
- Did not significantly upgrade the infrastructure in America

Trump's major downfall was his own petulant and erratic behavior. Though the media hounded him relentlessly he fought back just as vigorously mostly using his Twitter account. The problem was he picked on people with lesser standing and belittled them. Trump became seen as a bully and a bully does not win many public relations battles. He never understood that sometimes honey wins more battles than vinegar when dealing with those who don't agree with you.

Being apolitical, he summarily fired many people in the executive branch simply on a whim. No wonder the Deep State tried to take him out of power. Obama before him failed to heal the deep divisions inside America. Some of his rhetoric seemed to empower white power fringe groups and of course alienated some Blacks, though he did garner more Black and Hispanic voters than any previous Republican president. The racial divide is still real but exacerbated by a WOKE press that sees all social issues through a racial prism.

The schism in America may be best exemplified by Trump's selection of three new Supreme Court justices. In the old days there was honest debate but mostly all candidates of modern times—except Clarence Thomas—received overwhelming votes of approval. The only reason Trump's appointees became members of the Court was that the Senate had a Republican majority, but barely. Essentially there were party-line votes on the three candidates, all Republicans in favor of and all Democrats opposed. I do not foresee any president having the wherewithal to unite America. The goals of each side are diametrically opposed. Given his ignominious exit from the White House, it is likely that he, as well as Bill Clinton for that matter, will be judged in the long scope of history more for their transgressions, as opposed to their accomplishments.

The nadir of his presidency occurred on January 6th, 2021 just two weeks before the inauguration of the new president, Joe

Biden. Still insisting that the 2020 election was stolen from him, he encouraged Trump Nation to march on Washington, which they did, numbering more than 200,000. Trump's tone of voice, if not his exact words, gave license to the lunatic fringe of his supporters to use violence directed at the Congress, convening in the Capitol Rotunda to certify the electoral college vote.

Let history show that this was the first "assault" on the capital by American citizens. Acolytes broke through the outnumbered police lines and took control of the Senate chambers for a short period. Five people were killed but four of those suffered medical emergencies and the fifth was an unarmed former female veteran shot dead by the Capitol police. The name of the shooter has never been released by the government in yet another cover-up. There were over fifty injured in this historic assault on "the People's House." The only other time the Rotonda was breached was in 1814 by the British Army in the course of the War of 1812.

This riot led to a snap impeachment of Trump. He was charged with one article of insurrection. Trump now is the only president with the stain of two impeachments on his resume. Though private-citizen Trump was acquitted by the Senate, his legacy now has sustained permanent damage.

Regardless of who is the next president, a new election protocol must be put forth to avoid widespread fraud involved in the 2020 election, though you heard nothing about this from the mainstream media. There were thousands of questionable ballots tabulated that were either unsigned or indecipherable.

In the 2020 election, there was an unbelievable number of voters over the age of 100. One" voter" had died in 1823! [The 1960 "Graveyard Vote" from Chicago's Cook County is credited for JFK's victory over Nixon in the 1960 Presidential election.] There were hundreds of affidavits signed by poll workers witnessing fraud at polling sites yet the Supreme Court refused to look into these alleged abuses.

We need to get back to an Election Day, not an election season. Many millions of voters had already been cast two months before the election. What happens if a game-changing event occurs just before the election? On the opposite side of the coin, states allow votes to be counted up to two weeks after the election. That allows too much leeway for tampering with the process.

We need a 28th Amendment to the Constitution to prevent fraud in future elections. Common sense suggests that a potential voter has a recent photo ID and verifiable signature. Secondly, ballots need to be tabulated by midnight of Election Day with no exceptions! This proposal does not favor one political party nor the other and would return integrity and security into the system. As it stands now perhaps the main foundation block of democracy in America is severely at risk.

CHAPTER 56

China

CHINA POSES THE MOST SERIOUS EXISTENTIAL threat to the democratic nations of the world. The stated goal of communist China is global domination beginning with the subjugation of the U.S., whom they view as the major impediment to their goal of global hegemony. The Communist Chinese Party (CCP) is the authority in charge of the apparatus of the takeover. The CCP is relentless in achieving this stated goal. Before detailing that apparatus, a brief history of China would help to provide some context.

Throughout the many millennia of its existence, China has always had top-down authoritarian rule, mostly through its many family dynasties. Similar to European feudalism, China was composed of many small kingdoms, protected by barrier walls, against each other and the nomadic Mongolian Hordes, who came out of the Eurasian steppe region and overran China before the Great Wall was finally completed. In more modern times, the British defeated China in the Opium Wars of the 1800s and colonized sections of China, including Hong Kong on the island of Taiwan (nee Formosa) Hong Kong is the New York City of the Asian World, an important center of finance and trade. The U.S. Open Door Policy in the early 1900s prevented China from becoming divided up by multiple European nations. For a while, there were good relations between China and the U.S. but the world wars shattered that bond.

In 1921, the CCP was established by agents of the Far Eastern branch of the Soviet Russian-led Communist International. In 1949 the PRC (People's Republic of China) launched a Communist civil war against the new but weak Chinese nationalist government which was a democratic republic. The war-weary U.S. did not have the will to protect the new republic so the Communist takeover led by Mao Tse Tung (Chairman Mao) was successful.

Mao carried out the so-called Cultural Revolution in China using mass genocide of between 40 to 80,000,000 Chinese citizens who opposed Communism! As a comparison, Hitler's genocide of the Jews numbered 6,000,000 Stalin's genocide in Russia numbered between 12- 20,000,000. Mao "encouraged" the Chinese citizenry to dress in red and carry copies of the Little Red Book with them. This book was a compilation of Mao's philosophy, including his do's and don'ts. Communist China now was referred to as Red China by the free world. Chairman Mao was in total control of Red China until he died in 1976.

Today China is technically "one country, two systems" made up of mainland Red China and the Island nation of Taiwan that received its independence from England in 1997 and has had, up to now, democratic institutions. However, it is being systematically swallowed up by the CCP who are blatantly taking over the legislature and other institutions in Taiwan. Since Taiwan has a military alliance with the U.S., a confrontation could occur there and that would be bad news for the world. The Chinese Communist Party maintains control over its own mainland population by practicing autocratic capitalism, a hybrid of capitalism and totalitarianism. The people of China are allowed to amass personal wealth so long as they subjugate themselves completely to the government of

China. In short they have no individual rights and freedoms and are subject to the whims of a repressive de facto dictatorship.

Much of the following information concerning the evolving subjugation of the U.S. by China I gleaned from a special 2020 edition of the Epoch Times newspaper published in New York City. All of the writers are Chinese Nationals with detailed insight into the grand plan of the CCP.

With the successful takeover of China accomplished in 1949, the CCP quietly concocted its 100-year strategy: to replace the U.S. as the preeminent nation in the world by 2049. They realized they were in no position to challenge the U.S. in 1949, so they concentrated on constructing a new Chinese state ideology based on atheism, hate, conformity, and rejection of traditional values. Chairman Mao and succeeding dictators became "God," as organized religion was outlawed. Those who objected were executed. Problems within China were blamed on Japan, who had once colonized China, or on the U.S. which was a "threat to the existence of China." The younger generations were indoctrinated under this construct from birth. It is easy to hate another culture when all that you learn about that culture is negative. For example, Russian and Chinese children were only shown films depicting race riots from 1960s America and told this was still a common everyday occurrence in America. This narrative will be reinforced by the 2020 videos of American cities being torched by "social justice" warriors. The jubilant reactions expressed by most of the Chinese public following the 9/11 terrorist attacks on American soil indicate the progress made by the CCP in its anti-American propaganda campaign.

The CCP is utilizing a policy of "unrestricted warfare" against the U.S., infiltrating the U.S. culture and leaving no industry untouched. China is playing the long game in regards to taking over America. Where possible, they want to avoid an all out war, which would result in global annihilation. They are using the same initiatives against America that they are using to subjugate developing nations. In short, they are conducting a silent yet overt takeover of America and the world. According to Matthew Pottinger, a deputy national security advisor for the Trump administration, China has stolen enough data from the United States to compile a dossier on EVERY single American adult. During a Senate Intelligence Committee hearing, Pottinger stated that the Chinese use this information to "influence and intimidate, reward and blackmail, flatter and humiliate, divide and conquer." A good analogy would be of a cancer patient who is informed by an oncologist that their cancer has metastasized. This prognosis is on the near horizon for the American nation. Some of these initiatives are as follows:

Confucius Institutes (CCI's)

There are seventy five or more of these centers that operate under the pretense of promoting the Chinese language and history. Located mostly on college campuses, their real goal is to spread propaganda and recruit those of college-age to the Communist way of thinking. These institutes steal innovations and research ideas in their initial stages that are being developed on American college campuses.

United Front Work Department.

This is a global network that coordinates *thousands* of groups to carry out foreign political influence operations and suppresses dissident movements such as the Muslim Uyghurs in the Xinjiang Province of China. They have been interned in 380 detention centers housing over 1,000,000 Uyghurs. They have been "re-educated," abused, and tortured since 2016. Believe it or not, Google has been hired by the CCP to help surveil China's "rebellious" minorities. This department also gathers intelligence and transfers other countries' technology to China i.e industrial espionage.

Belt and Road Initiative (BRI)

This agency has invested billions of dollars in the infrastructure development of Third World countries. The Chinese create a "debt trap" charging these countries exorbitant rates on loan repayment thereby financially controlling these nations into submission to China.

One Belt, One Road Plan

This is a corollary to The BRI. In an attempt to intimidate and isolate the U.S., China is attempting to create spheres of influence in Oceania, Europe, Africa, and Latin, America, again utilizing the carrot of exorbitant loans.

Mask Diplomacy

Covid 19, Coronavirus, or Chinese Wuhan Flu, whatever you want to call it was no accident. Inside information from Wuhan suggests this virus was unleashed as a cudgel to weaken the U.S. and its allies. While the U.S. struggled with the epidemic, China continued to build artificial islands in the South China Sea that will one day be militarized. Trump has done what he can with the U.S. Navy in that area to counter this aggressive expansion. However retired four-star General Jack Keane, Vice Chief of Staff of the U.S. Army reports that current Pentagon generals have simulated war games vs. China in the area of the South Pacific, and the U.S. comes up on the short end!

Military Confrontation

The Chinese feel that the American satellites in space are our Achilles Heel. The Chinese plan to use lasers to knock out our GPS system that controls satellite movements as well as the electrical grid of the U.S and its allies. This is the reason Trump created the U.S Space Force to counteract this strategy of the CCP. Trump also authorized an executive order against some American companies that had been investing in the Chinese military. This is beyond belief! In December of 2020, it has been reported that Chinese geneticists are experimenting with genetic enhancement. The goal of the CCP is for scientists to ultimately spawn bigger and stronger soldiers of war!

International Groups

Current and former CCP officials hold key positions in twenty-eight international organizations. Please note the wide range of areas over which the CCP has some amount of control: World Health Organization (WTO), International Atomic Energy Commission (IAEC), Chemical weapons, World Bank, Asian Infrastructure Bank, Inter American Bank, International Court of Justice, and World Intellectual Property. This is only a partial listing!

The political divide in America has proven to be another back door entrance in reference to the infiltration of America. According to the NY Post, a former Facebook insider reports that Facebook hired half a dozen Chinese Nationals. So what? These technocrats were hired to install new and more sneaky computer algorithms that increased the censorship of information provided to Facebook users, especially content generated by the more conservative Republican Party who are more skeptical of Chinese motives.

Also, Alicia Garza, a co-founder of BLM has begun an advocacy group named Black Futures Lab, which is backed by the Chinese Progression Association. Their goal is to make policy for the black community and oppose American lawmakers who would reject these policies. This group went so far as to raise the Chinese flag over Boston's City Hall in 2019 to celebrate the CCP takeover in China sixty years before. Who authorized this!? Over the last two decades, the CCP has downed a U.S. military reconnaissance aircraft, used lasers to blind U.S. pilots, disrupted U.S. satellites, threatened to stop U.S companies from exporting antibiotics made in China (in response to Covid), and stole trillions of dollars in U.S. intellectual property.

The U.S. and the international community are now fighting back. FBI Director Christopher Wary stated that the U.S. has opened up over 2,000 investigations into CCP undertakings in America. Every FBI field office is working on trade secret cases involving China spanning almost every sector and industry in the U.S. with new investigations opening up every ten hours! Within the last year (2020) there have been more indictments under Trump than the entire eight years of Obama-Biden Administration. Not one Chinese National was charged as a spy under Obama, who viewed China as a benign competitor. In the year 2020, there have been twenty major FBI investigations by the U.S to counteract threats posed by the CCP just in communication and subversion alone.

This New Age Cold War has spawned a new alliance of democratic nations. The IPAC (Inter-Parliamentary Alliance on China) includes the U.S, England, the European Union, India, and Australia, a union of sixteen democracies pledged to stop the spread of Chinese influence throughout the world. This New Age Cold War may outlast the first Cold War, which lasted nearly four decades. Just before 2021, the European Union, unfortunately, broke with the U.S. and signed a long-term trade agreement with China. Trade agreements are susceptible venues for ideas being stolen.

Human Rights

The large-scale violation of human rights issues has been leveled at the CCP for decades. The response of the CCP to these allegations comes right out of the Saul Alinsky playbook—deny, deflect, ignore. To illustrate the depth of depravity occurring in China, for decades the Chinese regime has faced mounting allegations that it is killing prisoners of conscience such as Uyghurs, Falon Gong, and Christians en masse to sell their harvested organs for profit. Knowing the genocidal history of the CCP, this should come as no surprise. According to the Epoch Times, in June 2019 an independent London-based peoples tribunal, after a year-long GPS investigation considering testimony from more than fifty witnesses, found clear evidence that forced organ harvesting has taken place in China for years and "on a significant scale." And these barbarians have America in their crosshairs!

As you know history has a knack for repeating itself, often in a negative way. Earlier I related the story of Theodore Roosevelt's warning to America about an impending German invasion before WWI. Watching the videos of the large Chinese Army on the march, I get the feeling these maneuvers are not just for practice. I pray that our leadership has taken notice and is preparing for the worst.

CHAPTER 57

America...
or Amerika?

THE CALENDAR YEAR OF 2020 has been most challenging for everyone and our nation. There has been a breakdown of law and order, affecting both sides of the political divide not witnessed in decades exacerbated by a controversial president, the media, the Deep State that detests him, and a rampant pandemic that has enveloped America and the world.

Words and deeds have escalated to the point where we have to have two armed camps ready for battle, as evidenced by the burning of American cities and the destruction of monuments and statues representing traditional America, mostly by the hands of Far Left radical groups. To even the most casual observer it is clear that the United States of America is in trouble. There are many societal forces at odds with each other, forcing Americans to decide what kind of country they want to reside in going forward. Every nation faces an existential crisis during its existence. The decision Americans face today is do they want to live in a secular society or a traditional one?

A secular America is the goal of the New World Order globalists. The secular view of America is that America is evil, not exceptional, and therefore must be radically changed. This Neo-Communist New World Order scenario includes open borders and oligarchic control in America creating a trans-American nanny state while simultaneously taking steps to eliminate the Constitutional freedoms guaranteed to U.S citizens especially freedom of speech and religion and the right of citizens to own guns. Open borders and free health care for all would cause taxes to rise precipitously eventually leading to the crash of the economy. This would, in turn, open the door for the establishment of a new secular nanny state. If not a complete nanny state then perhaps a form of autocratic capitalism similar to the Communist China model. Sixty years ago, President John Kennedy said, "Ask not what your country can do for you, ask what you can do for your country." President Joe Biden is saying "Hey, look what your country can do for you!" It's a depressing measure of how far the Democratic Party has fallen. This slow walk toward a secular totalitarian state is abetted by the Cancel Culture and WOKE education in schools. A Gallup Poll from August 2018 showed that fifty-one percent of young Americans between the ages of eighteen to twenty nine have a positive impression of socialism.

What most people don't understand is that socialism is only a transient step on the road to a totalitarian Communist state where all democratic institutions will be eliminated. To paraphrase Alexander Solzhenitsyn, the author of "The Gulag Archipelago," in his 1978 commencement address at Harvard University, "Liberalism is inevitably pushed aside by radicalism, radicalism surrenders to socialism and socialism cannot stand up to Communism."

BLM is already assisting a soft Chinese coup of the American government and their website spells out their agenda: national defunding of police, prison abolition, and the destruction of the nuclear family, replacing it with a queer-affirming network that will dismantle cisgender privilege of the "straight" population. Gender is no longer biological but a decision to be made by the individual. There are no more mothers, only "birth people." Failed male athletes can now transgender and compete against biological females in order to amass "likes" on Facebook and assuage their bruised egos. Do not overlook the role the Big Tech social media companies play in this secularization of America. They have already run afoul of Congress in regards to censorship issues but until they are broken up they are a threat to American democracy as they attempt to ingratiate themselves further into the political power structure of our nation. Lastly, if violence is necessary, the George Soros-funded paramilitary group Antifa is lurking in the shadows, waiting to carry out their next mission of violence and anarchy.

Opposed to the secular vision for America stand the traditionalists. They believe in the Constitution and the rule of law giving firm support to the police and the military. For America to remain an exceptional nation it must have secure borders to keep out any agitators whose goal is to undermine the security promised to American citizens by the Preamble of the Constitution. Whereas socialism wants a nanny state where everyone fits a mold, the traditionalists realize that Americans are very competitive, our national DNA imprinted by our founders who used a strong work ethic to achieve success. They believe in the mantra put forth by Henry David Thoreau in his 1849 essay Civil Disobedience where he stated " the government is best which governs least."

Traditionalists oppose the unilateral bashing of America. They proudly salute and raise the flag and support the pledge of allegiance. They would never burn the flag nor spit and stomp on Old

Glory. They do not sit or kneel during the playing of the National Anthem. In a traditional society, change is seen as necessary but more effective and lasting in small doses. The clarion call of the secularists about "systemic racism" holds no water considering the myriad laws and amendments enacted from the Civil War to the 1960s, granting voting rights and citizenry to people of all persuasions. Women's rights have been solidified as well as the rights of the LGBTQ community. As to the issue of police brutality, government statistics show that the police are three times more likely to be killed as opposed to them killing an unarmed predator. Hundreds of police are assaulted and killed yearly as opposed to a handful of unarmed innocents yet which group receives ALL the negative opprobrium?

Traditionalists are no fans of the WOKE Culture and its attendant white privilege guilt-shaming. This is an ideological construct of the liberal university system that is presently expunging history back to ancient Greece and Rome, accusing them of White Privilege, if you can believe it. Traditionalists are the ones who stand up at school board meetings and loudly object to the Woke curriculum, which is looking to invalidate traditional education. By doing nothing, the country is lost. Fortunately parents are beginning to see through this radical agenda and are becoming much more vocal. Above all, the nuclear family, the backbone of America and the transmitter of culture from generation to generation, is to be revered and protected at all costs from a secular ideology that would put an end to it.

The 2020 presidential election is illustrative of one fact if nothing else—the defined lines that used to separate the two major political parties are now blurry. It is difficult to distinguish Democrats from Republicans. Easier to observe is the chasm that exists between the power groups (Big Tech, Wall Street, mainstream media, the educational bureaucracy, the Deep State, the Unions and professional sports including MLB,NBA,WNBA and NFL) versus everyone else. The former represents Amerika. The latter, America.

This is your choice, as the country assuredly is at a crossroads. As Americans bicker over gender identification, China scoffs at us while expanding its boundaries and insinuating itself into every facet of U.S. life. Meanwhile radicals torch American cities and demolish monuments and statues without recrimination. President Biden has seen fit to open the Southern border of the U.S. to any and all manner of illegal aliens who are now flooding America, up to a million strong with no end in sight. The Department of Homeland Security has become a resettlement bureau going so far as to utilize military transport planes to deliver thousands of illegals to unsuspecting cities,mostly under the cover of darkness. This is totally contrary to U.S. law yet nothing is done about it. The abyss beckons. I fear for the Republic.

This recitation of millennial American history has been the most prolonged and challenging intellectual endeavor of my life. For the record, I began writing on February 1, 2020 and the final revision was completed on the eve of Thanksgiving, 2021. In this book, I have invited you to walk in my footsteps as I explained history the way I learned it and, in more recent decades, the way I experienced it. To the best of my ability, I have minimized subjectivity in order to elaborate and elucidate the subject matter that was covered on an introductory level.

I hope that my tome has motivated you to learn more about history, perhaps now at the next level. It does not matter if you choose to pursue American history or world history. Just know there is an infinite amount of knowledge to be gleaned but only a finite amount of time to accomplish it. Good luck in your endeavors!

CHAPTER 58

Before I Go...
Did You Know?

THIS BOOK BEGAN ON A SCIENTIFIC NOTE so I thought it appropriate to conclude it with a few scientific vignettes.

Did you know that you don't need a wrist watch to tell the time during the daylight hours? I learned this trick in high school earth science class. And one disclaimer, this will not work on overcast days.

Here's how it works. Face north and spread both arms out straight out from your shoulders and parallel to the ground. Your body has now become a human sundial. Your head is 12 o'clock. Your extended right arm is 3 o'clock, your feet are 6 o'clock, and your left arm is 9 o'clock. The shadow cast by your head is the hour of the day!

In the 1970s in front of a disbelieving party, beach crowd, I had to prove my theory. Someone asked for the time and after setting myself up as a sundial, I replied "about 1:20." Catcalls were immediate and loud. A guy walked by with a watch and when asked the time, he replied "1:17." Silence, I felt like I could have walked on water at that moment.

Did you know that a common fish can help to predict the onset of stormy weather? I learned about this phenomenon from my father, who was an avid boater in the 1950s and 1960s. There is a certain cloud pattern referred to as a "mackerel sky" that is a surefire indicator of approaching foul weather, usually within twenty-four hours.

Go online and view a picture of a mackerel. Look at its dorsal (top) view as well as side views. It has a layered look of dark colors, eerily similar to a mackerel sky, which has rows of white, layered clouds, high in the sky. Eventually these clouds lower, and thicken and grow dark before the onset of rain. There are pictures of the 1938 hurricane known as the "Long Island Express" online that shows a panoramic mackerel sky. This hurricane was the most powerful hurricane of the 20th century, killing 500 people. Most mackerel skies are not panoramic, more in line with what I witnessed before Superstorm Sandy in 2012. Speaking of Sandy, did you know that our avian friends also predict the coming of storms? I had a difficult time believing that an unformed storm was moving quickly out of the Caribbean and rapidly approaching the New York Metro area in October, 2012. My fears were confirmed when I noticed all the shore birds- seagulls, terns and sandpipers-had gone elsewhere. Usually you notice birds flying inland a few hours before a storm. In the case of Sandy, the beaches were bereft of birds three days before the disaster struck. Many of us wished we could have taken our homes and flown away with the birds, the flood having ravaged thousands of homes in the area, some of which are still being rebuilt in 2021.

Bibliography

Alinsky, Saul. Rules for Radicals: A Pragmatic Primer for Realistic Radicals, 1971

Batchelor, John E., and James West Davidson. The American Nation, 1991

Brinton, Crane. Anatomy of a Revolution, 1938

Brookhiser, Richard. Founding Father, 1997

Casner, Mable. and Ralph Gabriel. Story of the American Nation,1967

Dimont, Max. Jews God and History, 1962

Epoch Times Newspaper,2020

Hofstadter, Richard. The American Political Tradition, 1948

How it Works Annual Magazine, 2020

Kilmeade, Brian. Sam Houston and the Alamo Avengers, 2020

Nader, Ralph. Unsafe at Any Speed,1965

NY Post newspaper, 2020-2021

NY Times newspaper, 2020-2021

Obama, Barack. Dreams from My Father, 1995

Paston, Amy. The Smithsonian Book of Presidential Trivia, 2013

Riesman, David. The Lonely Crowd, 1950

The Old Farmer's Almanac, 2020

Toffler, Alvin. Future Shock,1970

Trebek, Alex. The Answer Is, 2020

Turner,Frederick Jackson. "Frontier Thesis," 1893

Wall Street Journal, 2020-2021

Wikipedia, 2020-2021

Timeline Of World-Changing Events

1-Birth of Jesus Christ (Christianity)

476-Fall of Rome

570-Birth of Muhammad (Islam)

1096-The Crusades

1492-Columbus discovers America

1588-Defeat of the Spanish Armada

1607-First American colony (Jamestown,VA)

1754-French and Indian War

1760-Industrial Revolution(England)

1776-American Revolutionary War

1861-Civil War

1914-WWI

1943-Birth of Computer Age

1945-Atomic Bomb

1969-Man on the Moon

1989-End of Cold War (Soviet Union)

2020-New Cold War (China)

Acknowledgement

Big shout out to my typist, Bradley Berkowitz, whose facile fingers made the production of this book a reality.

Lightning Source UK Ltd.
Milton Keynes UK
UKHW021457230522
403390UK00007B/965